A HISTORY OF NORWAY

FROM THE ICE AGE
TO THE AGE
OF PETROLEUM

IVAR LIBÆK   ØIVIND STENERSEN

A HISTORY OF NORWAY

FROM THE ICE AGE
TO THE AGE OF PETROLEUM

TRANSLATED BY JEAN AASE

GRØNDAHL DREYER

Contents

Preface

A History of Norway – from the Ice Age to the Age of Petroleum was well received on its initial publication in 1991, but only three years passed before both publisher and authors felt a revision to be necessary, due to new findings in research. At the same time, the authors wished to place greater emphasis on Norway's place in Europe through the ages. The people's "No" to the EU in December 1994 marked a division in the country's history. This book attempts to explain why Norway, as the only nation in Europe, has voted "No" on the question of membership in *two* referendums.

A History of Norway – fom the Ice Age to the Age of Petroleum presents the main issues in Norwegian history from the earliest times and up to the present day. Something new in this edition are the framed texts which present special events and important people, such as the "Witch Craze", winter sports in Norway, the Nobel Peace Prize, Fridtjof Nansen, and Einar Gerhardsen.

An impressive number of illustrations show important characteristics of Norwegian art, society and commercial life. Fourteen thematic sections illustrate historical developments in selected areas. An interplay of text, pictures, maps and diagrammes presents the reader with information in an engaging manner. The sections on Fishing, Whaling and Sealing, Defence, Norway in the Age of Petroleum and Norway and the World have been brought up-to-date with new statistical material, texts and illustrations.

The publishers have engaged one of Scandinavia's foremost graphic designers, Roland Thorbjörnsson of Sweden, to design the thematic sections. He has used the very latest in modern computer technology and graphic production techniques for lay-out, cartography and graphic production. Most of the watercolours in the thematic sections are the work of Ulf Söderquist. Additional art work is by Lennart Molin and Lars Jödahl.

The authors have also acted as illustration editors and are responsible for the thematic sections. The idea and text for the section "A Golden Age in Literature" are the work of Anne Skalleberg.

The book is based on important works by Norwegian historians. We are deeply grateful to them all. We take this opportunity of thanking museums and archives all over the country for valuable assistance.

Ivar Libæk   *Øivind Stenersen*

From the Ice Age to the Iron Age

Hunter-gatherer Cultures in the Old Stone Age (the period prior to 4000 B.C.)

The last, long Age of Ice began approximately 100,000 years ago and lasted for nearly 90,000 years. During this period, Europe was settled from Africa by two species of man, the Neanderthal and the Cro-Magnon. That first species became extinct about 30,000 years ago but the other, also known as *Homo sapiens sapiens* (the thinking man), survived and reigned supreme. All people now living on the earth belong to this species.

The Scandinavian Peninsula was not completely covered by ice for the entire period of 90,000 years. Large areas became ice-free when the glaciers shrank, areas where animals and people could establish themselves. The oldest finds of ice age animal remains have been made in a mountain cave in Tysfjord, Nordland county, where bones of polar bear, wolves and birds over 50,000 years old have been found. Discovery of a mammoth tusk in Gudbrandsdalen in central Norway shows that these shaggy, elephant-like beasts also made their way to Scandinavia.

It is entirely possible that Neanderthal and Cro-Magnon hunters alike moved northwards tracking the migrating big game, but so far no trace of these ice age beings has been found. This is because northern Europe was covered by an immense glacier, 3000 metres thick in places, starting in about 20,000 B.C. This can have erased all signs of the oldest ice age hunters.

The ice-sheet began to melt again, however, and starting about 14,000 years ago the first areas along the Norwegian coast began to emerge. At this time dry land existed between Denmark and England, while the Viking Bank was an island in the North Sea. The Norwegian deep, or Gut, was the only body of water separating southwestern Norway from the mainland to the south. In cold winters even this strait must have frozen over. The climate was Arctic and the landscape covered with tundra vegetation such as heather, shrub willow and dwarf birch.

Towards the end of the ice age, the first human beings came to southwestern Norway from the mainland to the south. Although we will never know whether they crossed the Norwegian deep by boat or wandered over the ice one cold winter's day, we can be reasonably sure that they were lured northwards by the promise of plentiful supplies of food. The coast of Norway, with its countless islands and skerries, must have proved a far better area for hunting and fishing than the gentle, low-lying coastline of the mainland. This first immigration must also be seen in the light of the forestation of the North German plain, which caused herds of wild reindeer to range northward towards the Scandinavian glaciers. Some hunters must have followed behind.

The oldest probable Stone Age site discovered thus far lies in Blomvåg, near Bergen on the west coast of Norway. It is dated to approximately 10,500 B.C. Finds at this site include bones of whale, seal, reindeer, and sea-birds as well as snail shells. The position of these remains suggests that they are remnants of food, as examination of the flint material also shows. Flint tools and weapons found on islands off the southwestern coast near Stavanger and dated to about 9000 B.C., indicate that these first groups of hunters belonged to the so-called Ahrensburg culture established on the north German plain at about this time

At sites where these oldest Stone Age hunters lived, we can find arrowheads and other sharp pieces of flint that were used as axes, daggers, scrapers and augers. Occasionally we can discover stones used to weigh down

Opposite:
Wild reindeer have roamed the Norwegian mountains since the Ice Age. In our time the largest herd can be found on the Hardanger mountain plateau.

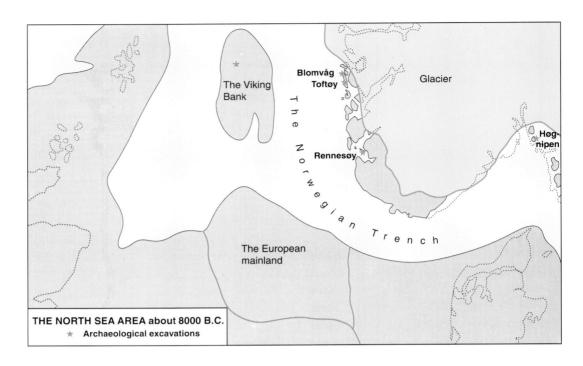

THE NORTH SEA AREA about 8000 B.C.
★ Archaeological excavations

tents or even traces of ancient cooking fires. As far as we know, these hunters lived in small family groups that moved often from place to place. They probably had lightweight skin tents and boats that were easy to carry as they ranged over large areas. By about 9300 B.C. some of them had reached as far north as Magerøya close to the North Cape in Finnmark county.

The span of time between 9000 and 8000 B.C. marked the last glacial period of the ice age. Once again a mighty sheet of ice covered most of the Scandinavian peninsula. Some areas along the coast of Norway remained ice-free, however, and it is entirely probable that descendants of those first ice age hunters continued to live alongside the glacier's edge. Starting in about 8000 B.C. the glacier began a rapid withdrawal, and from this time on the

entire coastal area was settled. The oldest Stone Age finds in Nord-Troms and Finnmark counties in northern Norway are called the Komsa culture, after a habitation site found on the Komsa Mountain near Alta. In the rest of the country, finds dated to around 7000 B.C. are called the Fosna culture, after a find site at Fosna near Kristiansund in south-western Norway. The weapons and tools used by both cultures were similar in form, but made of different kinds of stone: flint dominated in the South, while the Komsa hunters used quartz and quartzite.

The Fosna culture of southern Norway was replaced by the Nøstvet culture around 7000 B.C. This new culture is named after a habitation site at Nøstvet farm in Ås, south of Oslo. A characteristic of the Nøstvet hunters was their use of a long, narrow, oval axe with

Bear-hunting scene from the field of rock carvings at Alta, c. 4200-3600 B.C. During the Stone Age, the bear was a figure of cult worship in all of northern Scandinavia.

a honed edge, made of volcanic rock. The transition to this new type of axe can have been caused by a change in the natural environment. Much of Norway now had a climate comparable to that of present-day southern England. Trees such as elm, lind, ash and oak covered much of lowland Norway to the south, while pine and birch forests grew up in mountainous areas and in northern Norway. Deer, boar, bear and elk came in from the south. Felling trees and hunting in these great forests called for sturdier axes and different weapons.

The Nøstvet hunters chose to settle in sheltered inlets along the coast where they could fish, catch seal and hunt in the forests. Some also made the trek to the mountains to hunt reindeer and fish trout. Men probably had chief responsibility for hunting, while women and children, who remained closer to the settlements, gathered firewood, edible roots, berries, shells, mussels and eggs.

Stone Age rock carvings, or petroglyphs – hunters' carvings – provide an extraordinary insight into human existence in this period. The oldest carvings, which most often depict highly coveted big game, lie near ancient hunting grounds and fishing spots. In western Norway, pictures of deer predominate, while elk are most common in eastern Norway. Carvings of reindeer are chiefly found north of the district of Trøndelag while pictures of bear exist only north of the Dovre mountains in northcentral Norway. Whale, salmon, halibut and sea-bird figures can be found all along the coast.

These hunters' carvings can be interpreted as an attempt by those who made them to gain magical powers over game animals, so

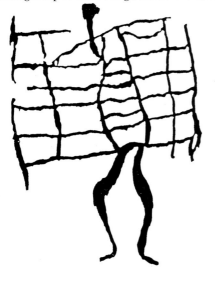

that they both increased in number and were more easily felled. The carvings were probably part of secret rituals whose content we can comprehend by observing Native American, Sami and Innuit ceremonies.

When people begin to appear in the carvings, however, the message becomes clearer. This is the case in Alta in Finnmark county. This largest collection of rock art in nothern Europe was placed on the UNESCO World Heritage List in 1985. The area can have been a meeting place for various groups of inland and coastal hunters, who came here for the express purpose of demonstrating their distinctive character and power to their neighbours. Figures of men hunting reindeer and bear are carved into the surface of the rock. They fish, sail, dance, use skis and snowshoes. In some places we can see figures of both men and women wearing masks and carrying drums. These probably represent *shamen*, or priests, who were in close contact with the supernatural and led the proceedings when the various rituals were performed.

About 4000 B.C. the people of the northern counties of Troms and Finnmark began using pottery and tools made of slate, innovations indicating close contact with the Stone Age cultures of Finland and Russia. The similarity between the rock carvings in Alta and those in northwestern Russia is another indication of such contact. The people of the North could travel hundreds of kilometres in a few months using skis, sledges and large skin-covered boats.

Bottom left and above:
Rock carvings at Alta

The Younger Stone Age. Agriculture appears (4000 - 1800 B.C.)

Analyses of pollen samples from bogs show that agriculture appeared in the districts near the Oslofjord about 4000 B.C., or about 5000 years after it had first been developed in the Middle East. Finds of thin-butted, honed axes and a special kind of ceramic vessel called *funnel beaker pottery*, suggest that knowledge of agriculture came by way of southern Scandinavia. The discovery of burial monuments made of large stone slabs (megalithic monuments) from the same period, shows that these first farmers were influenced by the European megalithic culture, of which Stonehenge in England is the most familiar illustration.

The first farmers practiced slash-and-burn agriculture, that is to say, they burned down the forest and planted grain in the ashes. When the soil was exhausted, they moved on to new settlements. Animal husbandry was probably more important than tillage to begin with, while in inland and northern districts, hunting and fishing long remained far more important than agriculture.

The final breakthrough for agriculture occurred sometime during the four centuries preceding 2500 B.C. During this period of time, people all along the coast as far north as Alta began growing oats or barley and raising pigs, cattle, sheep and goats. The same was true of the valleys in the south. This development is customarily regarded as coinciding with the arrival of the *Battle-axe people* in this country. These people have

been named after the beautifully polished stone axes they used as grave goods. The Battle-axe people brought with them a culture that included new burial customs, weapons and tools. In addition they probably brought the Indo-European language with them. Norwegian as well as most other European languages derive from proto-Indo-European.

The Bronze Age (1800 - 500 B.C.)

Decisive changes in agriculture occurred in this period. Ploughing with a wooden scratch-plow, an ard, became common, horses were used for riding and ploughing, and new flint sickles made harvesting easier. Farmers settled more permanently and began building whole farm complexes with permanent dwellings and yards. They now made their settlements in areas with dry moraine soil, such as on the great moraines near the Oslofjord, Lake Mjøsa, in Jæren in southwestern Norway and in the north-central district of Trøndelag.

Harvests were now so plentiful that some farmers could accumulate a surplus enabling them to acquire luxury items from far-distant places. This was most likely done by trading products that were sought after elsewhere in Europe, particularly furs and hides. The magnificent objects found at burial sites bear witness to this new affluence: elegant flint daggers, amber jewelry, bronze tools, weapons and decorative objects, and costly gold

Bronze Age rock-carving from Skjeberg, Østfold county. Ships are one of the most common figures in carvings from this period. Such depictions may relate to actual sea voyages; they can also symbolize the deceased's journey to the hereafter.

jewelry. Many of these status symbols were imported from Jutland in Denmark, which was an important centre during the Scandinavian Bronze Age culture. The metals of which bronze is composed were not found in Scandinavia. Tin came from England and copper from Hungary. However, many of the moulds used in casting bronze were made of soapstone quarried in the mountains of southern Norway.

Such luxury goods as the aforementioned had little impact on the lives of most people. They continued to use tools made of stone, bone and wood. Of far greater importance was the fact that women learned to spin and weave, so that clothing of furs and skins could be replaced by those of woolen cloth.

The monumental Bronze Age burial cairns are obvious proof of a socially stratified society in which chieftains held high status.

These bronze horns, or *lur*, were found sunken in a bog outside Stavanger. They were probably used in religious ceremonies. The clothes worn by the lur-players have been reconstructed on the basis of Bronze Age grave finds.

SAMI PRE-HISTORY

Starting about 1800 B.C., the hunting peoples of northern Scandinavia also began using bronze for weapons, tools and ornaments. This Bronze Age culture of the Arctic had links to Russia, and differed from the Scandinavian Bronze Age farming culture farther south.

The hunters of the North continued to receive impulses from eastern regions. About 800 B.C. they began using a distinct pottery ware tempered with asbestos imported from Finland. At the same time, they developed a settlement pattern based on seasonal migration between coastal and inland areas that followed after wandring herds of reindeer and also took advantage of fishing in rivers, lakes and fjords. This migratory pattern is in many ways similar to that which we can find among the later Sami.

It is quite possible that the cultural changes that took place in the far North were the result of migration from the south-east. Finno-Ugrian immigrants seem to have mixed with the indigious population, and with them developed the Sami language and culture.

The Sami began using iron about 500 B.C. Once again it was the close contact with Russia that influenced the North. But use of this new metal was not absolute. Stone and bone continued to be important raw materials for the production of weapons and tools.

The oldest written accounts of the Sami date to the first century A.D. The Roman historian, Tacitus, related in his work "Germania" of a hunting people called the "Fenni" dwelling in the far North. They lived on wild plants, wore clothing of animal skins, and both women and men participated in the hunt. This picture is elaborated upon by the Goth, Jordanes, about 400 years later. He refers to the Sami as skiers, as "*skridfinne*», a description that can be corroborated by archaeological finds: a typically Sami ski, pointed at both ends and dated to 600 A.D., has been excavated in Alvdal, Hedmark county, in south-central Norway.

It would appear that the Sami occupied much of the inland regions of Scandinavia at this time, from Østerdal valley in the south and all the way north to the Arctic coast of Troms and Finnmark counties.

These bone fish-hooks come from Kjelmøy in the Varangerfjord in Finnmark and are dated to the last centuries B.C. They come from the oldest culture classified by archaeologists as being Sami.

These cairns tend to lie on top of ridges or as landmarks on headlands along the coast.

Bronze Age rock carvings give tantalizing glimpses of these land tillers' religion. The symbols, ceremonies and rituals depicted on bare rock surfaces seem to have one main purpose: to secure the fertility of the fields, the animals and the people themselves. Crosses, cross-inscribed circles, wagons and ships suggest that worship of the sun or of a sun-god was primary. We find figures of women and men dancing and participating in ceremonies of frankly erotic content. In some places we see huge figures of men brandishing axes. This can be a sign that chieftains played a leading part in the cult of fertility. Several scenes are distinctly similar to those of the Minoan culture on Crete. This can mean that the religious beliefs of the Mediterranean peoples followed trade routes or accompanied migrating tribes to northern Europe.

The Iron Age (500 B.C.–800 A.D.)

About 330 B.C., the Greek sea-captain, Pytheas of Massilia (present-day Marseilles), sailed northwards. He reached a land he called Thule and his accounts are the first primary source concerning conditions in Scandinavia.

Gold jewelry from the Roman Iron Age, found on Haram Island near Ålesund. The armlet weighs 484 grammes, and the medallion, or bracteate, is an imitation of a Roman coin. The jewelry is made of 22 carat gold and has probably belonged to a chieftain.

Among other things, he wrote: «Thule lies six days journey to the north of Brittania. [....] The people live on oats and the like, namely greens, wild fruits and roots. Those who have grain and honey make themselves a drink thereof. But because they lack a clearly shining sun, they must thresh their grain in great houses after bringing the spikes thence, because the grain would become infertile if left to the mercy of pouring rain and lack of sun on open threshing grounds.»

Pytheas' account suggests that he went ashore somewhere along the coast of Nordland county. It confirms the impression of a climatic change in the last centuries B.C. The mean temperature fell and precipitation increased, until weather conditions became similar to those we have today. In western Norway and to the north, the warmth-loving, leafy forests were replaced by pine and birch, while spruce forests covered much of the eastern district.

The change in climate meant that farmers had to erect more buildings to provide shelter and warmth for people and animals alike. Because domestic animals now had to be kept indoors during the winter, it became necessary to collect hay, bark shavings and leaves for winter fodder. The new farm buildings were often built in places with dry, sandy loam. In this way farmers became even more attached to those areas that had been important to agriculture since the Bronze Age. This is where we find Norway's oldest farm names, most often based on the physical conditions of the site: Ås (Ridge), Haug (Hill), Åker (Field), or Sander (Sand).

This first period of the Iron Age, from 500 B.C. to the birth of Christ, is termed the Celtic Iron Age in southern Scandinavia. The term shows that it was the Celts who introduced iron to this part of Europe. This new metal was produced from ore that was easily found in bogs, enabling most people to acquire knives, sickles, axes, arrow-heads and other weapons and tools made of iron. Iron implements made it easier to work the soil. Harvests became larger and the population grew, making it necessary to clear even more land for farms.

Several generations lived under the same roof on these early Iron Age farms. When the sons took a wife, they remained on the farm with their families. A large extended family of this kind is called a clan. Each member was subject to the will of the clan father or mother, who were the heads of the farm. They were responsible for transmitting the old traditions to new generations, and they were the link to the deceased heads of the clan who were worshipped as gods. The clan gave security and protection to all its members. Each and every one could depend on assistance from the clan in case of illness, affirmity or old age, or in case of conflict with other clans.

When the farm population grew to the point where it was difficult to provide food for all, the youngest sons had to move out and clear new farms in the vicinity. In this way whole rural districts were populated.

If conflict arose between the clans in a district because of murder or theft, or because of uncertain boundaries between the farms, all freemen assembled at the *ting*. This was a sacred place where all use of force was prohibited. Many of the conflicts resolved at these tings led to some one person being fined to pay compensation to some other. These fines were usually reckoned in the form of grain, butter or cows. The criminal could be outlawed in more serious cases, which meant that all freemen could kill him at will.

The Roman Empire was the economic and political centre of power during the first four centuries A.D. Because the people of Scandinavia living outside the Sami areas were greatly influenced by conditions in Rome, this period is called the *Roman Iron Age*. Their set of written characters, the runes, is based on the Latin alphabet and their system of weights and measures also patterned on the Roman system.

A lively system of trade and exchange of goods between North and South was established during the Roman Iron Age. From trading centres near the mouth of the Rhine and along the coast of the Baltic Sea, quantities of Roman luxury goods were transported to Zealand in Denmark and then farther northwards. The graves of the local chieftains of the period contain Roman bronze vessels, gold and silver jewelry, glass beakers and swords. These goods were probably accepted in return for furs, feathers and down, animal skins and slaves. It is not entirely impossible that some Scandinavian chieftains themselves took goods of this kind home with them after having served as Roman mercenaries.

Finds in graves in the first few centuries A.D. show clearly that clans living on some of the largest farms, the *høvdingætten* or chieftain clans, acquired greater wealth and gained increasing influence in a number of fields. With the increase in population, the need for commonly accepted rules also increased. In addition, the production of iron was so labour-intensive and so complicated, that it had to be organized by an accepted leader.

The chieftains also functioned as priests when ceremonies were held in honour of gods such as Njård and Frey/Frøya. During such sacrificial ceremonies, or *blot*, farmers paid tribute to their chieftains in the form of produce from their farms. Some of these goods were used by the chieftains to pay their professional warriors, or *hird*. These private forces enabled the local chieftain to maintain his authority over the population of his territory. When he arrived at the ting accompanied by such a following of men, farmers most often

A bow brooch from Åker at Vang in Hedmark county, made of gilded silver inlaid with coloured stones and glass. The brooch, dated to the late 500s A.D., is part of Norway's most magnificent Merovingian Period finds. Its dominant motif is the crowned head of a man, with well-trimmed hair and mustache, encircled by two birds of prey and two wild boars. The artisan may have found inspiration in the royal line of the Frankians, the Merovingians, with their sacred hair.

had no choice but to submit to his wishes. The hird was also important in that they enabled the chieftain to conquer other tribes. A tribe was composed of the people of several districts within a certain *rike* or *land*, a petty kingdom or territory. We can find vestiges of such petty kingdoms in present-day place names such as Rogaland and Ringerike.

The mighty burial mounds found at various places in the country can have been political or religious assembly places for such petty kingdoms. Raknehaugen in Romerike in south-central Norway, dated to the latter part of 500 A.D., is the largest of these burial mounds.

The uneasy conditions of the *Age of Migration* from 400 to 550 A.D. may have led to farmers becoming more interested in giving the chieftains greater authority to organize and lead the district defences. One important element in this defence was the building of simple hill forts where both people and livestock could seek safety in times of unrest. These local defence works can have been built for protection against foreign tribes who wandered about after the collapse of the Roman Empire of the West, as happened in the British Isles. Two place names in western Norway are evidence of such invasion. Rogaland can be placed in connection with the *rhygi*, a tribe that lived on the Baltic coast and gave name to Rügen peninsula. Hordaland is linked to the *hord*, a tribe found in the German district of Harz.

Near the end of 500 A.D., parts of the country were hit by a catastrophe. Hundreds of farms in south-western Norway were abandoned and the population must have declined considerably. One possible cause can be epidemics, such as those related of in contemporary sources from both Gaul and the British Isles. It is quite possible that such epidemics could have spread to Scandinavia as well.

Beginning in the 600's a new period of growth set in. Abandoned farms were taken over once more, while new farms and *seters*, or mountain pasture farms, were cleared in the wilderness and new settlement grew up along the coast. The production of iron and soapstone increased again, and trade with other North Sea countries flourished.

This growth can be seen as a consequence of developments in the Frankish Empire, where the royal Merovingian line had built up a new and stable kingdom. The Merovingian kings became models for the petty kingdoms of northern Europe, making it easy to understand that the last prehistoric period, from 550 to 800 A.D., is called the *Merovingian Age* in Norway. Finds of both jewelry, helmets and ringed swords relate of good contacts with the Frankish realm. These Frankish luxury goods came via the large trading centres along the North Sea coast, with Dorestad in Friesland as the most important.

It is obvious that some clans increased their power and prestige during the 700's, at other clans' expense. One important condition for this development was that some clans increased their interest in and control over long-distance trade. The most powerful clans seem to have lived in Borre in Vestfold county, in Åker near Lake Mjøsa, in Ytre Namdalen in the district of Trøndelag, near Karmsundet in Rogaland county and at Borg in Vestvågøy, Nordland county. This laid much of the foundation for the economic expansion and political unification of the country that would take place in the centuries that followed.

The Viking Age 800–1030

A gravestone from Lindisfarne, carved just after 800 A.D. and showing a Viking attack. Two munks at prayer are depicted on the back of the stone.

«In the same year pagans from the northern regions came with a naval force to Britain like stinging hornets and spread on all sides like fearful wolves, robbed, tore and slaughtered not only beasts of burden, sheep and oxen, but even priests and deacons and communities of monks and nuns. And they came to the church of Lindisfarne, laid everything waste with grievous plundering, trampled the holy places with impure steps, dug up the altars and seized all the treasures of the holy church. They killed some of the brothers, took some away with them in fetters, [...]»

This is how an English priest described the attack on the monastery of Lindisfarne off the north-eastern coast of northern England in 793. This event is commonly regarded as the beginning of the Viking period. Starting at the end of the 8th century and continuing on to the mid-11th century, Scandinavians played an important part for the first time in European history. In this period

Swedish, Danish and Norwegian Vikings set off on voyages to distant lands and coasts. Their expeditions reached as far east as the Russian plains, as far south as the Mediterranean, the Black Sea and Caspian Sea, as far north as the Barents Sea and as far west as America.

The term Viking can be related to the Norwegian word *vik* meaning "bay" or "cove». This would suit the Vikings, who often hid in bays and inlets with their ships. But the term can also be derived from the Germanic word *wic*, which means market-place. Viking can have been a term used for the Scandinavian seamen who came to the trading centres lying on the southern coast of the North Sea, such as Lundenwic (London), Eoforwic (York) and Wic near Dorestad in Friesland.

In Byzantium, Scandinavians were called *væringer*. The Slavic people of the east used the term *rus*, while in Franconia they were described as *normans*.

In our age we do not consider the Vikings as having been mere murderers and robbers. Now Viking expertise in shipbuilding, in crafts, as seamen, explorers and merchants is equally emphasized. They colonized large areas, established towns and founded new realms.

Newer archaeological excavations and studies of written sources from western Europe, Arabia and the former Byzantium have given us a more varied view. Frankian and Anglo-Saxon chronicles, Arabian travelogues, runic inscriptions and Islandic sagas form the basis of a wealth of written material. This is so abundant that it gives grounds for regarding the Viking Age as the beginning of historic time in Scandinavia.

It is also clear that robbery and extortion of other peoples were common enough activities everywhere in the Europe of this period. To give just a few examples: the Franks oppressed the Saxons and the Friesians, the Anglo-Saxons rampaged among the Welsh, and the Arabs sacked Spain. Finno-Ugric horsemen, the Magyars, came out of the East to wage repeated attacks on Central Europe.

One important reason for the Vikings' having a poorer reputation than other marauders was that reports of their activities were written by men of the church. Priests and monks were among the few who could read and write at that time, and they were not sparing in their condemnation of the looting of churches and monasteries by those of a different faith.

Pre-conditions for the Viking Voyages

The Viking long-ship is the very symbol of the Viking Age, representing the climax of the Vikings' technical achievements. The ship had a solid keel, flexible hull and efficient sails, enabling them to cross long stretches of open sea regardless of the weather. Their knowledge of the use of sails probably came about through contact with the Friesian *wic*-merchants, who dominated trade in the North Sea area in the 7th and 8th centuries.

Even though the ships had relatively low freeboards midships, they were extremely seaworthy. Being shallow-draughted, they could be rowed up shallow rivers. Cooking equipment, tents and non-perishable provisions were stored on board, enabling the

Vikings to carry out long voyages to unhabitated wilderness areas. The ships could be run ashore on sandy beaches and, if necessary, drawn on log rollers from river to river and past waterfalls. Ships with such characteristics gave the Vikings a wide range of action. They could move swiftly, attack suddenly and make a quick retreat.

The Vikings were extremely competent navigators. They set their course by observing the stars and by measuring the sun's meridian. Accounts of sea routes were transmitted orally from father to son. Such knowledge of foreign shores, ocean currents, depths and prevailing winds enhanced a man's status.

We have previously shown how the population rose as a result of iron implements coming into general use. People cleared all available land for new farms, but towards the end of the 8th century, there was no more arable land left uncleared in western Norway. This must have been the most important reason why people from that region crossed the seas to settle in the thinly populated Shetland, Orkney, Faroe and Hebrides islands. The rest of Norway, however, still had room for new settlers. One trace of these new farms can be found in the many place names ending in -*stad*. Not all farm lads could clear and settle on their own land, however. Many of those who had no farm to inherit chose to seek their fortunes as Vikings on voyages to foreign countries.

The excavation of the Oseberg Ship was led by Professor Gabriel Gustafson (1853-1915), seen standing in the centre of the picture. The ship lay in blue clay and had been covered by stones, earth and turf in such a way that most air was kept out. It was therefore in an excellent state of preservation.

Opposite:
A wooden sculpture of Odin, from the Old Town in Oslo. According to Norse mythology, Odin had only one eye because he had forfeited his right eye to Mime, keeper of the well of wisdom lying beneath the roots of the sacred tree, Yggdrasil.

Many of these Vikings set off on such long voyages for the express purpose of gaining riches through trade. They used a special variety of ship, the *knarr*, which was especially well-suited to the transport of goods. New trade routes were opened over Scandinavia during the Viking Age, linking western Europe to the Byzantine Empire and the Caliphate of Bagdad. Swedish Vikings set up bases along the Russian rivers, and forced the inhabitants living there to pay tribute in the form of slaves and furs. They then sold these wares to the Arabs in exchange for silver coins, silks and other luxury goods.

The trading centre Birka on Lake Mälaren in Sweden was an important exchange market for eastern trade. Birka was closely linked to Hedeby in Denmark, the economic heart of the Viking Age. Trade routes ran from Hedeby to the Frankish Empire, to the British Isles and northwards to Skiringssal in Norway's Vestfold county. Skiringssal was Norway's largest trading centre in the 9th century.

Slaves did most of the actual hard labour on the largest farms. Digging the earth,

The Viking sword to the left is from Steinsvik in Lødingen, Nordland county. The other sword was found at Kongsgården in Åsnes, Hedmark county.

felling trees and milling grain were typical duties for slaves. The need for their labour increased when the men left on their long voyages. Management of the farms was then taken over by the women, with the mistress of the household in charge. Men without the urge to see the world were looked down on and called "stay-at-homes".

When Vikings went off on their long journeys they usually cooperated in acquiring a ship, crew, goods for trade and provisions. These *felag*, or joint ventures, were often led by rich yeomen or chieftains. The ships were probably owned by wealthy men like these, who also took the greater portion of the profits when the traders came home again.

It would appear that at the onset of the Viking Age, these Scandinavians had intended their voyages to foreign countries to be purely trading efforts. While on such journeys, they discovered that conditions were excellent for looting. They must have realized from the start that their ships were far superior and that coastal defences were poor. They realized too how easy it would be to rob churches and monasteries of their gold and silver treasures. Such news traveled fast once they were home again, tempting others to go off raiding.

It was not only due to their ships that the Vikings constituted a military menace. From childhood on, they had been trained in the use of weapons and in horsemanship. The weapons they used were formidable. Their favoured weapon was the sword, preferably of Frankish design and made in such a way that it would not break under combat. They also used razor-sharp battle-axes with long shafts, bows and arrows, and spears for both throwing and striking. The chieftains and their chosen men wore coats-of-mail fashioned of thousands of tiny iron rings, while the common soldiers wore heavy leather coats. They also wore conical helmets with nasals and carried light-weight wooden shields with iron shield-bosses to protect the grip.

The Vikings' effective military organization was both feared and admired. They banded together in companies of warriors led by their chieftains. They were professional soldiers who were death-defying to the extreme and who valued strength, skill with weapons, courage and self-sacrifice above all else. They worshiped Odin, god of war, believing that he had the power to decide the outcome

A Viking helmet from Gjermundbu in Ringerike, Buskerud county. Such helmets were probably worn by chieftains, while ordinary soldiers may have had to make do with pointed leather caps.

Eirik Blodøks' ("Blooded-Axe") silver coins, minted in York about 950 A.D.

of a battle. A Viking would far rather die an honourable death doing battle for his chieftain than die of old age in his own bed.

The Vikings believed that if they were killed in battle, Odin would transport them to Valhalla, the heavenly kingdom of death. Here they could fight all day and in the evenings, beautiful maidens would serve them meats and mead. This optimistic view of death may have given the Vikings a psychological advantage when doing battle with Christians. After all, priests in their churches preached the doctrine of eternal damnation of the dead in blackest Hell.

Norwegian Expansion in the Viking Age

Norwegians were most interested in sailing westwards to the islands of the North Atlantic, but they also took part in raids along the Russian rivers together with Swedes and Danes. Vikings often fought amongst themselves and were quite ready to ally themselves with Christian rulers in order to defeat other Vikings. On several occasions chieftains from different areas of Scandinavia banded together in large armies in order to conquer wealthy towns or larger territories.

During the early 9th century the Viking invasion technique was to launch a series of quick attacks along the coast and up the rivers. These raids remained an important feature of Viking tactics, but starting in the mid-9th century, they began wintering on islands whose strategic placement benefitted further operations. In 843, for example, Vikings from Vestfold raided Nantes in the Frankish Empire. After plundering and firing the town, they built a base on the island of Noirmoutier near the mouth of the Loire River. From there they set off on raids to the inland, forcing the inhabitants to pay duty on their wine and salt trade. Still later, Norwegian Vikings joined forces with the Danes and went off raiding in Spain and from there farther on into the Mediterranean.

The British Isles became the main objective for Norwegian Viking operations. From the newly colonized Shetlands, Faroes, Orkneys and Hebrides, they penetrated ever southwards, settling in northern Scotland, on the Isle of Man and on the eastern shore of the Irish Sea. Innumerable place names bear witness to the Norse settlements in these areas. People living on the Shetlands and the Orkneys spoke Old Norse until the 18th century. On the Faroes they do so to this day.

The Danes, who had conquered much of England, competed with the Norwegians for control of York. During the Viking Age, this town was one of the most important trade centres north of the Alps.

When the Vikings arrived in Ireland shortly after A.D. 800, they found the country easy prey. The island was split up into puny kingdoms engaged in constant warfare with each other. The Vikings settled along the coast, founded the first towns, introduced coinage and started trade with the rest of Europe. The Vikings' brutal conduct led the Celtic inhabitants to unite against the invaders, however. The Irish were especially enraged by Turgeis, who founded Dublin. He attempted to replace Christianity with worship of Thor, god of thunder, to the extent of building a heathen temple in Armagh, the headquarters of the Christian church in Ireland. The Celts captured Turgeis and put him to death by drowning.

The Celts were quick to learn from the Vikings how to build better ships and weapons. The petty kings of Ireland allied themselves with the Danes and by 900 had driven out the Norwegians. But they returned. It was only towards the beginning of the 11th century that the last Norwegian Viking kingdom in Ireland was overwon.

When an Irish chronicler referred to the Vikings about one hundred years later, he

Leif Eiriksson discovers America, painted by Christian Krohg (1852-1925) in 1893.

still emphasized the looting of the land: "Many were those whom they carried off to oppression and slavery on the far side of the great, green sea. Alas! Many a bright eye filled with tears and darkened with grief and despair, when father was torn from son, mother from daughter, brother from brother and family from clan and people."

In the latter part of the 9th century, some Vikings who were driven off course while sailing from Norway to the British Isles discovered Iceland. The country was already inhabited by Irish monks, who left when the Vikings began to settle there. The majority of the colonists were from western Norway. Some of them had left Norway because they refused to submit to King Harald Fairhair who was attempting the unification of the country. However, many came from the Norwegian settlements in Scotland and Ireland.

By about the year 930, the whole of Iceland had been divided amongst some four hundred chieftains. They established their own *Allting*, or assembly, based on the laws of the Norwegian *Gulating*. The majority of the inhabitants were, however, slaves of Irish or Scottish origin who had had to renounce their Celtic culture.

Iceland became a centre of Norse saga litterature. The sagas are a principal source for our knowledge of the Vikings and of the society of the Middle Ages. Even though they were written down several centuries after the events they describe took place, they contain a wealth of reliable information. The Sagas of the Kings are based on a number of heroic poems composed by the Viking kings' skalds. The poems were in verse, and they were preserved verbatim from generation to generation until being written down by Snorre Sturlason and other saga authors.

The sagas relate that the first Vikings settled in Greenland in the 980s. This colonization was led by Eirik Raude of Rogaland in southwestern Norway, who had been outlawed after committing a murder in Iceland. From Iceland, he set off for the new land with 25 ships fully laden with people, livestock and equipment. Only 14 ships arrived safely. In the years that followed, over 250 farms were established in the Eastern District (*Austbygda*) and nearly 80 in the Western District (*Vestbygda*). These settlements survived until about 1500, by which time the inhabitants had died out of causes still unknown.

About the year 1000, Eirik's son, Leiv, led an expedition along the coast of North

THE OSEBERG FIND

An animal-head post from the Oseberg find. Archaeologist Haakon Shetelig (1877-1955) called the artist who carved it, the "Academician», because of the traditional and fixed style he used.

In 1904 a Viking long-ship was excavated in Vestfold county. The ship, named the Oseberg Ship after the farm where it was found, contained grave goods of a quality and quantity unparalleled in Scandinavia. The ship itself was made of oak and was 22 metres long, just over 5 metres wide and had had a crew of 35. Newer studies indicate that the burial mound in which the ship was found was built up in the 830s.

The woman who lay interred in the ship had received a noble burial. Every effort had been made to make her journey to the kingdom of the dead as comfortable as possible. A female slave had been sacrificed together with several horses and dogs. In addition the ship contained kitchen utensils and weaving equipment, a ceremonial cart, three sledges, chests, caskets, tapestries, furniture, clothing, and agricultural implements. Many of these objects were decorated with rich carvings of the highest quality, and bear witness to the style of life in a Viking Age chieftain's household.

There is great disagreement amongst archaeologists and historians as to exactly who lay buried in the ship. According to Snorres *Ynglinge Saga*, the woman was Queen Åsa, paternal grandmother to Harald Fairhair.

The woman may have been a priestess in the cult of Frøya, goddess of fertility. The beautiful Oseberg cart can have been used to transport idols or sacrificial priests round about in the fields. One of the tapestries in the find contains a scene which can represent a procession of this kind. We see also a sacred grove with the bodies of sacrificed humans hanging from the trees. Ritual killings such as these could be carried out to the greater glory of Odin, god of war.

Odin riding his horse, Sleipner, accompanied by two ravens, Hugin and Munin.

The Viking Age

The period from the end of the 8th century to the mid 11th century in Scandinavia is known as the Viking Age. Over the preceding century the population had increased rapidly, and in western Norway all the arable land was under cultivation. Ground was cleared for new farms inland, but that was not sufficient. And so, skilful shipbuilders as they were and armed with good weapons of iron, many set off overseas in search of land and wealth. Soon the warriors from Scandinavia were feared far and wide in Europe.

Those who went on the voyages were called «Vikings». Danes and Norwegians tended to head westward, to islands in the Atlantic and to the Frankish

On the band above the map is shown the alphabet used by the Vikings. These symbols are known as runes.

Vikings in the west

Eirik Raude's son Leiv was the first European to reach the coast of North America. He called the land he came to Vinland. People on Greenland needed timber, and this may have been why they sought new land to the west. In the 1960s Norwegian archaeologists found the remains of a Viking settlement at L'Anse aux Meadows on Newfoundland. The settlers abandoned Vinland after a time, presumably because they were attacked by Indians.

On the band below is a runic inscription of c.1020 from Galteland in Evje in the Setesdal valley. *«Arnstein raised this stone for Bjor his son. He met his death in battle when Knut attacked England.»*

Colonisation of Iceland began in the 870s. Chief Eirik Raude sailed further westward, and around the year 985 he discovered a new land he named Greenland.

GRØNLAND

Vestribygd

Austribygd

Brattalid

MARKLAND

L'Anse aux Meadows

VINLAND
(Newfoundland)

A reconstruction drawing of the Viking farmstead Jarlshof on Shetland. Th island was only a day's voyage from Norway. The house were built of stone, earth and turf.

The excavations at L'Anse aux Meadows were conducted by Helge and Anne Stine Ingstad. Leiv Eiriksson's house may have looked like this.

Empire, while Swedes sailed east to Russia. At this time Scandinavia really became a part of Europe.

The Vikings were expert warriors who sacked and pillaged. They took prisoners and sold them as slaves. But they were also efficient merchants, craftsmen and farmers who established new states. Norwegian Vikings settled first in the Shetlands, Orkneys, Hebrides and Faroes. Later they colonised parts of Scotland and northern England, the Isle of Man, Ireland, Iceland and Greenland. They also reached the coast of Newfoundland. Moreover Norwegian and Danish Vikings went on expeditions to the Frankish Empire to trade and plunder; there they were known as the Northmen. Led by the chief Rollo they founded a Viking state in Normandy. Rollo became a duke recognised by the French king, and Normandy became an important centre of power and influence in 11th-century Europe.

The Vikings brought Christianity back with them to Scandinavia. Administrative concepts gleaned in continental Europe played an important role in the evolution of the Norwegian monarchy in the Middle Ages.

The largest and most important Viking town in England was Jorvik (York). Norwegian and Danish chiefs fought for supremacy in the town, and against the inhabitants they found there.

York now has an impressive Viking museum illustrating life in the town's homes, workshops and streets over a thousand years ago. Several street names in York derive from Viking days.

Jarlshof

Map labels:

Bjarkøy

ISLAND
Tingvellir

Færøyene

KVENLAND

BJARMELAND

Dvina

Frosta
Lade

SVITJOD

Hjaltland
(Shetland)

Gula

Skiringssal

Birka
Helgö
Gotland
Seeburg

VIRLAND
Holmgard

LIFLAND
Isborsk
Dúna

GARDARIKE

Rostov

Volga

Bulgar

Orknøyene
Hafrsfjord

Sudrøyene

Lindisfarne

Aggersborg
Fyrkat
Trelleborg
Ribe
Hedeby

KURLAND

STORE SVITJOD
Gnyozdova

Dublin
Man

Jorvik (York)

DANE-
LAGEN

Dørestad
Hamburg

Truso
Jomsborg?

Njemen

KIEVRIKET

Kønugard

Limerick
Cork
Waterford

BRETLAND

Lundun

Quintowic

SAKSLAND

VENDLAND

Wisla

Volga

Ural

Atil

NORMANDIE
Bayeux

Rhinen

Elben

Don

Paris

Lyon

Donau

Beresan
Dnepr

Tmatarakhan

Noirmoutier

VALLAND

Nimes

Pisa

Bordeaux
Toulouse

Tortosa

Romaborg

Miklagard
(Bysants)

JAKOBSLAND

Lisboa

SPANLAND
Sevilla

Palermo

Sikeløy

DET BYSANTINSKE
RIKET

SERKLAND

Norva   sund

STORE SERKLAND

JORSALALAND

Alexandria

Women in the Viking Age had considerable authority. House-wives carried a bunch of keys at their waist, a sign that they were responsible for running the house-hold. When the men of a settle-ment were away on expeditions, the housewives directed the farm work, too.

▢ The Viking homelands

▢ Areas often raided by the Vikings

▢ Principal areas of Viking settlemen

● Important trading place

Vikings in the east

Some Norwegians went on ex-peditions to the east. The Emperor in Constantinople had a body-guard of Vikings. Harald Hard-råde, who became king of Norway in the 11th century, was for a time colonel in this guard.

York bustled with life, and a wide range of merchandise was sold there. It included walrus tusks from north-ern Norway, silk from Byzantium and wine jars from Germany.

America. He wintered near the northern tip of Newfoundland, at a place now called L'Anse aux Meadows. This area was given the name *Vinland*, which probably means "the country of fine grassy meadows». Several more expeditions made for Vinland, but no permanent settlement was ever established there. Attacks by agressive Native Americans may have been the reason for this.

The Unification of Norway

In the 880s, Ottar, a chieftain and merchant from the district of Hålogaland in northern Norway, visited the court of the Anglo-Saxon king, Alfred. Ottar told of both his homeland and his voyages, and the king had this account written down. This account is the oldest written source to relate of the Norwegians and their land *Nordweg* (the northern route), which later would become Norway. It is obvious from the account that the Norwegians of this time felt themselves to be a people different from the Svea and the Danes.

The ninth-century population, from the Oslofjord in the southeast to the northern district of Troms, spoke their own language, Old Norse, which was different from that of the neighboring peoples. Despite the fact that the various districts were separated from one another by mountains, forests and fjords, a network of trade and kinship ties bound these different parts of the country together.

The country was still split up into petty kingdoms led by powerful chieftains, however. They not only owned the largest farms, headed the wealthiest clans, and dominated the affairs of the assemblies, they were also military and religious leaders.

The latter half of the 9th century saw the beginnings of a struggle for complete power among the chieftains. One of those participating in the conflict was determined to gain control over the whole of Norway. His name was Harald Fairhair who, according to Snorre, belonged to the Ynglinge clan from Vestfold, who had a leading position in eastern Norway. Several historians have linked Harald Fairhair's family to the impressive burial mounds of Oseberg and Gokstad.

Harald's motives for unifying the country are hidden by time, but like most Vikings he must have been interested in increasing his personal power, honour and wealth. We might reasonably assume that Harald was concerned with protecting trading activities along the coast. He probably had responsibility for defending trading centres such as Skiringssal and that merchants and craftsmen paid tribute for this protection. The sea route along the Norwegian coast was far from safe, however. Vikings in western Norway constantly attacked ships sailing north from Skiringssal to the districts of Trøndelag and northern Norway. It was probably with the aim of stopping this piracy that Harald journeyed to Trøndelag. There he formed an alliance with the mighty earldom of Lade, which had important trading interests in the North. Thus allied, they waged war against the petty kings of western Norway. Towards the end of the 9th century, Harald won a decisive victory at Hafrsfjord in Rogaland.

Harald did not establish an extensive system of government. Accompanied by his warriors, the *hird*, he travelled about the kingdom on *veitsle*, or journeys of state. When the king and his following arrived in a district, the local yeomen were duty-bound to provide accomodation, food and beer. Harald also stayed at his own royal farms, many of them former properties of chieftains who had been killed or had fled during the battles for unification. The king appointed *årmenn*, or bailiffs, to administer the estates and the law. They had charge of maintaining law and order in the districts; they punished criminals and collected fines from those who had broken the laws. In this we can observe the king usurping the clans' ancient right of avenging crimes.

Harald also made efforts to secure his kingdom against foreign countries. He attacked the Vikings of the Western Isles and sent one of his sons, Håkon, to be fostered by King Athelstan of England, where the lad also converted to Christianity.

Harald had several sons and at his death about 930, a bitter conflict arose among them as to who would inherit the kingdom. Håkon was victorious and was acclaimed king at the *Øreting* in Trøndelag. He promised to respect and to improve the laws of the land. Keeping his promises, he gained the by-name of "the Good", this too because he gave up his attempts to introduce Christianity.

Working closely with the yeomen in western Norway and in Trøndelag, Håkon established a new system of assembly. These *lagting*, the Gulating and Frostating, were

assemblies of deputies from the two areas of the country. The royal bailiffs chose the deputies and the king attended sessions to discuss current issues. The assemblies passed judgement and formulated laws, presided over by a lagman, a person especially well-versed in lawgiving. He recited the laws and interpreted them before the assembly reached its final decision.

Håkon got the assemblies to agree to the development of a naval defence system known as the *leidang*. The laws decreed that yeomen were to provide long-ships, and also the men, their equipment and enough provisions to last two months. The ships were under royal command and were to be called up by a system of coastal beacons.

Both the assemblies and the naval defence system strengthened the monarchy and the Hårfagr (Fairhair) clan, but there were still those who would not accept that *one* clan could dominate all the others. After the death of Håkon the Good in 960, the earls of Lade formed an alliance with Danish kings in an attempt to gain control of the districts around the Oslofjord. This alliance to counteract the Hårfagr clan's attempt to gain full

supremacy in Norway lasted until 1030.

The unification of Norway is part of a larger pattern. Princes and kings in various parts of Europe built up new nation-states. Scandinavians who came into contact with these state systems on their Viking campaigns could not help but bring these ideas of a stronger, centralized royal power home with them. Both Sweden and Denmark were unified as separate kingdoms at about the same time as Norway.

Olaf Tryggvason and Olav Haraldsson, both of the Hårfagr line, attempted to assume the legacy of Håkon the Good. Both were mighty warriors who had amassed great fortunes on Viking campaigns, especially those to England. They used their wealth to pay hirdmen and to buy the support of the Norwegian chieftains. The opposition was fierce, however. Olav Tryggvason was defeated after only five years. In the year 1000 he fell at the battle of Svolder.

These two Olavs had converted to Christianity on their campaigns through Europe. When they came home, they attempted to introduce Christianity by force. Even though the new faith had gained followers along the coast towards the end of the 900s, there were still many who opposed it, especially in the eastern districts and in the North.

Neither chieftains nor common yeomen can have found it easy to reject the old faith which was part of the very fabric of centuries of daily life and ceremony. They were accustomed to performing sacrificial rites and various other rituals in order to satisfy the gods. Such sacred acts were carried out in special groves, in the fields, at burial mounds and stone alters, and in buildings housing sacred idols (*hov*). Great sacrificial ceremonies in honour of the gods, *blot*, were held several times a year. During these ceremonies, leading men and women from the great clans officiated as sacrificial priests and priestesses, called *goder* and *gydjer*.

It was customs like these that Olav Haraldsson wanted to end when he arrived in the country in 1015 to seize royal power. The time was ripe. The king of Denmark, Olav's mightiest enemy, was occupied with major campaigns in England. It was, therefore, relatively easy for Olav to defeat the earls of Lade and to build up a new kingdom.

Olav persuaded several of the assemblies to pass a special law of Christianity in order to prepare the way for Christianity. The new

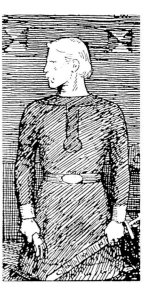

Olav Tryggvason, drawing by Erik Werenskiold.

Death of King Olav Haraldsson at Stiklestad on 29 July 1030. The day became an important holy day in the Middle Ages under the name "Olsok». The drawing was done by Erik Werenskiold (1855-1938) for an edition of *Snorre's Sagas of the Kings.*

legal regulations meant that religious power was transferred from kin and home to the Church. The king tore down the sacred *hov* and destroyed the idols. He built churches in their place and appointed clergymen with himself as leader. Those who refused to submit, risked being put to death or having their farms burned down.

Many of the chieftains feared that Christianity would deprive them of their positions as religious leaders and heads of the clans. Their role as priests had great influence on their status at the assemblies and as military leaders. It should not, therefore, come as a surprise that Olav had many enemies in the districts around Lake Mjøsa and in Trøndelag where the old religion was most deeply entrenched.

Olav had to get the most powerful clans in the country to join his side. He offered them the incomes from his farms and allowed them to take over the duties of the bailiffs. In return they had to swear allegiance to him. A chieftain who pledged himself in this way was called a *lendmann.*

The majority of the chieftains were not satisfied with the prestige offered by this position of *lendmann.* Even though several of them were Christians, they still feared that Olav would assume too much power over them. It was not difficult for the Danish king, **Canute** the Mighty, to gain the support of these Norwegian chieftains in 1025 after he decided to incorporate Norway into his North Sea realm. Many others were tempted by substantial gifts of money from Canute's treasury.

Olav was forced to flee the country, but he returned to do battle. In 1030 he met his opponents at Stiklestad in Trøndelag. This is how Snorre describes the crucial moment:

"Torstein Knarresmed smight King Olav with his axe, that blow falling on the left leg just above the knee. [...] Thus wounded, the King leaned back against a rock, cast off his sword and prayed to God for deliverance. Now Tore Hund thrust at him with his spear. This blow went in under the mail coat and to the stomach. Then Kalv struck at him, and that blow was against the the left side of the neck. [...] Thus fell the three blows that killed King Olav."

It would appear that the Hårfagr line had lost the struggle for the throne of Norway.

The Middle Ages 1030–1537

King and Church in the Century of Peace 1030-1130

"Pray to Olav
that he might grant you
power in his land,
God's man is he;
from God Himself
he can procure
life and peace
for all men."

These lines were chanted by skald Torarin Lovtunge to young Svein Alfivason, who succeeded to the throne of Norway after King Olav Haraldsson's death. Svein was a son of the Danish king, and being only ten years old, had been accompanied by his mother to help him govern. Danish rule was soon felt to be a burden. New taxes were levied on peasant families, while poor harvests reduced many to eating bark bread. Svein's reputation suffered accordingly, because a ruler who did not bring prosperity and happiness was considered a disaster for the

Life and Death of Saint Olav, c. 1300, an altarpiece from Haltdalen Stave Church in Trøndelag. After the Reformation in 1537, the altarpiece was sent to Denmark but was given back during the Olav Millennium in 1930. It is now in Nidaros Cathedral in Trondheim.

Heddal Stave Church was built about 1250 and is the largest stave church in Norway.

country. There was good reason for Torarin's advice that Svein seek help from Olav, the man of God.

Svein's rule was challenged even by Olav himself. After the battle of Stiklestad, a group of yeomen had spirited away his body in great secrecy, burying it in the sand near the Nid River. Rumours soon circulated telling of the miracles that had taken place near the king's grave. The bishop to Olav's *hird* journeyed northwards to Nidaros, and a year after the king's death his body was exhumed in the presence of the most prominant men in the country. According to legend, Olav was as handsome as the day he had been buried and his beard and hair had continued to grow. The body was laid in a casket and placed in St. Clement's Church and the bishop declared Olav as a saint. In this way the kings of Norway had a direct connection to God, and Olav's descendants gained a special right to the throne. Olav had become *rex perpetuus Norvegiae* - "Eternal King of Norway", and the country had acquired a national saint.

In the centuries that followed, hordes of pilgrims wandered to Nidaros. They came from all parts of Norway, from Scandinavia, from England and the Continent. They came

burdened by sin and infirmity, seeking remedy and consolation at the grave of the saintly king, and many felt their prayers were answered. Nidaros became a principal centre for pilgrimage in the Middle Ages, on a par with Rome to the south, Jerusalem to the east and Santiago de Compostella to the west. Both pilgrims and ordinary people living along the pilgrim routes spoke of the king's deeds amongst themselves. About 1100 these tales were recorded by the priests at Nidaros in a manuscript entitled *Passio Olavi* (The Passion of St. Olav). Transcriptions of this manuscript have been found in Finland, England, France and Austria, indicating just how widespread the cult of St. Olav became in the Middle Ages. The many legends about Olav provided inspiration for artists, and pictures of the royal saint were painted, drawn, woven and carved in wood by pious men and women. The life of St. Olav has continued to inspire artists right up to our own time.

St. Olav became a rallying-point, and even the king's enemies accepted the fact that his influence continued after his death. By 1034 dissatisfaction over Danish rule had grown to the extent that one of Olav's slayers, Kalv Arnesson, journeyed to Gardarike (Novgorod) where the king's 11-year-old son, Magnus, resided. He came to Norway the following year to be the new king. Svein and his mother left Norway without offering resistance.

The hundred years following the battle at Stiklestad can rightly be termed "the Century of Peace". Peace reigned in the country until after King Sigurd Jorsalfar's death in 1130. The country entered into a period of growth and prosperity,and the first cities were founded.

After the conversion to Christianity, churchmen described the relationship between God and mankind in simple terms. The conflict, they said, was between Satan, who ruled in Hell, and Christ, who was the key to salvation and eternal life with God in Heaven. The Lord Jesus Christ comman-ded an army of angels. One had to choose the right side, where saints now filled the pagan gods' former role as helpers to man. St. Olav took over Thor's role as he who warded off trolls and the power of evil. St. Nicolaus succeeded Frøy as protector of the fertility of nature. His name lives on in the word *nisse*.

KING HARALD HARDRÅDE AND THE STRUGGLE FOR THE THRONE OF ENGLAND

Harald Hardråde was half-brother to St. Olav. At the age of 15 he had fought at Stiklestad and after the defeat there, had fled through Sweden and Gardarike to Constantinople. There he entered the service of the Byzantine emperor, whose Life Guard was made up of Scandinavian warriors. Harald fought in Sicily and Bulgaria, earned the rank of colonel and gathered great wealth which he took with him on his return to Norway. He became co-king with Magnus in 1046. When his nephew died the following year, he was chosen to be king.

After King Edward of England died in 1066, he was succeeded by the English earl, Harold Godwinson, who was promptly crowned at Westminster. Tostig, a brother of the new king, became jealous. He therefore sent a message to King Harald Hardråde in Norway, offering to support him as king of England. Harald leapt at the chance. He made claim to England's throne, set up an army and invaded the country by way of Northumbria. His venture was short-lived. On 25 September, while fighting in battle at Stamford Bridge outside York, he was struck down by an arrow shot from Harold Godwinson's army.

William, duke of Normandy, descendant of Rollo the Viking, had better luck. On 14 October he defeated Harold Godwinson at the Battle of Hastings and won the throne of England. This segment of the famous Bayeux Tapestry, which was worked in memory of the Duke's victory, shows the death of Harold Godwinson at the hands of the Norman cavalry.

Old customs lived on in new forms. The festivities at *jól*, at the time of the winter solstice continued, but now peasants drank to Christ and the Virgin. Christianity took over the functions previously filled by the clans and the heathen gods. Divine services replaced sacrificial rituals, and although people understood but little of what took place in the churches, the mysterious ceremony seemed attractive, with its Latin preachings, beautiful pictures and exotic odours. Each one had acquired a new fellowship – the Christian.

By studying lawmaking, we can see that the new teachings influenced community life.

Relationships between men and women are one example. Sexual morality had to be improved. The laws regarding the Church forbade sexual relations on about half the days of the year. Before Christianity had been introduced, married noblemen had kept concubines, called *friller*. Because the Church wished to end this practice, priests proclaimed the sacred nature of marriage established by God. But the Church opposed the woman's age-old right to divorce if her husband mistreated her. Man was not to dissolve that which God had joined together. Women also lost the right to be priestesses which they had enjoyed in pre-Christian times.

The King was head of the Norwegian Church in this Century of Peace. It was not until 1152 that Norway became a separate archdiocese with an archbishopric at Nidaros. The Church needed the authority of the king to ensure the country's final conversion to Christianity. The king for his part availed himself of the well-organized administrative system of the Church. In addition, there was no disadvantage in the Church declaring that the king had been given his power by God. Common people, too, gradually found a place in this new organization. When a priest was to be appointed, yeomen proposed a candidate to the bishop who usually followed their advice. The yeomen themselves paid the priests and had a common responsibility in the maintenance of the parish church. In this way the Norwegian

Top, right:
This crucifix from Horg Church, North Trøndelag county, depicts Christ as a victorious king.

The Virgin Mary, Queen of Heaven, was regarded as the most powerful of the saints. Wooden sculpture from Enebakk Church, Akershus county.

Church grew to be not only the church of the king, but also of the people during the Century of Peace. Norwegian noblemen and peasants built more than 800 churches during the Middle Ages, most of which were stave churches of wood.

By the mid-12th century the power of the king and the authority of the Church were undisputed. But when king and Church advanced their demands and regulations, someone had to pay. It is against this background that developments in peasant society during the Middle Ages must be regarded.

Peasant Society in the Early Middles Ages

Between the years 1000 and 1300, the population of Norway increased from 150,000 to about 400,000, necessitating new land being brought under the plow all over the country. Som 5000 farms were cleared in eastern Norway as is shown by the large number of farmnames ending in *-rud* (clearing). The population rise also led to the partitioning of farms. This was particularly the case in western Norway where little arable land was available.

During the Viking Age, independent yeomen had owned their own land, but 300 years later much of this land had changed ownership. A majority of the yeomen had become tenants under king, church or nobility, who owned about 70 per cent of the land between them. Potent forces had led to this change in ownership. When Norway was unified, the kings had confi-scated the land of anyone defying them. The kings also claimed ownership rights to any untitled lands, which automatically led to all who cleared new lands becoming tenants of the Crown. The pressure of a growing population increased during the 12th and 13th centuries. If crops failed, yeomen were forced to borrow from the king, the church or a nobleman in order to support their families through the winter. If they could not repay their debts, their creditor acquired ownership rights to all or part of the farm. The yeomen continued to work the land, but now as tenant. It also became customary for king and noble, and sometimes common peasants as well, to donate land to the Church,so that the priests would pray for them. Such spiritual gifts led to the church becoming Norway's largest landowner.

Norwegian peasants still had a freer position than peasants living on large estates elsewhere in Europe. Norwegian landowners owned individual farms only often lying miles from each other, or they might own smaller portions in such farms. The country was large and roads few, so that farm families did not see their landlords often. Norwegian peasants were legally free throughout the Middle Ages. A peasant was never looked down upon because he was a tenant. Indeed, many such tenant peasant who worked farms in good agricultural districts could become more prosperous than their fellows on freehold land. In addition, a great many peasants were both tenant and freeholder at one and the same time, in that the peasant himself together with some other peasants, and even the Crown or Church, could own shares in the farm.

The toil of the farming families provided a living for the upper classes. Landlords insisted on receiving rents, the Crown demanded payment of taxes and the Church received its tithes. Peasants were responsible for maintaining the churches and for providing transport for the king's men on their way through the district. Both Crown and Church levied fines on those who broke the laws.

The result was that the average peasant in the 13th century had to make over about 20 per cent of his farm produce to King, Church and nobleman.

The Civil War Period 1130-1217

Shortly after 1120 an Irishman called Gilchrist ("Christ's servant") arrived in Norway, claiming to be the son of King Magnus Berrføtt and demanding to be named king. To prove his claim, he walked barefoot over nine red-hot ploughshares and, according to the sagas, his feet appeared completely uninjured three days later. Sigurd Jorsalfar was king at this time. He accepted the result of this trial as God's judgement in the case, while Gilchrist on his part promised not to press his claim to the throne until after both Sigurd and his son, Magnus, were dead. This promise proved of little value. After Sigurd's death in 1130, Magnus and Gilchrist, who now called himself Harald Gille, were acclaimed joint kings. Harald went so far as to have Magnus maimed and killed, but was himself later murdered by yet another pretender. Norway now entered into a period of civil war. We must not, however, dramatize the effect of civil warfare in this century. There were long periods of peace, as shown in the marked increase both in population, in clearance of new land, and in revenues to Crown and Church.

The system of royal succession was one reason for the outbreak of civil warfare in Norway. Every son of the king, whether legitimate or illegitimate, had equal rights to the throne. They ruled together in a kind of "joint monarchy". Thanks mostly to kind fate, inner strife had not broken out in Norway during the Century of Peace. But in the years following 1130, many of the pretenders were mere children. Each was supported by powerful noblemen from different areas of the country, who were equally interested in promoting their own interests. This was another important reason for civil warfare.

The power of the church increased during this period of extreme unrest. Demands had arisen for freeing the church from worldly control – *libertas ecclesiae* - and had also reached Norway.

Several of the Edda poems relate of the Germanic mythic hero Sigurd Fåvnesbane (Siegfried), who killed the dragon, Fåvne. This portal from Hylestad Stave Church in Setesdal, carved in about the year 1200, depicts several scenes from the saga. This is one showing Sigurd and his step-father forging the sword.

Far right: The Blaker chair from Lom in Gudbrands-dalen, dated to about 1200.

This reform movement had started in the priory of Cluny in France, and was based on the assumption that the state could neither act in the best interests of the Church nor ensure peace in society. This could only happen when the Church freed itself and managed its own affairs. Pope Gregory VII (1053-1085) was the powerful leader of the movement. He maintained that the Church ranked superior to kings and princes, because even they could be threatened with excommunication, expelling them from the communion of the Church.

With the establishment of the archbishopric at Nidaros in 1152, the Norwegian Church gained a strong leadership of its own. Under Archbishop Øystein (1161-1188), attempts were made to create a monarchy that could be influenced and controlled by the Church. The Archbishop chose to support Lord Erling Skakke from western Norway, whose wife, Kristin, was a daughter

of King Sigurd Jorsalfar. Their son, Magnus, was a legitimate child of this marriage. Magnus had no real claim to the throne, not being a direct male descendant of a king, but because he was legitimate, the Church wished to see him as king. Erling himself was respected among churchmen because he had taken part in a crusade to the Holy Land as a young man, in the company of the Earl of Orkney. He got his by-name "Skakke" ("Crooked") from a wound to the neck suffered while fighting the Arabians in Sicily.

Erling Skakke, who saw the possibilities for his own personal political gain, defeated the other pretenders. In 1163 the Archbishop anointed and crowned seven-year-old Magnus as King of Norway. At the same time, a law was passed prohibiting joint monarchy and reserving the right to the throne to the king's eldest legitimate son. 60 yeomen from all over the country were to choose the king, but their choice could be rejected by the bishops if they found the man chosen to be unsuitable as king. The events of 1163 were a victory for the Church and for Erling Skakke.

Erling and Magnus were not left in peace, however. They were engaged in constant warfare with rival pretenders. In 1176 a man called Sverre arrived in Norway. He had grown up in the Faroes and had been trained for the priesthood. He claimed to be of royal blood. Most historians agree that this could not have been true, but that he could have believed it himself. Sverre became the leader of a group of rebels called the *Birkebeinere* («Birch-legs»). This nickname came of their being so poor that they could not afford proper footwear, but had to wear shoes made of birch-bark.

Sverre and his followers were supported by many of Erling Skakke's enemies. In 1179, Erling was killed in battle and five years later King Magnus lost his life the same way. Sverre was not yet ruler of the country, however, meeting especially strong opposition from the Church. In 1190 the Church and a number of noblemen banded together as the *Bagler party* (of the Old Norse word for bishop's croisier: bagall). There were two main reasons for Sverre's conflict the Church. In the first place he challenged the monarchy of the crowned and anointed Magnus Erlingsson, and in the second an acceptance of Sverre would destroy the agreement reached in 1163. But Sverre's struggle with the Church must be seen in a larger perspective. The reform demands for more freedom for the Church was a source of struggle between the sacred and the worldly powers in several European countries. Sverre's conflict in Norway was one of many such examples in Europe of kings fighting to maintain and to regain their influence over the Church.

During the winter of 1202 Sverre lay on his deathbed in Bergen. The Bagler Party controlled most of the coast of northwestern Norway, the bishops had fled the country and the King himself had been excommunicated. That is why Sverre advised his son, Håkon, to try to reach an agreement with the Church when he became king. Håkon followed this advice and a gradual rapprochement was established between Sverre's descendants and the Church. Nonetheless, one king from the Birkebeiner group and one from the Bagler Party each ruled a part of the country until 1217, when both died. Now 13-year-old Håkon Håkonsson was chosen as king. His mother, Inga of Varteig, had attested to his being Sverre's illegitimate grandson. The following year she bore red-hot iron seven paces to prove her son's royal blood. She, too, had God on her side, as had Gilchrist a century earlier. Young Håkon ruled alone.

The Age of Norwegian Greatness

Thirty years were to pass before the Pope blessed this illegitimate king, and even then the price was high. After being granted a large sum of money, the Pope disregarded Håkon's illegitimacy and in addition agreed to recognize the king's descendants as rightful heirs to the throne. The hereditary monarchy of Norway was secured.

In June of 1247, the papal legate, Cardinal William of Sabina arrived in Bergen for Håkon's coronation. This took place in Christ Church on 29 July, the anniversary of St. Olav's death. The procession was led by 80 hird-soldiers, followed by the King, the Royal Family and the country's foremost noblemen. Cardinal William's reception of the King at the church door was witnessed by crowds of peasants and townspeople in the churchyard. Then as now, it often rains in Bergen and to protect the prominent guests, a pavilion-roof of red and green cloth was stretched between the palace and the church. After the ceremony was finished, 500 of the guests retired to a huge boathouse to dine. Tents had been set up for the remainder of the guests. The Royal Family, the clergy and the hird-soldiers were seated according to their rank. As the meal ended, Cardinal William held the following speech of thanks:

"Thanks be to God Almighty, and thank Him, too, that I did not turn back as I was advised. It was said that I would here meet a multitude, and that all I met would behave more like animals than like men, but all have conducted themselves most courteously. Many foreigners are here also, and more ships than I have seen in any other harbour, all loaded with fine goods. Men frightened me by saying I would receive but little food here, and that little would be vile, and that no drink other than watered milk would be offered me. But praise God for showing me all manner of fine goods here, such as are better to own than to want."

The Cardinal probably exaggerated somewhat, but the coronation shows that Håkon Håkonsson did pattern his court on foreign examples and that the ceremonies and festivities also conformed to European custom. Labelling the 13th century an "Age of Greatness" may be a form for nationalistic vanity, since the country was almost entirely a rural society and the Norwegian state a poor one compared to most others. Nevertheless, the 13th century was the age in which Norway took its place among the kingdoms of Europe.

In this period, the kings of Norway ruled over more territory than ever before, to the extent that one usually speaks of a Nor-

wegian empire (*Norgesvelde*) in the 13th century. England was the main commercial partner, and Norwegian long-ships sailed to English ports loaded with salt herring, dried cod and timber. The most important return cargo was grain, but woolen cloth, weapons and luxury goods were also imported.

Commercial activity in the 13th century led to a strengthening of cultural influences from the West and the South. Norwegian craftsmen learned to build churches in England and France, while castles built in this period were modelled after the French. Akershus Castle in Oslo and Vardøhus Castle in Finnmark county are typical examples. French romances and tales from the Orient were read aloud at the Norwegian court, gradually spreading more widely. Such foreign examples intermixed with the native Norwegian, resulting in a specifically Norse folklore. People sang and danced to such folk-songs, while folk-tales were passed on from generation to generation in the centuries that followed. Great authors also arose in other parts of the empire. The most famous was the Icelander, Snorre Sturlason, who wrote the sagas of the Norwegian kings up to and including King Sverre. This monumental work is our primary source of knowledge concerning older Norwegian history.

Towards the end of the 13th century the Germans became Norway's most important commercial partner. Due to a rapid increase in population, the country had an insufficient supply of grain. The German cities on the Baltic Sea had ample quantities, however, and the ships of the Hanseatic merchants proved to be better-suited for the transport of grain than the old Norwegian long-ships. In the 14th century the King was forced to grant Lübeck and Bremen and other cities of the Hanseatic League higher privileges than those enjoyed by Norwegian tradesmen. A special community of German merchants and craftsmen grew up in Bergen, the most important city during the Age of Greatness.

The royal governing system in Late Medieval Norway made the country into what can be called a *state*. The king built up a country-wide governing system both locally and nationally. The country was divided into 50 *sysler*, or districts, where royal *sysselmenn*, or bailiffs, collected revenues, led the defence system and enforced law and order. Ten court districts were established, each with

its *lagmann*, or judge, while meetings of the *lagting* (assembly) were held each year. In the 1270s King Magnus Lagabøte (Lawmender) created a new legal system for the whole country based on the old district laws. This *Law of the Land* was submitted for approval at each annual lagting-meeting. This indicates that the King still showed some consideration for the yeomen at the *tings*, but that judicial powers in reality were now under royal control. The king appointed the lagmen, who became the real judges. The king reigned supreme, but could not make all decisions alone. In order to ensure that these decisions would indeed be carried out, and also because he needed advice, he conferred with the lords and the bishops. From the 1280s on, these "good men and true" functioned as a permanent royal council. One must not forget that the yeomen were the backbone of the Norwegian Mediaeval state. Without their support, the king would have been unable to rule effectively. In addtion to paying goods and money to the king, yeomen had wide-spread duties in the local community.

The old Norwegian state had a weak foundation, however. Håkon Håkonsson's

Nidaros Cathedral in Trondheim is the largest mediaeval building in Scandinavia, and built according to western European style. The cathedral was built on the remains of King Olav Kyrre's Christ Church, c. 1075. Construction started shortly after the archbishopric was established in 1152. The illustration shows the west wall of the building as it appears in our day.

Opposite:
Håkon Håkonsson was crowned in Christ Church in Bergen on 29 July 1247 by Cardinal William of Sabina, and witnessed by the country's foremost religious and secular leaders. Watercolour by Gerhard Munthe from 1910.

Law of Succession of 1260 decreed that the king's eldest legitimate son was to inherit the throne after his father. Håkon V Magnusson, who reigned at the beginning of the 14th century, had no sons. His daughter, Ingebjørg, married the Swedish duke Erik of Södermanland. A son, Magnus, was born to this couple. At the deathbed of Håkon V in the spring of 1319, the most prominent men in the country swore that no foreigner should ever own castle or fiefdom in Norway, and that the country should remain forever free. The dying king must have had a foreboding of what was to come.

Union and Depopulation in the Later Middle Ages 1319-1537

When Håkon V died, three-year-old Magnus succeeded to the throne of Norway. That same year he was elected King of Sweden, and the two kingdoms were joined in a personal union. In Norway the royal council, now known as the *Council of the Realm*, was to govern together with the Queen Mother, Ingebjørg, until Magnus came of age. Both Magnus and Ingebjørg came into conflict with the council, however. When Ingebjørg attempted to take over the Danish province of Skåne, the council excluded her from the government. Magnus continued Ingebjørg's policies from the time he came of age and until he was deposed in 1343.

The Swedish and the Norwegian councils forced the king to agree to his two sons inheriting one country each as soon as they came of age. The councils tried in this way to repair the damage that had been done by joint rule. But Norway was soon to suffer a greater disaster. The plague came to the country, according to the Icelandic chronicles on board an English ship that reached Bergen in the summer of 1349. Other parts of Norway were hit at about the same time, while newer research indicates that Oslo's inhabitants probably had been struck by the plague during the previous autumn. This was carried to the town by a ship from England or Germany.

The infection spread rapidly. During the autumn and winter of 1349-50, one-third of the population was wiped out by the Black Death. Other and lesser epidemics struck the country in the following decades, so that by 1400 the population had been halved compared to that of the Age of Greatness.

The catastrophic plagues led to an improvement for ordinary people. After 1350, peasant families who had survived could take over the best farms. Whole districts had been laid waste, and people moved in from the smaller farms. It was not until 1500 that these deserted farms were reclaimed, and the memories of the crisis are still retained in family names such as *Ødegård* and *Aunli* (both mean "deserted farm»). Land rentals also became cheaper, and peasants paid less in taxes and tithes. In 1500 taxation revenues were half of what they had been in the Age of Greatness. The lack of manpower resulted in many farms changing from grain production to cattle farming, leading to people eating more protein-rich food than before.

The State fared less well. The loss in revenues weakened the power of the king, while peasants in many rural districts took on added responsibilities. One example is the legal system. The old district assembly, where peasants themselves passed judgement in private court cases, flourished once more.

The nobility was also weakened. The lesser nobility sank down into the ranks of the yeomanry because the land they owned produced less income. The higher nobility, who held the King's fief, managed better and a weakened royal power gave these lords more room for manoeuvring. The *sysler*, or districts, of Medieval times began being called *len*, or fiefs. The cornerstone of the system that now evolved were the royal castles ruled by a noble *lensherre*. This nobleman ruled in the name of the king in the larger areas, called *hoved-*

len, adjacent to the castle. Compared to the nobility in the neighboring countries, however, Norwegian lords were few and far from wealthy. Swedes and Danes soon began marrying into the Norwegian aristocracy.

The Church managed fairly well. Even though its incomes were reduced, it remained the country's largest landowner. In the late Middles Ages people feared death more than ever and donated land to the Church in an attempt to save their souls. The Archbishop of Nidaros became Norway's most powerful man and the undisputed leader of the council. Most of his tithes were paid in dried cod, which he sold to the Hanseatic merchants in Bergen.

Norway was inferior to Sweden and Denmark, whose populations were larger and amount of arable land far more extensive. The Swedish and Danish nobility could exert pressure on their peasants harder to compensate for loss in incomes. When the Hanseatic League gained control of Norwegian foreign trade during the 14th and 15th centuries, this German economic and political expansion caused growing concern in Scandinavia. This is the background against which we must see the Union of Kalmar (1389-1521).

In 1343 the Norwegian council chose Magnus Eriksson's younger son, Håkon, as king, thus bringing the personal union with Sweden to an end. King Håkon VI married Margrete, daughter of King Valdemar Atterdag of Denmark. This marriage alliance created antagonism in Sweden. The Swedish council deposed Magnus Eriksson and chose Albrecht of Mecklenburg as king. This began the struggle between two dynasties for power in Scandinavia.

Håkon VI and Margrete had a son, Olav, who was elected king of Denmark when Valdemar Atterdag died in 1375. Olav also inherited the Norwegian throne at his father's death in 1380, signalling the start of the long period of union between Denmark and Norway which was to last until 1814.

When Olav IV died in 1387, Margrete managed to have her young relative, Eric of Pomerania, elected king of both Norway and Denmark. After Sweden was attacked and vanquished, she had King Albrecht deposed and in 1397 the union between the three Scandinavian kingdoms was ratified in the town of Kalmar. Here Eric of Pomerania was crowned King of Scandinavia, but it was Margrete's firm hand which ruled the three countries.

Her policies were intended to strengthen royal power and to weaken the councils. Sweden and Norway were to be subordinate to Denmark. Full sessions of the council were no longer called in Norway and the Great Seal – symbol of sovereignty – was carried off to Copenhagen, residence city of the king of the union. The queen's supporters received fiefs and bishoprics in Norway. Eric of Pomerania continued Margrete's anti-German policies, resulting in warfare with both German princes and the Hanseatic League. Bergen was attacked and plundered, and German ships, *koggs*, destroyed the Norwegian defence fleet. German blockades and heavy taxation affected Norway deeply. Swedish and Norwegian peasants, and while the Swedish nobility used this opportunity to withdraw their country from the union, the Norwegian council proved too weak for such action. It was impossible to recreate a separate Norwegian kingdom.

Hamburg's harbour pulsed with life in the late Middle Ages. The illustration shows Hanseatic ships, *koggs*, which were excellent vessels for trading and for war. Illumination from a German manuscript dated to 1494.

In 1507 or 1509, Duke Christian, the later Christian II, visited Bergen. He fell in love with a beautiful Dutch girl, Dyveke, whose mother, Sigbrit Willums, kept a tavern in town. Dyveke became his mistress, and the duke had a house built for mother and daughter in Oslo. When he became king in 1513, he brought them to Copenhagen. Here Dyveke died suddenly in 1517, and rumours spread that she had been poisoned. There were many who disliked the king having a mistress in addition to his young queen. Portrait by Wilhelm Rosenstand, 1885.

Christian II became King of Denmark and Norway in 1513. The Norwegian council was set aside, the king gave fiefs to his untitled supporters, while his private secretary became the Archbishop of Nidaros. Christian tried to restore the Union of Kalmar, but his conquest of Sweden proved to be the beginning of the end. After his coronation in Stockholm, he had 82 noblemen and clergy murdered in a move to spread general fear. At this, both Danish and Swedish noblemen rose against "Christian the Tyrant», and in 1523 he fled to the Netherlands.

Norway took no part in this struggle. But now a powerful politician, Olav Engelbrektsson, became archbishop in Nidaros. Martin Luther's teachings were well-known in Denmark and the archbishop realized that they soon might pose a threat to the Catholic Church of Norway. As leader of the council, he made every effort to keep the country free of "Lutheran poison›, but with little success. An alliance with the German kaiser and the exiled Christian II having failed, the Archbishop's uprising ended in total defeat. In 1537 King Christian III's forces reached Norway. The newly elected king was a Lutheran who had introduced the Reformation in Denmark the previous year. He now laid claim to the Norwegian throne.

The Norwegian Kingdom founders

On Easter Sunday, 1 April 1537, Olav Engebrektsson sailed out along the Trondheim fjord bound for the Netherlands. Norway's last archbishop had lost the struggle for the Catholic Church and for the independence of the Norwegian state. He must have reminisced as he watched the mainland vanish on the horizon. What had gone wrong? The plague and the loss of population had been a disaster for both church and state, while Sweden and Denmark had been far stronger in the period of the union. His most bitter thoughts may well have been of Christian III's deceit. The king had betrayed the true faith, so that he, Primate of the Church and head of the council had to flee the country. The joyous tidings of Easter could hardly have lessened Olav's dejection. And when Olav died in the Netherlands the following year, Christian III gained firm control of both realm and church, a control which his descendants were to retain for 280 years.

On 3 February 1388, Queen Margrete was chosen by a combined meeting of the Council and the nobility as "Norway's mighty Lady and lawful Master". She was to govern "to the end of her days», while the right to Norway's throne would emanate from her. These decisions set the law of royal succession aside, leading King Albrecht of Mecklenburg to call her, contemptuously, «King Trouserless". The illustration is of Queen Margrete's sarcophagus in Roskilde Cathedral in Denmark.

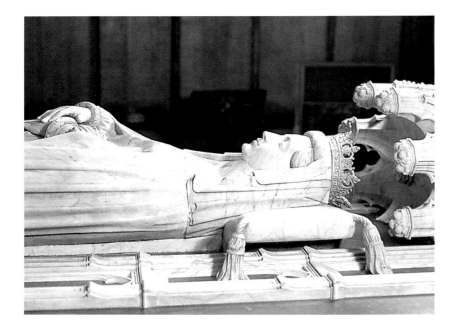

ITALIANS IN THE FAR NORTH

In 1432 a Venetian merchant ship was wrecked during a violent storm in the Atlantic. Eleven of the crew of 68 managed to get a lifeboat ashore on uninhabited Sand Island, outermost in the Lofoten Islands. After a few days they were found by fishermen from nearby Røst, who shared food and housing with them over the winter. In May, when the fishermen sailed their cargoes of dried cod to Bergen, their Italian guests went with them. Their leader, nobleman Pietro Querini, later wrote a report about the crew's experiences in the Far North. This is one of our very few primary sources concerning ordinary people's lives in the remote areas of Medieval Norway.

«There were 120 souls living on the island, and at Easter 72 received communion and thereby professed themselves as being pious and faithful Catholics. They have nought but fish with which to nourish themselves, for nothing can be cultivated in this remote region [...]. In the length of a year they fish endless quantities of fish, and of these two kinds only. The one [...] is named 'stockfish' [cod] and the other 'flounder' [halibut]. The stockfish are exposed to sun and wind without being salted, and because these fish have but little fatty fluid, they become as hard as wood. When they wish to eat thereof, they beat it with an axe-back, and make it sinewed, after which butter and herbs are added to give taste. These are goods for trade of infinite worth in the sea of Germany

[...]. In May they leave the island in a fairly large boat of fifty tonnes, and loaded with fish they sail to a place in Norway of more than a thousand miles distance called Bergen. There other ships of three hundred to three hundred fifty tonnes also arrive from many places, loaded with wares of all types such as are made in Germany, England, Scotland and Prussia, all that is needed to live and to clothe oneself. And those who come with fish (and this is a numberless quantity of ships), barter these for wares they need [...]. The men of these islands are the most honourable of men, and of pleasing countenance, as are their women. So innocent are they that they never lock a door, nor do they guard their women. And this was easily seen, for in the same room that man, wife and child lay to sleep, there abided we also, and in our presence they undressed themselves to lay naked in their beds [...]. Their dwellings are round and made of wood, with only one opening for light and that high in the middle of the roof. The cold of winter is so intense that they cover the opening with great fish-skins, that are prepared so as to allow much light to pass. They wear thick woolen clothes from London and other places, and use but little furs. To accustom small children to the cold and make them better able to endure it, they take their new-born babes when but four days of age and lay them naked under the opening, remove the fish-skin and let the snow fall upon them.»

The Middle Ages

GRØNLAND 1261 - 1814

After the fall of the saintly King Olav in 1030, the Norwegian population increased, reaching about 400,000 in the mid-1300s. The king gained control of the whole country in the eleventh century and the first towns appeared. Norway was converted to Christianity and controlled by the Church, the king and the over-lords. There was widespread unrest in the twelfth century and the period from 1130 to 1217 is known as the Civil War Period. Pretenders to the throne fought to win the kingdom. The thirteenth century is often called the «Golden Age». At this time the King of Norway controlled more territory than in any other period. In 1349 the country was ravaged by a plague known as the «Black Death» and about one third of the population died.

In this drawing by Erik Weren-skiold we see bishops and over-lords paying homage to Magnus Erlingsson after his coronation in 1163. This was the first coronation in Scandinavia.

The child-king Magnus needed the support of the Church because he was not a king's son. He was killed by Sverre Sigurdsson, another pretender to the throne, when he was only twenty-seven years old.

The Baldishol tapestry from Nes in Hedmark county may have been woven as early as the 13th century. The knight with his lance and shield is thought to symbolise the month of May. Although knights such as this were common in the rest of Europe, there were few of them in Norway.

Gol Stave Church, dating from the thirteenth century, is one of approximately 800 wooden churches that were built by farmers in the Middle Ages. Today it stands in the Norwegian Folk Museum in Oslo.

This drawing shows life on a farm in the Middle Ages. The farmers had to give one fifth of their production to the king, the Church and the overlords. The Church owned about 40 percent of the land and was the biggest landowner in the country.

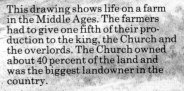

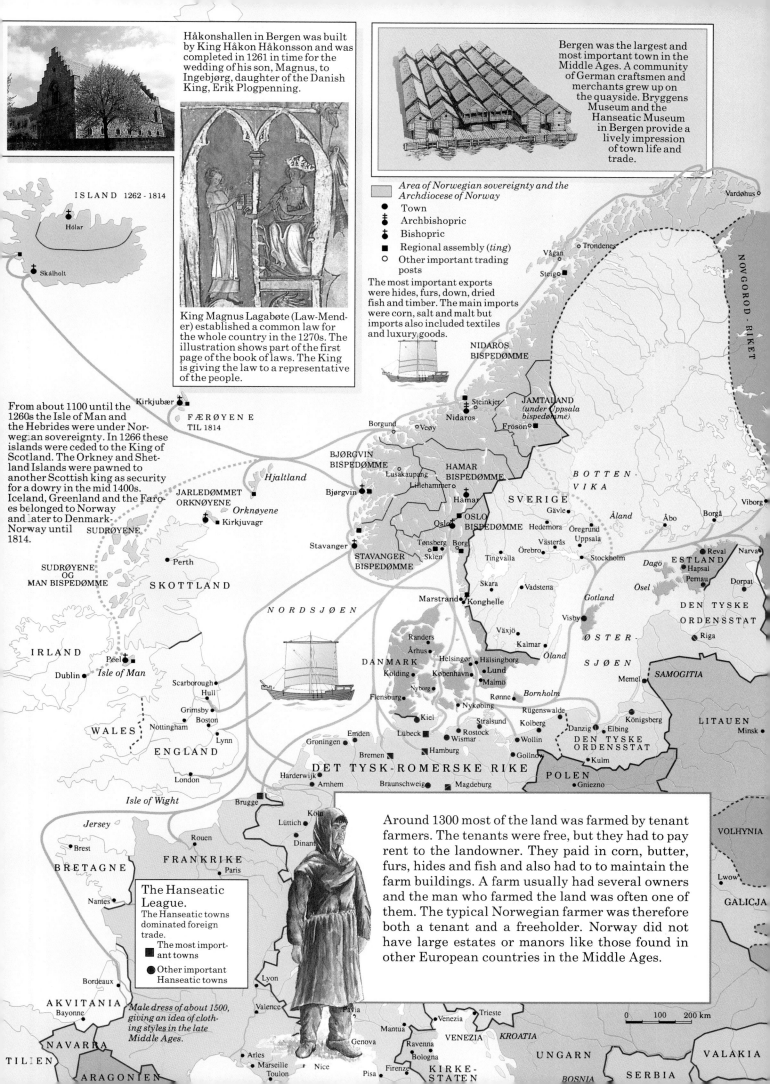

Håkonshallen in Bergen was built by King Håkon Håkonsson and was completed in 1261 in time for the wedding of his son, Magnus, to Ingebjørg, daughter of the Danish King, Erik Plogpenning.

Bergen was the largest and most important town in the Middle Ages. A community of German craftsmen and merchants grew up on the quayside. Bryggens Museum and the Hanseatic Museum in Bergen provide a lively impression of town life and trade.

Area of Norwegian sovereignty and the Archdiocese of Norway
● Town
‡ Archbishopric
† Bishopric
■ Regional assembly (ting)
○ Other important trading posts

The most important exports were hides, furs, down, dried fish and timber. The main imports were corn, salt and malt but imports also included textiles and luxury goods.

King Magnus Lagabøte (Law-Mender) established a common law for the whole country in the 1270s. The illustration shows part of the first page of the book of laws. The King is giving the law to a representative of the people.

From about 1100 until the 1260s the Isle of Man and the Hebrides were under Norwegian sovereignty. In 1266 these islands were ceded to the King of Scotland. The Orkney and Shetland Islands were pawned to another Scottish king as security for a dowry in the mid 1400s. Iceland, Greenland and the Faroes belonged to Norway and later to Denmark-Norway until 1814.

ISLAND 1262 - 1814
Hólar
Skálholt

FÆRØYENE TIL 1814
Kirkjubær
Hjaltland

JARLEDØMMET ORKNØYENE
Orknøyene
Kirkjuvagr
SUDRØYENE

SUDRØYENE OG MAN BISPEDØMME
Peel
Isle of Man
Dublin
IRLAND
SKOTTLAND
Perth

NORDSJØEN

NIDAROS BISPEDØMME
Vardøhus
NOVGOROD · RIKET
Vågan
Trondenes
Steigo
Steinkjer
Nidaros
Borgund
Veøy
JAMTALAND (under Uppsala bispedømme)
Frösön

BOTTEN-VIKA

BJØRGVIN BISPEDØMME
Bjørgvin
Lusakaupang
Lillehammer
Hamar
HAMAR BISPEDØMME
SVERIGE
Gävle
Åland
Åbo
Viborg
Borgå

OSLO BISPEDØMME
Oslo
Hedemora
Öregrund
Uppsala
Västerås
Örebro
Stockholm
Tønsberg
Borg
Skien

STAVANGER BISPEDØMME
Stavanger

Tingvalla
Dagö
Reval
Narva
ESTLAND
Hapsal
Pernau
Ösel
Dorpat

Skara
Vadstena
Gotland
Visby

DEN TYSKE ORDENSSTAT
Riga

ØSTER-SJØEN

Marstrand
Konghelle
Växjö
Kalmar
Öland

Memel
SAMOGITIA

DANMARK
Randers
Århus
Helsingør
Hälsingborg
Kolding
København
Lund
Malmö
Nyborg
Rønne
Bornholm
Flensburg
Nykøbing
Rügenswalde
Kolberg
Königsberg
LITAUEN
Minsk

Kiel
Stralsund
Kolberg
Danzig
Elbing
DEN TYSKE ORDENSSTAT

Emden
Lübeck
Rostock
Wismar
Wollin
Groningen
Bremen
Hamburg
Gollnow

Harderwijk
Arnhem
DET TYSK-ROMERSKE RIKE
Braunschweig
Magdeburg
POLEN
Kulm
Gniezno

SKOTTLAND
Scarborough
Hull
Grimsby
Boston
Nottingham
Lynn
WALES
ENGLAND
London
Isle of Wight

Brugge
Köln
Lüttich
Dinant

VOLHYNIA

Jersey
Brest
Rouen
FRANKRIKE
Paris

BRETAGNE
Nantes

Lwow
GALICJA

The Hanseatic League.
The Hanseatic towns dominated foreign trade.
■ The most important towns
● Other important Hanseatic towns

Male dress of about 1500, giving an idea of clothing styles in the late Middle Ages.

Around 1300 most of the land was farmed by tenant farmers. The tenants were free, but they had to pay rent to the landowner. They paid in corn, butter, furs, hides and fish and also had to to maintain the farm buildings. A farm usually had several owners and the man who farmed the land was often one of them. The typical Norwegian farmer was therefore both a tenant and a freeholder. Norway did not have large estates or manors like those found in other European countries in the Middle Ages.

AKVITANIA
Bordeaux
Bayonne

Lyon
Valence
Arles
Marseille
Toulon
Nice
Pavia
Mantua
Genova
Pisa
Firenze
Bologna
Ravenna
Venezia
Trieste
VENEZIA
KROATIA
KIRKE-STATEN
BOSNIA
SERBIA
UNGARN
VALAKIA
NAVARRA
TILIEN
ARAGONIEN

0   100   200 km

Norway in Union with Denmark 1537-1814

"Under Denmark's crown for evermore"

Norway's fate was formally sealed in 1536. In the autumn of that year, Duke Christian with his army of mercenaries had conquered Denmark and, as Christian III, had introduced the Reformation. The coronation charter he entered into with the Danish council in order to be elected, stated:

"Because Norway now is much reduced in power and fortune, and the subjects of the realm of Norway no longer are capable of supporting a Ruler and King [...] and because most members of the council of Norway, and most especially Archbishop Olav, twice now have failed to fulfill their obligations towards Denmark, we have therefore sworn and promised Denmark's council and nobles that [...] the realm of Norway hereafter shall be and remain under the crown of Denmark in like manner to the other lands of Jutland, Fyn or Skåne, and hereafter shall neither be nor be called a separate kingdom, but be part of the realm of Denmark and under Denmark's crown for evermore."

After the defeat of the Catholic Church, the few remaining Norwegian noblemen had proven too weak to uphold the country's independence. Hereafter Norway would be governed from Copenhagen where the king and his council of noblemen shared power. When one king died, the council would elect a new monarch, who then automatically

King Christian VI (1699-1746) and his German-born queen, Sofie Magdalene of Kulmbach-Baireuth, together with Crown Prince Frederik and Crown Princess Louise – good representatives of the exalted power of the absolute monarchy in Denmark-Norway. Painted by C.M. Tuscher, German-born portrait painter to the royal court.

became king of Norway. The Norwegian council was to all intents and purposes wiped out.

Norway never became part of Denmark, as had been determined in the coronation charter, because the ties binding people with country were too strong. Even though Danish became the written language, Norwegian dialects and Norwegian customs survived. Norwegians were extremely conscious of being Norwegian, and the kings called themselves King of Denmark *and* Norway. Coins minted in Norway bore the Norwegian coat of arms, and the Danes themselves never had any doubt but that Norway was a separate realm. The article concerning Norway in Christian III's coronation charter was in reality only a paper provision, and the decision itself was never made public. Danish noblemen had little reason for complaint even though the king never put the decision into effect, because they were granted fiefs in Norway which

This reliquary from the Church of St. Thomas on Fillefjell and formed like a church, was probably made in Bergen in the 13th century. St. Thomas' Church was built in the 12th century and dedicated to the English archbishop, Thomas á Becket (1118-70), who was murdered by King Henry II's men in front of the high altar in Canterbury Cathedral. He was canonized in 1173.

Bærum's Works, founded in 1610, was one of the first iron works in Norway. Flames shoot out from the top of the blast furnace hut where ore was smelted. Painted by C.A. Lorentzen in 1790.

brought them sizable revenues. Norway kept its status as a separate realm, and the Norwegian nation lived on. Norway experienced a period of expansion with a rapid increase in population in the centuries that followed. Norwegian products, such as fish, timber and minerals, were in great demand and were exported to many countries. Norway was, however, primarily a country of peasants, and this peasantry existed under difficult circumstances. Their struggle for the daily bread was of far greater concern to them than was the independence of the Norwegian nation.

Norway, the Reformation and the Power of the King 1537-1660

The Reformation strengthened the power of the king. The head of the Church was now the king in Copenhagen instead of the Pope in Rome. Norway had not experienced a Lutheran revival as had Denmark, but Norwegians were given no choice save that of adopting the new faith. It must have seemed strange when saints, relics and monasteries disappeared and Danish became the language of the sermons in the new church services.

It took time to find qualified ministers, however, and many of those chosen in the first decades after the Reformation were ignorant, intemperate and quarrelsome. Nevertheless, the ministers gradually became a useful instrument of the state. They could preach the king's business "to simple, foolish commoners".

The Reformation also had an economic aspect. Prior to 1537, the Catholic Church had been the largest landowner in the country, with over 40 per cent of the land. All this now became the property of the king. The gold and silver treasures of the Church were sent to Copenhagen to be melted down. In 1540, 125 kilos of gold and silver, including St. Olav's reliquary, were shipped from Trondheim to Copenhagen.

The king increased his power in other areas as well. Norway was divided into five main fiefdoms and a number of smaller ones, most of which the king granted to Danish noblemen. At the beginning of this period, the overlord had been responsible for most administrative tasks, but the king gradually increased his power at the expense of the overlords. Historians speak of a transition of government by noblemen to government by royal officials in the century prior to 1660. By the end of the 16th century, the overlords were required to present proper accounts and were in reality put on a fixed salary. The bailiff, who had originally been a personal servant to the overlord, became a royal official. It was the bailiffs who collected taxes and who were responsible for law and order in their districts. Control over those who were in daily contact with his subjects was of paramount importance for the king.

Society became increasingly complex in the century after 1536, with a corresponding need for specialized knowledge. One of the duties of the overlords had been to lead their armies into battle, but starting in the 1620s the king engaged professional officers. In this way regular soldiers came to lead Norwegian peasants. The judiciary system also had need of control and specialized knowledge. District magistrates, who originally had been yeomen's secretaries at the district assemblies, soon became royal judges. With the rise of custom revenues due to the increased export of timber, one more responsibility was taken from the overlords. In 1620 the king organized a separate customs service.

Most important was the king's appointment of a viceroy for Norway as early as in 1572. Being the king's foremost representative, his residence was at Akershus Castle. Even though the viceroy had relatively little power, these appointments showed that the king sought better control over the country, and most importantly, that he regarded Norway as a separate realm. We find, therefore, stronger royal power and an enfeebled nobility in the first half of the 17th century. Christian IV (1588-1648) is regarded by many observers as the most influential of the kings who reigned during the century after the Reformation. He was "the King who discovered Norway". He had great expectations for the resources of Norwegian forests and mountains, visiting the country all of thirty times. The king also entertained hopes for Norway as a military resource. But Christian IV died a broken man, his foreign policy having failed and the crown prince having died a year before his father. The council elected the younger son, Frederik, as king, forcing him to accept a strict coronation charter that guaranteed the power of the council and the privileges of the nobility. But only twelve years later, Frederik III was to win a resounding political victory over both council and nobility. Scandinavian political history can provide an answer as to why Christian was defeated and Frederik succeeded.

The Evangelical Lutheran Church retained only two sacraments, communion and baptism. At the same time, sermons in the native language were made part of the church services, but in Norway ministers preached in Danish. Painting of Torslunde Church in Denmark, dated to 1561.

④ A busy King

Between 1536 and 1814 Denmark-Norway had ten kings called either Christian or Frederik. Only one of them, King Christian IV, is generally remembered today. He reigned for 60 years and stories of his marriages, his women and numerous legitimate and illegitimate children are well known. The King was fond of feasting and drinking, but he also wanted to govern his realm well. He was well-educated and trained to lead from an early age. As King, he was highly interested in everything that went on, both at court and throughout Denmark-Norway.

In Norway the King was primarily known for his interest in developing the country. Christian regarded Norway as a rich country. He brought in iron and mining experts from Germany. There was iron ore in the Norwegian mountains, and possibly copper, silver and gold too! The state could also earn revenues from forestry and fishing. They would be welcome in the struggle against the main enemy, Sweden, since King Christian intended to strengthen the position of Denmark-Norway as a great power in the North.

Christian IV was a warrior king, but he had bad luck in war. At the Peace of Brømsebro in 1645 he had to cede the Norwegian districts of Jemtland and Herjedalen to Sweden. When the King died three years later the country was deeply in debt and Sweden was on the way to becoming the main power in Scandinavia.

Christian IV (1577–1648) became king when he was 11 years old and governed Denmark-Norway from the time he came of age in 1596. This portrait was painted by Peter Isaacz just after the Kalmar War (1611–13), when Christian had experienced some success. The King is wearing the sash of a field marshal.

The King often took part in meetings of the Supreme Court in Denmark and Norway. He was the supreme judge and took his work seriously. He had the common law of Magnus Lagabøte translated from Old Norse to Danish in 1604.
In this drawing by Karel van Mander of 1648 King Christian is seated at the end of the table.

Christian IV visited Norway about 30 times. The map shows some of the places he visited most often. He was particularly interested in mining.

- Vardø (1)
- *Kildin*
- JEMTLAND
- HERJE-DALEN
- IDRE OG SÄRNA
- Bergen (5)
- Akershus (11)
- Kongsberg (3)
- Flekkerøy (6)
- Båhus (6)

In 1599 the King sailed along the Norwegian coast as far as the island of Kildin, now in Russia. He wanted to ensure control of Northern Norway.

700 △ 1000 riksdaler

- ☐ Customs duties
- ▨ New taxes
- ▤ Income from the fiefdoms

600 — 500 — 400 — 300 — 200 — 100 — 0

1600-1620 | 1621-24 | 1625-29 | 1630-40 | 1641-48 | 1649-1656

State revenues from Norway 1600–1656

Norwegian farmers were heavily taxed during the reign of King Christian IV. The King imposed new taxes and they were particularly high when Denmark-Norway was at war, i.e. in 1625–1629 (the Imperial War) and in 1643–1645 (the Torstensson War). Customs duties accounted for an increasingly large proportion of state revenues in Norway and Christian IV employed more customs officers so that collection would be more efficient. Income from the fiefdoms included land rent, ground rent, land taxes, fines and tithes. The statistics are from Øystein Rian, 1984.

In 1623 two goatherds, a boy and a girl, found pure silver in the forest in Sandsvær. Christian IV declared the find to be the property of the King and mining commenced in the autumn. In spring 1624 the King inspected the new mines and founded the mining town of Kongsberg. The King is said to have designed the town plan himself. In the mid-1700s the mine was the biggest employer in Norway, with over 4,000 workers.
This detail from an engraving shows Kongsberg in the 1600s. The silver mine was closed in 1957. Today the Norwegian Mining Museum is located in Kongsberg.

Akershus was the main fortress in Norway. The King had new walls and embankments built and the old castle was modernised. This painting by Jacob Coning dates from 1699.

Christiania in 1645

Bjørvika

Akershus festning

Akersneset

A fire broke out in Oslo on 17 August 1624. After three days there were few buildings left. The King decided to move the town closer to Akershus Castle and he came to Norway to lead the construction work. He named the town Christiania.

The castle would provide protection and brick houses would prevent fire. The map shows that the King wanted a network of straight roads. Christian IV also founded the town of Christiansand in southern Norway in 1641, laid out on a similar pattern.

THE 'WITCH CRAZE' IN NORWAY

The hysterical persecution of witches also spread throughout Norway starting sometime in the mid-1500s. Old Norse laws had imposed the death penalty for 'black' witchcraft, and after the Reformation, the state showed a zealous ability and will to increase punishment for old violations against the laws and to criminalize new ones. The decree issued by King Christian IV in 1671, on "Witches and their fellow Conspirators", was in keeping with the tendencies of the age. The decree prescribed the death penalty for all types of black witchcraft, and also forbade healing, or 'white' witchcraft. Historians believe that this decree accelerated the process of witch-hunting in Norway. Most Norwegian witch trials took place between 1570 and 1670. Experts estimate that approximately 2000 witches were tried during this period. 500 of the accused were put to death. The great majority were impoverished women, most of whom were burned at the stake, often after having undergone illegal torture to make them confess and to denounce others who had entered into a pact with the devil. The law did not allow torture until after judgement had been passed, but in these Norwegian witchcraft trials officials often ignored the rules, to the extent of every fourth accused being illegally tortured. In 1663 a witch-wife in Finnmark county was "torment'd and pinc'd with glowing Tange, and Sulfur put upo' her Broest upo' the Tortur-Benk". Many others had to endure trial by water in order to have their guilt confirmed. The accused was tied up and thrown into the sea. If she floated, she was considered guilty because water had been made holy through Christ's baptism and would reject all things evil. If she sank instead, she was considered innocent.

There were several reasons why women, and especially poor women, were the victims of persecution. The Original Sin had proved women to be more susceptible than men and therefore more likely to enter into a pact with the devil. Women nursed the sick and if they became known as 'wise women' or even healers, they risked quick accusation. If any family lacked food, it was the womenfolk who went out begging. How tempting it must have been to *damn* those who gave nothing, with persecution as a result. It was in closely-knit communities – among "people like us" – that fear of witches was strongest. There were fewer executions resulting from witchtrials after the 1670s. One important reason was that judges in the period of absolute monarchy had stricter requirements as to the evidence presented to the assemblies.

Woman cooking medicines as shown on a 17th-century, stained glass window from Årdal in Sogn.

The Struggle for Power in Scandinavia in the First Half of the 17th century

Early in the 17th century, Denmark-Norway had the upper hand over their arch-rival, Sweden, as a glance at the map clearly shows. The Swedes' only access to the North Sea was in the area around the mouth of the Göta River. The Danish king controlled the Øresund and exacted duties from every passing ship. The so-called "naval stores" from the Baltic states – linen, hemp, tar, pitch and timber – were shipped through this bottleneck overlooked by Kronborg Fortress. The importance of these goods to the naval powers, England and the Netherlands, brought Øresund into political focus. In the far north, however, the borders between states had never been defined. Norwegians, Swedes and Russians all collected taxes from the Sami. Sweden aimed both at gaining control of the North and freeing itself of the the Dano-Norwegian obstruction.

When Christian IV had Magnus Lagabøte's law translated from the Old Norse in 1604, he had changes made concerning defence because the old *leidang*-arrangement no longer was effective enough. The king still retained the right to conscript common people when war threatened, but such soldiers were now required to furnish their own weapons. Each farm was to have a musket with powder and bullets, a sable, and a battle-axe available. Peasants were to assemble for annual inspection and control of both weapons and men by king's officers.

During the Kalmar War (1611-1613), Christian IV tried to halt Swedish advances in the Baltic and in the North. He demanded that Norway raise a conscripted army of 8000 men. This proved a dismal effort. The Danish lords had little experience as military officers, and the peasant soldiers lacked both food and sufficient weapons. They drank, fought and shot wildly about them. Their officers could not prevent mass desertions by peasants who simply left and went back to their farms.

This mass desertion has been forgotten in Norwegian tradition, but the battle of Kringen in Gudbrandsdalen is still remembered. Here a Norwegian peasant army defeated a Scottish mercenary army of some

3-400 men, of whom only 113 survived. Most of these prisoners were massacred the next day. This victory over the Scots, after being somewhat revised in folk tradition over the centuries, has beeen an important element in Norwegian national pride.

The Kalmar War must be said to have ended satisfactorily for Christian IV. The peace treaty stated clearly that the northern coastline between Tysfjord and Varanger was Norwegian. This outcome was influenced both by the victories of the Dano-Norwegian fleet and of the Danish army on Swedish soil. The war also proved one thing about Norway as a military resource: it *was* possible to raise a large peasant army.

Acting against the will of the council, Christian IV entered into the Thirty Years' War (1618-48) in Germany, on the Protestant side. As a German duke he declared war in 1625, but suffered disastrous defeats and only just managed to keep the kingdoms intact when peace was declared four years later. Sweden fared far better, winning great victories on German soil.

SWEDEN AS A GREAT POWER

Duch of Holstein-Gottorp

SWEDISH CONQUESTS

1500-1611

During The Thirty Year's War

From Denmark-Norway 1645-1660

From Denmark-Norway 1658 Returned 1660

▲ Ironworks

■ Copper mines

○ Silver mines

Norwegians were also affected by the war. Over 3000 of them were conscripted to serve in the fleet, while about 350 men were sent to garrison the border forts. In 1628 the king issued a war order for Norway that formed the foundation for the Norwegian army. The country was divided into areas of four farms each, each area being required to provide and equip one soldier. The system would have provided more than 6000 intantry soldiers. Because a peace treaty was signed in 1629, the system was never implemented. Christian IV did not remain passive in the following years. Because of an acute need for increased revenues, he raised the level of the Øresund customs duties. This action, however, led to an alliance between Sweden and the Netherlands in 1640. The fortunes of war had placed Sweden among the great powers of Europe. It was this situation that faced the Danish nobleman, Hannibal Sehested, who came to Norway as viceroy in 1642. He was both son-in-law and confidant to the king and was, despite his mere 34 years, an experienced linguist and diplomat. He had the task of organizing the army according to the order of 1628. In addtition the aristocracy, clergy and burghers were directed to provide 520 armed and mounted cavalry soldiers. He negotiated with the burghers concerning their equiping of *ships of defence,* armed merchant vessels that could be used in battle if necessary. He also arranged for officers and weapons to be brought in from abroad. All this led to even heavier taxes on the peasantry. Never before had the authorities made such demands on them.

Just before Christmas 1643, veteran Swedish troops marched up through Jutland, quickly occupying it. Christian IV gathered his troops to defend the rest of the country. Hannibal Sehested's Norwegian army did not win any decisive victories, but the Norwegian forces' skirmishings in enemy territory near the borders of southern Norway kept Swedish troops busy. At the peace negotiations in 1645, the king was forced to give up the islands of Gotland and Øsel and Jemtland and Herjedalen in Norway, while the Netherlands obtained reductions in the Øresund duties.

The war of revenge conducted by King Frederik III from 1657 to 1660 also proved a catastrophe. Norway lost Båhuslen while Denmark had to give up the provinces east of Øresund. This happened despite considerable Norwegian efforts in which Jemtland was retaken for a time. By 1660 Sweden held an undisputed position as the leading power of Scandinavia.

After the peace of 1660, Denmark-Norway faced an acute financial crisis. The kings had borrowed money for the war from wealthy burghers of Copenhagen, and it was left to Frederik III to resolve the crisis.

Norway and the Absolute Monarchy

The downfall of the council and the aristocracy had been many years in the making. Aristocratic power had gradually weakened during the century following the Reformation, and wars had proved that lords were ill-suited as leaders of troops. It was, however, the financial crisis of 1660 that led to their collapse. At a meeting of the three estates in Copenhagen that autumn, the king joined forces with the Danish bourgeoisie, who thirsted for political power. The nobles now agreed to pay taxes, but to avert attack on other aristocratic privilege, also proposed extensive taxation on the other estates. After dramatic negotiations between the burghers and the clergy on the one hand and the nobility on the other, the king confined the council and nobles in a hostile Copenhagen until they gave up. Frederik III took over the charter that had guaranteed noble privileges, and he and his descendents gained hereditary rights to the throne. The council was dissolved and all power lay in the hands of the king. He had become an absolute monarch.

Norway was not affected by the events of the autumn of 1660 and was not represented at the homage ceremony in Copenhagen in October. A separate homage ceremony was held in Christiania the following year, however, even though the kings had always considered Norway to be a hereditary kingdom. Frederik III was represented by his son, Prince Christian. The fact that 408 of the 543 Norwegian representatives were peasants indicates their strong position as compared to their opposite numbers in Denmark. In Copenhagen only a handful of peasants had participated, and only one of them was allowed to kiss the king's hands.

Both central and local administration were reorganized after 1660. Previously only one administrative office had worked with state affairs. Now a system not unlike present-day ministries was introduced, in which business was divided according to subject matter. These *collegia* also included representatives for the burghers, showing that the nobility had lost their monopoly of power. In addition Frederik III established a new aristocracy of earls and barons. Such titles were granted to members of the old nobility, while burghers whom the king wished to reward were now also elevated to the nobility. Norway had two counties and one barony in the period of absolute monarchy: Jarlsberg and Larvik counties in present-day Vestfold county, and Rosendal barony in Sunnhordland county.

The king also imposed a new administrative system where fiefdoms were replaced by counties administered by a salaried governor. These counties were further divided into bailiwicks. Because the king did not wish these governors to become too powerful, the army was now put in charge of military officials. There were approximately 1600 different public officials in Norway during the period of absolute monarchy, all of them appointed by the king. These included governors, judges, bailiffs, clergymen, officers and customs officials. Local administration was administered by the collegia in Copenhagen, with the king and his advisors at the very top. The capital was far-distant, however, and Norwegian officials often determined the handling and outcome of matters under consideration. Local administrators or even common people in Norway often took the initiative in a great many of these cases.

Peasant Society, Rural Life

Between 1500 and 1600, Norway's population increased from about 150,000 to 900,000, ninety per cent of whom got their livelihood from the land. The population increased because epidemic plagues no longer raged, but mortality was still very high, particularly among small children. As late as in the 18th century, almost a quarter of all infants died in the first year of their lives.

Dwellings were small and humble and even though there were two-storey houses on many farms in southeastern Norway by 1660, the draughty open-hearth cottages typical to the Middle Ages were still the most common. Diet was very simple, and most people's everyday meals consisted of porridges, crisp-bread and meal pancakes. There was no public medical system to cure or prevent illnesses. As a cure for typhus, one clergyman advised eating a mixture of manure and milk. A society of this kind was extremely vulnerable to epidemics and famine, and a bad harvest or bad luck in fishing could have catastrophic results. All families were familiar with death, but in spite of such setbacks, the population continued to rise and by the 18th century a certain over-population became noticeable.

Towards the end of the 17th century, Norwegian peasants became owners of the land they cultivated. When the absolute monarchy was established in 1660, only 20 per cent of the land was owned by peasants, but by 1800 the majority of farm families lived on freehold land. To reduce the state debt after the wars with Sweden, King Frederik III had alloted land to townspeople to whom he owed money. They quickly resold the land to peasants against a mortgage, thus freeing capital for investment in other ventures, such as shipping and mining. The peasants were interested in purchase. Title to the land gave security and the right to cut timber in the farm's forests, raising enough money to pay off the mortgage. It was only in northern Norway that landowners retained title, because hunting and fishing rights followed ownership of the farms.

The increase in population after 1500 led to a need for new means of livelihood. Farms that had been abandoned in the later Middle Ages were now reclaimed. Any farm owning enough land was partitioned. With needs still unsatisfied, a large lower class of *husmenn* (crofters) grew up in rural areas. A crofter family was permitted to clear and rent land on a larger farm. In eastern Norway and in Trøndelag, larger farms often had many crofter farms because so much manpower was needed for work in forests and fields. The whole family participated. Women and children cared for cattle while the crofter himself cut timber. During spring ploughing and sowing, and at haying, harvesting and threshing time, they all worked together. Their limited spare time was used on their own land. With virtually no contracts, crofters' families were at farmers' mercy. Many were turned off because of sickness or

«Rose-painting" is the name given to this decorative country art form, which developed in Hallingdal and in Telemark in the 18th and 19th centuries, but enjoyed popularity in other districts as well. Inspiration came from the work of professional urban artisans, as well as from 15th-century church decorations, when several church interiors were decorated with the acantus boughs and flowers of the Renaissance. Later European styles such as baroque and rococo also became important sources of inspiration for rural artists. Rosepainting was not only used to decorate smaller items, such as drinking cups, bowls and chests, but also whole rooms with walls, ceiling, beds, doors and cabinets. This interior is from Rygi cottage in Telemark, decorated by Ola Hansson in 1782.

old age. There were fewer crofters in western Norway and they enjoyed higher status. Their duties were lighter because the need for their labour was not as great. Many crofters in these districts were fishermen or craftsmen. The number of crofters rose from 17,000 in the 1600s to 48,000 in 1800. There were then just as many crofters as freehold farmers in Norway.

Crofters and their families were not the farmers' only source of cheap labour. Servants were common all over the country. In the mid-18th century, the king commanded that all unemployed people enter into annual service "for meager Wage". This was undoubtedly done to ensure farmers of a stable, year-round labour force, reducing the need to hire expensive help at harvestime. Farm servants were usually young and unmarried. Work on farms gave them necessary experience before marrying and, possibly, taking over a croft.

The farmer and his wife were dependent on each other's efforts for the survival of the family. If one died, this could lead to the children being put out and the farm not being properly run. Re-marriage was therefore common in both farmer and crofter families.

What did the state demand of farmers in the period of absolute monarchy? Naturally enough, they had to pay taxes on the land they farmed. The level of taxation in Norway was low compared to Denmark, however, and although the authorities made repeated attempts to increase tax rates, they were unsuccessful. The Skåne War (1676-79) is a good example. During the preceeding years the whole country had been struck by crop failures and famine. Defence demands had also become more stringent. Now only two farms shared responsibility for equipping a soldier, whereas in 1628 four farms had had that same burden. During this war of revenge, the king's half-brother, viceroy Gyldenløve (1638-1704), had led the Norwegian army to important victories over the Swedes. Denmark-Norway had not won back any territory, but the war proved that the Norwegian army put up as good a show as the fleet or the enlisted troops of Denmark. Now the question of taxation was raised. Could more taxes be squeezed from Norwegian farmers? Gyldenløve thought not. Nothing and no one should be allowed to destroy the morale of this strong army, and the king gave way. A militarily trained population with an

Starting in the 17th century, many Finns immigrated to Norway, settling in Lyngen and Alta in the far north. An important area of Finnish settlement in southern Norway was in Finnskogene, Hedmark county. The illustration shows the Finnish farmyard set up at the Glåmdal Museum in Elverum.

agressive Swedish neighbor had to be taken seriously. The 17th-century tax system remained unchanged until the 1800s. In addition farmers were helped by an inflation which lightened tax burdens. In the late 1700s, Norwegian farmers paid between four and 10 per cent of their gross income in taxes and tithes. French farmers paid between 60 and 70 per cent.

Similar tendencies can be found in other areas as well. The large number of beggars in the 1730s led to more efficient poor relief. The introduction of confirmation in 1736 meant that all children were required to learn to read. Since farmers bore the full economic burden for these reforms, poor relief was of little help to the majority of the poor, while the school system was in a miserable state for the rest of the period of absolute monarchy. The state had few means of exerting pressure on farmers, and the farming community itself was too poor to care for those who most needed help.

Towns and Urban Occupations

Although farming was the livelihood of most of the population, the timber trade, mining, fishing and shipping were also important, providing an essential economic basis for townspeople's business activities.

During the 17th and 18th centuries most European countries conducted a mercantilistic trade policy, and Denmark-Norway was no exception. In order to make the state as powerful and self-sufficient as possible, trade

and business were assisted by restricting imports, imposing protective duties, and encouraging monopolies. Town burghers had a key position in this policy, as indicated by the town charters of 1662 which gave them a monopoly on carrying on business and trades. Towards the end of the period of absolute monarchy this pro-bourgeois mercantilistic policy was modified by the king.

The timber trade grew in importance during the 17th century. Water-powered saw-mills produced boards and planks, the most sought-after wood products in continental Europe. England was the most important market for timber, and exports increased, despite efforts by the authorities at regulation to prevent deforestation. Farmers and crofters earned money by cutting, transporting and selling timber, but it was the upper-class merchant princes who earned the greatest profits. In 1688, the king decreed the closing of a large number of saw-mills, and restricted production at each remaining mill. This was done to raise the price of timber and to prevent deforestation. Farmers were hardest hit by these restrictions, since they owned the small mills most affected by the closure and were now excluded from the most profitable sector of production. By the mid-18th century, the country's upper class consisted of some few timber exporters in those towns where timber was shipped out. Eight timber exporters were among the wealthiest men in Christiania, foremost among them was Bernt Anker (1746-1805). He had interests in iron founderies, mining operations and shipping, and estimated himself that 20,000 people were dependent on his business activities.

A mug of beer hit the spot when sharpening a saw-blade! Stained glass window from 1715.

Mining was another lucrative field for wealthy merchants. In the 16th century Norway had had few mines and works, but Christian IV's active support helped greatly in the next century. Self-sufficiency and ample supplies of precious metals were good, solid mercantilistic policy. With the wars against Sweden having proved so costly, the king relied on the Norwegian mountains. He brought in mining experts from Germany, and by 1660 several mines produced at a profit. The Kongsberg silver mines and the copper mines at Røros are good examples.

When ore was discovered, the king granted exclusive privileges to the mine-owner, including extensive rights over the area within a 40-kilometre radius from the mine. Everything and everyone within this *circumference* was to benefit the mine. Farmers were obliged to produce charcoal, cut wood and transport ores for a mere pittance. Tens of thousands of free farming families thus spent large parts of the year as forced labourers and suppliers. Mine workers' living conditions were also sub-standard, as indicated by infant mortality at the Kongsberg silver mines, where 4200 men were employed in 1769, being by far the highest in the country. Workers' wages were deducted under illness. Child labour was common, with every tenth worker at Kongsberg a boy under age 15 by 1800. Circumference farmers and mine

Damsgård, in Bergen, built in the rococo style in 1770.

workers alike rebelled against oppression and poor living conditions. The uprisings at Røros in the late 17th century and the unrest at Kongsberg in the 1770s are well known. Common grievances were that wages were not paid on time and that poor and expensive foodstuffs were given instead of money.

About two-fifths of the population had fishing as a livelihood in the 17th and 18th centuries. Most fishermen's families also farmed but fishing provided a vital addition to farm incomes, particularly on the west coast, in Trøndelag and above all, in northern Norway. The big seasonal fisheries, such as in Lofoten, provided most of this income. 15,000 men took part in this regional fishery in 1800. Bergen and Trondheim were the main ports exporting fish to central and southern Europe.

The traditional method for preserving cod was by drying it on racks. This was cheap and easily managed by fishermen themselves. Northern Norway had excellent, stable drying conditions. Combined salting and drying became common about 1770, and this method of producing *clipfish* was used farther south in Norway. Cheap salt was readily available from southern Europe, but purchase of large quantities of salt required capital and capital had to be provided by town merchants. The fisherman remained a producer of raw materials.

The "farming fishermen" from northern Norway had a special position. They caught and prepared the fish, and then sailed their catch southwards in open boats. Merchants in Bergen and Trondheim bought the fish, selling fishing equipment, grain and liquor in return. The price of grain rose for each passing year while the price paid for fish remained constant. The well-organized merchants also tricked and cheated fishermen, with stones on the scales and false measurements. Debts incurred were passed on from father to son. Because the authorities were incapable of intervention, the merchants kept their position of power for the entire period of union.

Norwegian shipping grew as a result of increased trade and industrial activity. Appreciable quantities of goods had been exported from Norway since the Middle Ages but most of these had been shipped on foreign ships owned by the Hansa, Dutch, British and Danes. Following good mercantilistic principles, the authorities attempted to stimulate Norwegian shipping in the 17th century. One example is the customs reductions enjoyed by the ships of defence. The English Navigation Act of 1651 closed freight markets between England and Norway with adverse effect. Norwegian ships got their first real chance during the European wars of the late 1600s, and the years between 1690 and 1710 are called the first "Golden Age" of Norwegian shipping. Denmark-Norway had kept neutral, but conditions worsened after King Frederik IV involved the kingdoms in the Great Scandinavian War in 1709. After peace returned in 1720, foreigners again assumed control.

Norwegian shipowners did not get a new chance until the revolutionary wars in the second half of the 18th century. Neutrality was again profitable, and when the Union was drawn into the Napoleonic wars in 1807, Norway had become one of the great shipping nations of Europe. The Norwegian fleet was half again as large as the combined fleets of Denmark and Schleswig-Holstein. 12.000 Norwegians sailed in foreign trades. And once again it was the merchant princes who reaped the profits. Bernt Anker alone owned 27 ships in 1799 and had an annual income of some 100,000 Norwegian *daler*. He was the wealthiest man in Norway.

The growth of towns and of business prosperity were closely interconnected. At that time a town was called a *kjøpstad* (marketplace). In 1660 only eight towns had this status, but by 1800 there were 23 *kjøpsteder* in Norway. The medieval towns were still the most important: Bergen had 14,000 inhabitants in the mid-1700s, and was twice as large as Christiania and Trondheim together.

A town was a complex society with wealthy merchants and public officials at its top. Such grandees lived in great luxury,

Scandinavia's largest wooden building, the Stiftsgård in Trondheim, was built for Cecilia Christine de Scholler in the 1770s. It received its present name when it was bought by the state as a residence for the *stiftamtmann*, or diocesan governor, in 1800. The style of the building is rococo, with traces of the baroque. It has about 70 rooms and a total area of some 1150 m². Since 1906 the building has been one of the royal family's residences.

building magnificent dwellings such as *Stiftsgården* in Trondheim. An English visitor wrote in 1799, "Although built entirely of wood, it is the grandest palace in all Scandinavia". And social life flourished. This same Englishman wrote after a visit to John Collett (1759-1810) at Ullevål Gård in Christiania: "Such was the magnificence of the feast to which we had been invited, that it would hardly be possible for our own Sovereign to afford a more sumptuous entertainment." Public officials were far less wealthy than the merchant class, but their office gave them status and authority, and many married into "the best society".

Tradesmen and artisans were also burghers of the towns, although their standard of living was far lower than that of the upper class. There were great differences within this social group, such as those between a master baker with many apprentices, and a huckster or a cobbler who scraped together an existence in the back streets. Over half the inhabitants of a town had no rights of citizenship whatsoever. As servant girls, day labourers, soldiers, prostitutes and alms-folk, they made up the lower class which was one basis for the upper classes' luxurious wealth.

The Post master of Larvik and his family, gathered round the punchbowl. Engraving on a goblet by Villas Vinter, c. 1780.

The runebom was a drum used by the Sami people to contact the animistic gods.

The Sami

people

A missionary preaching to the Sami people in the 1700s.

These drawings of 1555 by the Swedish historian Olaus Magnus show that the Sami people were good at hunting and skiing.

The Roman historian, Tacitus, was the first to write about the Sami people. In *Germania,* he wrote that the Sami people were good hunters. From the Viking Age onwards the Sami people had to pay taxes to Norwegian chieftains and kings.

From the Middle Ages the Sami people lived in *siidas.* A *siida* was an area around a fjord or a river. People in the *siida* cooperated in hunting, trapping and fishing. From the 16th century some of the Sami began to keep herds of tame reindeer, while others ceased their nomadic existence and gained their livelihood from farming and fishing. In the 18th and 19th centuries the Sami lands were divided among Denmark-Norway, Sweden and Russia. In Norway the conversion of the Sami people to Christianity began at the beginning of the 18th century and the old animistic religion disappeared. At the end of the 19th century the Storting decided that Sami children should be taught in Norwegian. An Act passed in 1902 made it difficult for Sami people to buy land. Only after the Second World War were these policies changed.

Elsa Laula Renberg (1877–1931) tried to organise the Sami people in the early 20th century.

In 1989 King Olav V opened the first popularly elected Sami assembly. It is called the *Sameting* and meets in Karasjok. The aim of the *Sameting* is to protect the Sami language and culture, and the assembly cooperates with other indigenous populations all over the world.

Njåemel
Douij
Gærhkoeve
Troàn'din *Ladtieb*
(Trondheim) ● *Tjohkeleh*
(Kristiansund) ●

(Ålesund)

(Røros)

Sami language areas

The Sami people speak nine different dialects. Many of them differ so greatly that the Sami cannot understand each other. The map shows the various language areas, which cross national borders.

In 1990 there were between 30,000 and 40,000 Sami living in Norway. There were approximately 17,000 in Sweden, 6000 in Finland and 2000 in the Soviet Union.

In 1986 the Sami Conference in Åre, Sweden, passed a resolution that the Sami territory should have its own flag. In this illustration a woman in Karasjok dress and a man in Tana dress are hoisting the Sami flag.

In the 1970s the Storting passed a resolution to build a power station on the Alta river in Finnmark. Many Sami believed that this took away their right to control land and water. They organised a popular movement. The illustration shows Sami women demonstrating outside the Storting in February 1981. Their protests were unsuccessful.

◀ This is a French scientist's impression of a Sami settlement on Magerøya in Finnmark at the end of the 1840s.

Today the snow-scooter is an important aid for Sami people who keep herds of reindeer. ▼

Map labels:
Ávákki (Honningsvåg), Várgát (Vardø), Trömsa (Tromsø), Jiek'kevárri 1833, 1560 Vággevárri, Álahæddjo (Alta), Ráste-gái'sa 1067, Áccejákka, Buol'bmát, Gir'konjár'ga (Kirkenes), Baec'cán, Guoladat (Murmansk), Kárásjåkka, ANÁRS.G., GIELDDAS.G., DARJJLS.G., Njellim, Likkavárri 1503, Njunis 1713, Guovdagæi'dno (Kautokeino), Avvil (Inari), NUORTALAŠŠ.G., Rlehppecöhkka 1456, DAVVISÁMEGIELLA, Vuotso, Ippocöhkka 1727, Ábeskåvvo, 2117 Giev'dnegái'se, Girun (Kiruna), Gihccecöhkka 1381, Gaskacohkka 1512, Rago 1512, 2090 Sárekčåk'ka, LULEVUS.G., Olm.maiallojiekna 1290, Suličælbma, Guol'kajákka, Bår'jus, 1768 Nuortasávlu, 1369 Dåhttarcöhkka, Gálás (Kalix), Giebma (Kemi), bicåk'ke 1120, Vuog'gåcoal'bme, Duordnos (Tornio), 1311, Ballunai'vi, Sarvestjahke, 1387, Gåptesbåk'ti, BIHTÁNS.G., Árjapluovvi, Árviejav'ri, (Oulu), 1525, Bro.resenåelkie, Aarpoevaartoe (Hattfjelldal), UBMIS.G., Bitun (Piteå), Vcænjelåelkie, Urrehksdurrientjahke, Liksuo, Skiellet (Skellefteå), OARJIELSÁMEGIELLA, Upmeje (Umeå), (Pietarsaari), (Vaasa), (Östersund), (Sundsvall)

OCKELBO

Stability and Growth in the 18th Century

«Norwegian society seems to me to be the most liberated that I have ever seen.»
(Mary Wollstonecraft, British author in 1795)

The first twenty years of the 18th century was an unpeaceful period in Scandinavia. The Great Scandinavian War broke out in 1700, but Denmark-Norway were not drawn in until 1709. This was after Sweden's young warrior-king, Karl XII, had suffered a serious defeat at Poltava in the Ukraine. King Frederik IV now opened war in order to win back old Danish-Norwegian territory. His attack on Skåne was unsuccessful and Karl once again took the offensive. The Swedes invaded southern Norway in both 1716 and 1718. King Karl XII was killed during the siege of Halden in December 1718, when struck by a Norwegian or a Swedish bullet.

The war cost both kingdoms dearly. The citizens of Halden had set fire to 330 houses to halt the enemy advance. Sweden was forced to give up its exemption from duty at Øresund, and lost all her possessions in the Baltic states and Germany. Denmark-Norway did not regain any territory, but Sweden's day of glory was over and the balance of power was restored.

The aim of the absolute monarchy was to join the two kingdoms together, economically, politically and culturally, with Copenhagen at the centre. The results of this single-state policy became obvious in the late 18th century, when between one-half and two-thirds of the Norwegian state revenues were transferred to Denmark. All sectors of the state administration of Norway were directly subordinate to the authorities in Copenhagen. Norway was governed as a group of counties - not as a separate kingdom. While Copenhagen expanded and became a centre for politics, trade, art and science, Christiania languished. It was not until the 19th century that the citizens of Christiania experienced what it meant to live in the capital city of an independent kingdom. Then there was growth, expansion and activity!

However, the authorities heeded the advice given them by public officials in Norway, and most Norwegians did not feel oppressed. Norway retained its own legal system during the entire period of union with

The body of the warrior-king, Karl XII, being carried home to Sweden by faithful soldiers in December 1718. Painted by G. Cederström in 1878.

Denmark. Property rights were respected and legal security was maintained. Regardless of status, everyone had the right to present his case directly to the king, by means of a petition, or *supplikk*. The district magistrates were even obliged to assist common people write their petitions, thousands of which were sent to Copenhagen every year. The petitions covered every possible subject, from pleas for pardon and requests for tax exemption to complaints about officials. Farmers placed their trust in the king, expecting him to deal justly with the matter and protect their rights. The authorities in Copenhagen considered the petitions, and surprisingly often adopted a policy satisfactory to the seekers' demands and wishes. Historian Jens Arup Seip terms this ‹opinion-controlled monarchy».

Conflict did occur, of course, as in the previously mentioned unrest at the Kongsberg and Røros mines. During the last twenty years of the 18th century, farmer Chistian Jensen Lofthus (1750-97) and evangelist Hans Nielsen Hauge (1771-1824) opposed the authorities in other fields. Lofthus complained to the king about public officials' exploitation of farmers and about towns-people's misuse of monopolies to force farmers off their land. He became the leader for a wide-spread farmers' rebellion. Imprisoned in Akershus Castle, he died in 1797 after having been enchained for 11 years. Two years later his life sentence was upheld by the Supreme Court. Lofthus' demands were taken into consideration by the authorities, however, resulting in the dismissal of several public officials and

An Evening at the Norwegian Society is the name given by Eilif Petersen to his painting from 1892. Johan Nordahl Brun recites poetry while Johan Herman Wessel raises his glass of toddy, and tavern hostess, Madame Juel, brings in renewed refreshments.

The Haugians, painted by A. Tidemand in 1852.

revision of regulations. Hans Nielsen Hauge fought for the right to preach the gospel freely, a privilege given solely to ministers of the State Church. His following increased rapidly, becoming a popular, nation-wide movement. Hauge suffered years of imprisonment without sentence, but the movement he inspired could not be stopped. Both Hauge and Lofthus opposed local authorities in Norway, however, not the king and the Union. Ordinary people did not oppose the union with Denmark.

The bourgeoisie and the public officials criticized centralization, comparing Copenhagen to a bloodsucking leech. Demands for a national bank and a national university were made on several occasions, but refused by the king. This may have been due to fears of splitting the union. The upper classes kept well-informed about events in continental Europe and it should not be surprising that nationalism flourished in these circles. National identity was also expressed through The Norwegian Society in Copenhagen, a meeting ground for Norwegian authors and students. Johan Nordahl Grieg's rousing song, «To Norway, Home of Giants», shows that Norwegian self-assertion was widely encouraged in these circles.

Despite this self-assertion and growing nationalism, however, there was little danger of Denmark and Norway parting company in the 18th century. Government policy was liberalistic in the 1790s, resulting in several measures that tempered criticism from the bourgoisie. Owners of the largest saw-mills were permitted to sell unlimited amounts of timber, while various import and export restrictions were lifted. The excellent economy at the turn of the century lessened the burghers' discontent even more. It was only when both countries became involved in the Napoleonic wars that the Union showed signs of splitting.

Nevertheless, Norway's situation towards the end of the 18th century was entirely different than when it became "part of Denmark's realm" in 1536. Growth of population and of trade and industry had strengthened the country's economy. Social injustice was relatively slight. A cultural elite of public officials and bourgeoisie had grown up during the period of absolute monarchy, while the fact that Norway had been considered a separate kingdom even after 1536 would ease the rebuilding of a Norwegian state in 1814.

1814 – Independence and New Union

The Constituent Assembly at Eidsvoll, painted by O. Wergeland in 1855. The leader of the Independence Party, Christian Magnus Falsen, stands by the table. Seated on his right is the secretary of assemby, Wilhelm F.K. Christie, and between them on the other side of the table is Count Herman Wedel-Jarlsberg.
The painting now hangs in the Storting in Oslo.

«It was called a year [...], but centuries have run their course and been far less remarkable than this one year. I do not think the history of any other nation can demonstrate its equal. Even Napoleon's catastrophic fate is less amazing.»

This diary notation by Claus Pavels, chaplain to Akershus Castle, in 1814 was most relevant. As the year began, Norway and Denmark were still joined in a union ruled by an absolute monarch. For a few hectic summer months Norway was independent, with a king of her own and a constitution based on the sovereignty of her people. By autumn, the country was forced into a new union - this time with Sweden.

Denmark-Norway chooses Napoleon

In 1792 France had declared war on Austria and Prussia, and war still raged in Europe in 1814. Balancing nicely between the belligerent parties, Denmark-Norway had managed to remain neutral. Both kingdoms had exploited the trade conditions brought about by the war and the Norwegian bourgeoisie made fortunes. The times were described as a "golden age" for shipping and export.

It proved difficult to withstand the pressure. Country after country had been forced to support either Emperor Napoleon Bonaparte in France or the naval power Great Britain. To prevent neutral ships from

The British frigate *Tartar* participated in the blockade of Norway. Here it is seen in battle with Norwegian gunboats in 1808, off the gunpowder factory at Alvøen near Bergen.

carrying goods to France, British warships also searched Dano-Norwegian merchant vessels. The Danish king then had the ships sail in convoy protected by warships. This defiant policy led to a British naval attack on Copenhagen in 1801. After a brief yet bloody battle, the British forced Denmark-Norway to cease sending ships in convoy. British warships could now freely inspect cargoes on Dano-Norwegian merchant ships.

The British attacked again in September of 1807, when troops went ashore in Zealand and warships bombarded Copenhagen. The British confiscated most of the Dano-Norwegian fleet, 37 large and some smaller ships, to prevent them from falling into Napoleon's hands. This marked the end of a century of peace for Denmark-Norway. Eleven days after this so-called "Fleet-robbery", King Frederik VI entered into an alliance with Napoleon. Norway faced great difficulties now that the kingdoms were committed to joining in the blockade of Great Britain. The king had prevented Napoleon from attacking Denmark and Schleswig-Holstein, but the agreement brought Norwegian imports to a halt.

War and Blockade

Once war was declared, the British prevented Norwegian ships from carrying timber, fish and iron to foreign ports. Import of grain from Denmark, on which Norway was completely dependent, was also reduced drastically. This forced the king to abandon his single-state policy and establish a governing commission in Christiania for the duration of the blockade. Norway became completely isolated in 1808 when hostilities were opened with Sweden. Earlier that same year Russia had won Finland from Sweden, and King Gustav IV Adolf of Sweden hoped to gain Norway as compensation. This proved more difficult than expected. Norwegian peasant troops put up a strong defence, defeating the Swedes in several minor battles in southern Norway. A ceasefire was signed later that year, and when peace was concluded in 1809 conditions between the two realms returned to normal.

Dissatisfaction with the king was widespread in Sweden. The loss of Finland and the failure of the campaign against Norway forced Gustav IV to give up the throne. When his aged and childless uncle was c hosen king, as Karl XIII, it was obvious that Sweden needed a vigorous heir to the throne. The choice fell on one of Napoleon's generals, Jean Baptiste Bernadotte. Arriving in Sweden in 1810 and taking the name of Karl Johan, the crown prince became Sweden's undisputed leader, whose goal was the conquest of Norway.

The years following the "Fleet-robbery" of 1807 had been harsh for all Norwegians. During this one year Norwegian shipowners lost 553 vessels, either to confiscation in British ports or to seizure by British warships. Timber exports sank drastically, from nearly 900,000 tons in 1805 to under 9000 tons by 1808. Exports of fish were reduced correspondingly. South-eastern Norway was hardest hit due to the region's dependency on grain supplies from Denmark. In the county of Akershus, with 40% of of the country's population, the death rate rose markedly, from an annual average of 8278 between 1803 and 1807, to 12,679 in 1808 and 21,391 in 1809. "Nothing is heard save desparate pleas for grain and foods, and soon all supplies will be gone," one merchant wrote in 1809.

The governing commission had made several requests to the king to alter his foreign policy, but Frederik VI continued his alliance with Napoleon and blockade of Great Britain. During the summer of 1809 the king finally realized that famine and discontent in Norway could shatter the Union. He therefore permitted Norway to resume export of timber to Great Britain if Britain allowed grain ships to sail freely between Norway and Denmark. This "trade by license" saved Norwegian merchants from ruin and the south-eastern districts from famine. The crisis was overwon for a time.

In 1812 Napoleon attacked his former ally Russia. This expansion of the war forced Frederik VI to relinquish trade by license. The summer that year was exceptionally cold in south-eastern Norway and harvests were minimal. Fishing failed in the north and grain froze. The entire country was hit by famine, need, and death. Peasants revolted in several districts, but as was the case with the Lofthus and Hauge rebellions, their anger was directed at merchants and officials, not against the king and his foreign policy.

Napoleon's defeat in Russia was the beginning of the end for both the emperor and for the Dano-Norwegian Union. Sweden joined Napoleon's enemies, and the Great Powers promised Norway to Karl Johan provided he helped crush France. After his victory at the battle of Leipzig in 1813, Karl Johan turned and marched on Denmark. Frederik VI was forced to admit defeat after brief hostilities. On 14 January he accepted a peace treaty at Kiel in which he ceded Norway to the king of Sweden. The 434-year-long union between Norway and Denmark had ended.

Jean Baptiste Bernadotte (1763-1844), the son of a solicitor from Pau in southern France, enlisted as a soldier at age 17. During the French revolution he rose rapidly through the ranks, and in Napoleon's service he was appointed Marshal of France and Prince of Ponte Corvo in Italy. When relations between him and Napoleon became strained, he resigned. In 1810 he was chosen crown prince of Sweden, taking the name Karl Johan, and was adopted by King Karl XIII. This painting by Justinien Clary from 1841 shows Bernadotte at the battle of Halle in 1806.

UNIVERSITAS REGIA FREDERICIANA, 1811

Demands for a separate Norwegian university grew towards the end of the period of union with Denmark. King Frederik VI refused, however, due to his single-state policy. As late as in 1810, he wrote, «A University in Norway will confirm to a greater and greater Degree, that harmful Tendency towards Separation of the two Kingdoms, which already prevails.» The king's later decision on 2 September of that year to establish a university in Norway reflected the weakened condition of the dual monarchy, and leading citizens' extreme interest in the matter. The Royal Norwegian Society for Rural Development, founded in 1809, had held a successful country-wide subscription. Donations were large, especially in Akershus diocese whose population had suffered under the blockade of 1808-09. The king could not disregard this popular interest, and he decreed that "a complete University" should be established in the

kingdom of Norway. Kongsberg was first choice of locations, but in 1812 it was decided that Universitas Regia Fredericiana – The Royal Frederik's University – would lie in Christiania and have four faculties: theological, medical, judicial and philosophical. When classes began in 1813, the university had five professors, one lecturer and 17 students. Celebrations were arranged all over the country by the Royal Society. Members in Alta to the far north, gathered at the local vicarage where "Toasts were proposed to the Health of the Royal Family and to the both swift and complete Establishment of the University; the Assembly not dispersing until the Light of Day». Classes were first held at different locations around town. In 1841 the foundation stone was laid for the university buildings still standing on Karl Johan Street in Oslo. In 1939 the name of the institution was altered to the University of Oslo – Universitas Osloensis.

Lithography c. 1850, after a painting by Joachim Frich.

Prince Christian Frederik and the Constitution

When news of the treaty of Kiel reached Norway, the country fortunately had the perfect man as its leader. This was Prince Christian Frederik, heir to the throne of Denmark-Norway, whom the king had appointed as viceroy in the spring of 1813. The prince, only 26 years of age, lacked both administrative and military experience but was gifted, hardworking, handsome and charming. His most important task was to secure the union with Denmark for the king and for himself.

Christian Frederik, refusing approval of the treaty of Kiel, immediately set about strengthening his own position in Norway. Although officially opposed to these actions, being bound by the agreement he had signed at Kiel, Frederik VI privately supported the prince's plans, still hoping that Norway could still be saved. A few days after the treaty had been signed, the king gave secret orders to have cargoes of grain shipped to Norway, taking extreme care to conceal this double-dealing from the Swedes and the British.

Christian Frederik's foremost opponent in Norway was Count Herman Wedel-Jarlsberg (1779-1840). During the blockade and the years of crisis, he had done his utmost to effect a union between Norway and Sweden. He maintained that a lasting peace with Sweden and Britain was vital to foreign trade and the all-important grain imports, thus benefitting both townsmen and country-folk. Wedel and his supporters wished that Norway should remain a separate nation and that a joint king with Sweden should not hinder substantial Norwegian independence.

Christian Frederik's ideas triumphed, however. The bonds with Denmark were still strong, and the prince controlled the state administration and its loyal public officials. Although Karl Johan's agents tried to influence the public, the prince's propaganda proved more effective. He spoke and wrote of "the beloved Norwegian people" and of Norway's "fortune and glory». Towards the end of January, he travelled from Christiania to Trondheim to win support.

On 16 February, Christian Frederik summoned twenty-one of the country's most influential citizens to meet at Eidsvoll. This "convention of notables" was to consider

Christian Frederik (1786-1848) was the son of the Danish heir presumptive, Prince Frederik and his wife, Sophie Frederikke of Mecklenburg-Schwerin. Because none of the sons of his 18-year-older cousin, King Frederik 6, grew up, Christian Frederik became his heir. Painted by J.L. Lund in 1813.

the prince's claim both to the Norwegian throne and to absolute power, in keeping with the Norwegian Monarchy Act of 1661. But the convention was of a different opinion. They favoured a liberal constitution and the election of the new king by the people. While it was clear that the prince would be the obvious choice, he on his part would have to accept that his royal power derived from the people. During a private conversation with the prince, Professor Georg Sverdrup (1770-1850) pointed out that since Frederik VI had relinquished Norway at Kiel, the Norwegian people had "regained their natural and indisputable Right to determine their own Constitution".

Christian Frederik agreed to the demands of the convention. One reason lay in the strength of Sverdup's arguments, another in the prince's need for the support of these men. The prince was well aware that both public officials and bourgeoisie in Norway were influenced by the ideals of liberty prevalent in the revolutionary, Napoleonic period. He could ill afford to challenge powerful men in the difficult situation in which he found himself. For these reasons, Christian Frederik and the convention resolved that the people were to elect representatives to a constituent assembly to meet at Eidsvoll. The electorate and their representatives were to swear a "people's oath" to the effect that they would defend Norway's independence. In the meantime, Christian Frederik was to rule the country as regent.

The first representatives arrived in Eidsvoll in early April. On Easter Sunday, 10 April, the prince regent and the representatives attended church services. The next day Christian Frederik opened the national assembly. A total of 112 representatives were present – 18 townsmen, 37 farmers and 57 civilian and military officials. The prince did not participate in the sessions, but because he lived at Eidsvoll he was able to influence the decisions reached. He had real grounds for making demands. If the constitution was not to his liking, he could refuse to accept the crown.

The representatives at the national assembly divided into two factions. The clearly larger Independence Party supported Christian Frederik. Its leader, magistrate Christian Magnus Falsen (1782-1830), was loyal to the prince regent. Count Wedel was the leader of the Unionist Party, most of whose members were townspeople. They meant that the treaty of Kiel could not be disregarded and that some arrangement acceptable to Sweden was inevitable.

The representatives at Eidsvoll used six weeks to compose a constitution for Norway. As models they used several of the foreign constitutions which had been drawn up during the revolutionary period. The most influential of these was the French constitution, which had been translated into Norwegian at about the time of the assembly.

Sovereignty of the people was the essential principle of this constitution. In accordance with Montesquieu's principles, power was divided between the *Storting* (the national assembly), the judiciary, and the king. Characteristically, the king was accorded wide-reaching powers. He was supreme military commander with the power to declare war and conclude peace. The king also levied taxes, appointed officials and had a delaying power of veto on legislation. It was the duty of the Storting to originate legislation and to appropriate funds, but it would assemble for only three months every third year, unless the king decided differently. When considering legislation, the Storting was to divide into two chambers, the *Odelsting* and the *Lagting*. The rules of franchise were liberal by the standards of the day, with nearly half of all men over age 25 given the vote. This gave farmers political influence not only as voters, but also as possible representatives to the Storting. No other country compared to Norway on this point. The constitution adopted at Eidsvoll was thus a compromise between absolute monarchy and democracy.

When work on the constitution was completed on 17 May 1814, the national assembly unanimously elected Christian Frederik as king over a free, sovereign and independent Norway. On 19 May the newly elected

The news that Christian Frederik had been chosen king of Norway did not reach Bergen until 27 May. In this gouache by J.F.L. Dreyer, riders attract the attention of the onlookers by blowing trumpets, while an officer announces the great event down by the wharf. The Church of St. Mary is seen to the right.

king appeared in the assembly to swear his oath on the Consitution. On the following day, the assembly held its final meeting. Linking hands and forming a ring, the representatives swore themselves to everlasting unity and loyalty.

Into Union with Sweden

People all over the country enthusiastically celebrated their constitution and their newly elected king. When Christian Frederik entered Christiania on 25 May, he was received by a company of grey-clad peasant soldiers who escorted him to what was now the capital city of Norway. At the city boundary the king's carriage passed beneath a triumphal arch, while young ladies cast flowers and the crowd "cheered and hurra'd ceaselessly». But danger was close at hand. The great powers, suspecting Christian Frederik of double-dealing, set up a new blockade between Denmark and Norway. Napoleon was now defeated in continental Europe, allowing Crown Prince Karl Johan to effectuate the provisions of the treaty of Kiel.

Christian Frederik's attempts to have the great powers recognize an independent Norway were unsuccessful. Towards the end of July, Karl Johan attacked southern Norway with an army of 40-50,000 experienced soldiers. Christian Frederik's forces consisted of about 30,000 poorly trained troops. The war was short and the Norwegians retreated. On 14 August the two parties met in Moss and agreed to a ceasefire. Karl Johan accepted the constitution of Eidsvoll as the basis for negotiations, promising that Sweden would not propose any amendments other than those necessary for the union between Norway and Sweden. He demanded that Christian Frederik convene an extraordinary session of the Storting, renounce the throne and leave the country.

And Karl Johan had his way. He avoided occupying Norway, with all the bitterness that would have caused. Christian Frederik summoned a special Storting to convene in Christiania on 8 October. Two days later the king abdicated, leaving the country that same evening.

The Storting resolved immediately that Norway would enter into a union with Sweden, and negotiations began. The Norwegian negotiators achieved some success, in that the Norwegian government was to be divided into two parts, with one part in Christiania and the other in Stockholm, but that Norway would not be allowed an independent foreign policy. But even though Norway obviously was the lesser partner in the union, the powers of the king were limited in comparison to the constitution of Eidsvoll. He no longer had the right to declare war or to conclude peace without the approval of the Storting. Nor was he allowed the right to appoint Swedes as public officials in Norway. Norway was to have her own flag and national bank and, in the words of the first paragraph of the revised constitution: "The Kingdom of Norway is a free, independent, indivisible and inalienable Realm, joined to Sweden under one King." Much had been won during these ten dramatic months.

The revision of the constitution was completed on 4 November, at which time the Storting elected Karl XIII as king of Norway. President Christie concluded the election with the fervent prayer: "May Almighty God grant that this Union be lasting and fortunate for both Kingdoms."

Norwegian troops from 1808, equiped with snowshoes and skis, drawn by A. Bloch.

From 1814 to 1905

Crisis and the Struggle for Independence

An economic crisis struck Norway after the end of the Napoleonic wars. Even though the blockade had been lifted, the timber trade with Britain was slow in getting started. In addition, the British had imposed a high toll on Norwegian timber in order to protect their own imports from Canada. The timber crisis affected shipping as well, while a huge fire in the lumber yards in Drammen added to the misery. Many wealthy burghers with "old money" went bankrupt in these years. This was, however, a crisis affecting the upper class.

Because export duties were of such extreme importance, the post-war crisis also affected national finances. And as if that were not enough, the young nation experienced a severe inflation. Prior to 1814 King Frederik VI had printed banknotes to finance the war, and Christian Frederik had followed this example in 1814. The Swedish crown prince, Karl Johan, kept a close eye on events in Norway. He may have hoped that the Storting and the government of Norway would not be able to solve the financial crisis. Would the Norwegian state prove too weak to survive? Leading politicians in Norway knew that well-ordered finances were a precondition for national independence.

The Norwegians did succeed, if but slowly. In 1816, the Storting introduced the *speciedaler* as a monetary unit and established the Bank of Norway. This national bank was to have exclusive rights to issue banknotes, to be assured by a capital fund of precious metals worth 2 to 3 million speciedalers. It was intented that citizens make voluntary contributions to the fund, but their generosity was weak. The Storting therefore imposed a "silver tax". People of wealth were to pay a special tax to the bank, using silver instead of banknotes. All over the country townsman and farmer alike had to give up their heirlooms to the national bank, but payments were slow in coming, and time passed before the problems had been overcome. The economic situation improved in the 1820s, but it was not until 1842 that the Bank of Norway had collected sufficient silver to redeem the banknotes.

Despite financial crisis and virtual national bankruptcy, the Storting managed to preserve Norway's independence. The question of settling the debt to Denmark caused especially strained relations with Sweden, however. By the treaty of Kiel, Karl Johan and Frederik VI had agreed that Norway was to pay her share of the joint national debt of Denmark-Norway, and by 1820 the Danes were pressing their claim. The Storting was unwilling to pay, both because Norway had never ratified the treaty and because the state was poor. Europe's great powers supported Denmark, while Karl Johan, who had become king in 1818, threatened the Storting: «*If you wish to remain independent, pay the debt to Denmark. If you prefer becoming part of Sweden under the Swedish constitution, then do not pay!*» In May of 1821, Karl Johan announced that he intended to deploy 6000 soldiers to Christiania on military manoeuvres. The Storting yielded, and a large majority voted that Norway was to pay.

Opposite page:
Bark in a storm, by Håkon Kaulum (1863-1933). Undated.

During the night between 1 and 2 May 1817, fire broke out in the lumberyards in Drammen. Two years later the lumberyards in Christiania also burned down, and this intensified the crisis in the timber business. Painting by H.P.C. Dahm.

The headquarters of the Bank of Norway was located in Trondheim in 1816. A new building was raised for the branch in Christiania in 1830 (to the right in the illustration). The building to the left is the Christiania Theatre, opened in 1827. Painted by Chr. M. Grosch in 1836-37. The headquarters of the Bank was moved to Christiania in 1897.

In the autumn of 1814, Karl Johan had been most concerned with enacting a peaceful settlement with the Norwegians. Shortly after succeeding to the throne, however, he decided to revise the Constitution in order to strengthen royal power at the expense of the Storting. An anti-democratic reaction swept the political climate of continental Europe, and Karl Johan hoped to win support for his Norwegian policy among the great powers. In the autumn of 1821, he proposed several amendments to the Constitution, among them the right of the king to dismiss all officials except judges. Further, that the Storting would not assemble oftener than every five years, the king would have the right to dissolve the Storting and to appoint its presidents. Most startling of all was the king's demand for an absolute veto on legislation. These amendments were put forth several times to the threat of military action, but the Storting stood firm and rejected them all. The members regarded the Constitution of 1814 as a safeguard against oppression and excessive royal power. Public officials, who dominated the memberships of the Storting, were not pleased by the king's attack on their positions. Nor did the great powers support Karl Johan, as they prefered a balance of power in Europe. A relatively independent Norway posed no threat to stability, while increased royal power in Sweden was considered a definite threat by Russia.

Another controversial matter was the celebration of 17 May. Since 1814 the day had been marked sporadically, but celebrations became more widespread in the 1820s. Karl Johan was displeased by this. He considered 17 May a day of rebellion, regarding 4 November as a far better date for celebra-

tion. The Storting tried to moderate festivities in order to placate the king, but on 17 May 1829 there was a violent conflict in Christiania. The steamship *Constitution* came to town on this warm Sunday, people appeared to cheer the event and a large crowd gathered in the main square. The town authorities sent soldiers to disperse this peaceable company. No one was killed, but this "Battle of the Marketplace" had lasting effects. The Swedish viceroy, Balthazar von Platen, was made to feel the wrath of the public for this scandalous military action. He himself said that he was "soiled and spat upon from every side». After this it became impossible for the king to appoint a Swede to be viceroy of Norway and in the years that followed, celebrating 17 May became accepted practice. Karl Johan had been bettered once again by the Norwegians.

Government by Public Officials with a Storting of Farmers

The Norway of the decades after 1814 is often referred to as having been controlled by public officials. Officials who had served under the absolute monarchy kept their positions. As governors, bailiffs, magistrates, clergymen and officers, they were also undisputed leaders of local communities. To their number were added professors at the new university, top civil servants in the new goverment and above all, the royal ministers. Norway had only about 2000 such officials in the first half of the 1800s, but their solidarity, class feeling, self-recruitment and influence belied their small number. The Constitution of 1814 was in large part the work of these same public officials, and it was they, as members of the Storting, who had defended it against Karl Johan in the 1820s. Defence of the Constitution also defended their positions in public office. The provisions of the Constitution as to two-thirds of the members being elected from rural districts did not hinder the influence wielded by public officials. Farmers, having little interest in politics, often elected officials as their representatives. The fact that Norway completely lacked an aristocracy and a bourgeoisie who could challenge the officials socially and politically emphasizes the unique position they occupied. Noble titles and privileges had been abolished by the Storting in 1821, quite contrary to the king's wishes.

A cultural gap existed between farmers and public officials. Most of the latter had been educated in Copenhagen, and mastered both Latin and the behaviour favoured in polite society. Quite often they regarded farmers as "coarse», forgetting how they had praised "the free, Norwegian yeoman" in the first, heady flush of independence.

In the late 1820s the farmers began to advance. Before the 1832 elections their leaders had urged that they elect their own kind, not officials, as members of the Storting. This agitation gave results. The Storting that assembled in 1833 had a majority of farmers and has since been called the "Farmers' Storting". After the next election the majority was also made up of farmers.

Two issues were of special importance to these farmers. One concerned the reduction of state expenditures in order to cut taxes.

Many of them spoke contemptuously of government officials who while producing nothing lived off the labour of others. The Farmers' Storting reduced taxes and increased import duties on a number of goods. This transferred much of the burden of cost from rural districts to the towns. Farmers felt that they had little benefit of more state government. Better roads and more efficient government meant little to people whose daily lives were based on self suficiency. Military service was also resented because only men from the agricultural classes were subject to conscription.

The other issue concerned local selfgovernment. In 1833 a farmers' group proposed that towns ought to be governed by a small committee of representatives called the *formannskap*, or Board of Aldermen. They hoped this would reduce public officials' influence in local communities. The farmers were again successful and an act establishing local boards of aldermen was passed in 1837. A popularly elected town council was given authority on certain matters, such as school buildings, teachers' wages, local roads and care of the poor. The national government could also impose certain duties on the councils, something that happened with increasing frequency in the following years. Participation in local elections was negligible to begin with, but increased in the latter half of the century. Local self-government gave farmers valuable political experience.

The farmers lost their majority in the elections of 1838, when they reverted to electing public officials. This new generation of officialdom dominated both Storting and government.

Rector Niels Hertzberg: *Farmhouse interior. Wedding in Kinsarvik in Hordaland,* about 1820. The wedding festivities usually began with a solid meal before the bridal couple and their guests went to church.

A Golden Age in Literature

When in the autumn of 1814 Norway entered the union with Sweden, she was permitted to keep the Constitution. Norwegians saw it as a defence against Sweden. Great challenges faced the newly-fledged nation in most spheres of life. In the field of the arts, identifying what was quintessentially Norwegian became of prime importance. What should be the written language in the land? Had there during all the years of Danish rule been anything one could call Norwegian literature? Was there typically Norwegian music? What did Norway and its rural population look like? The artists set off from the towns on journeys of discovery, and brought back with them to the urban public their impressions of Norwegian landscape and folk life.

The drawing shows the manor at Eids voll where the Norwegian Constitutio was adopted. 112 officials, merchants and farmers assembled here in the spring of 1814. Together they gave Norway one of Europe's most democratic constitutions.

Peter Christen Asbjørnsen (1812–1885)

Together with the clergyman Jørgen Moe (1813–1882) he collected and wrote down folk tales and legends. The language of these tales was remarkable for the Norwegianness of its vocabulary and syntax.

Ivar Aasen (1812–1896)

A farmer's son from the Sunnmøre district of western Norway, Aasen objected strongly to the fact that ordinary Norwegians had to write Danish. He decided to create a written Norwegian language based on the spoken language. For four years he travelled around the country researching the spoken language. His written language is now known as New Norwegian.

Rana
Kristiansund
Troudheim
Molde
Alesund
Bergen
Kristiania (Oslo)
Stavanger
Kristiansand

The trolls in the folk tales were wealthy, an could obtain power ov human beings – prefer ably beautiful princess Fortunately the trolls were also stupid and easily to trick.

The 1820s and 1830s	1840s	1850s
The illustration shows Henrik Wergeland (1808–1845). He was a Romantic, devoted to Norway and the Norwegian landscape, and one of the country's most prolific lyricists. He was also an educationalist and a keen user of a more Norwegian form of language. He worked tirelessly to open Norway's borders to Jews. They acquired that right only in 1851, six years after his death. Wergeland is little known in other countries though he ranks as one of Norway's greatest poets.	In the 1840s many collectors of folk songs, folk tales and folk music were active. The drawing shows a talented folk musician, Myllarguten, who imparted a lot of his knowledge to the famous violinist Ole Bull. At this time, too, artists discovered Norway as a source of motifs, and some of the best-known paintings of Norwegian landscape and folk life date from the 1840s. «Birch Tree in a Storm» by J.C.Dahl (Bergen Art Gallery) and «Bridal Journey in Hardanger» by H.Gude and A.Tidemand (Nasjonalgalleriet, Oslo) are good examples.	This decade was a period transition in Norwegian literature. The nation's f life and history were still interest but authors also became increasingly awa of contemporary problem The bank note (right) sho Camilla Collett, whose n famous novel The County Governor's Daughters (18 was a powerful statemen women's rights.

Synnøve and Torbjørn outside the church: a scene from *Synnøve Solbakken,* a short novel by Bjørnstjerne Bjørnson (1857). The story is set in the countryside of his day, but it is no idyll. Bjørnson exposes the struggle between good and evil.

Henrik Ibsen (1828–1906)

(Portrait by Erik Werenskiold) Ibsen is Norway's best known playwright. He suffered many disappointments while working as artistic director in the theatre. He lived abroad for 30 years and became an acknowledged writer both in and outside Norway.

The photograph above shows Ingrid Bergman as Hedda Gabler and Claude Dauphin as Eilert Løvborg in Henrik Ibsen's play of 1890, *Hedda Gabler* (Theatre Montparnasse, Paris, 1962). The character Hedda Gabler is typical of her time: a woman whose talents are unused and who therefore becomes destructive of herself and others. The play dates from Ibsen's last period as playwright.

Ibsen is best known for his plays of the 1870s and 1880s which were critical of contemporary society. He attacked all forms of bourgeois hypocrisy. *A Doll's House* (1879) is particularly famous. It has been interpreted as putting the case for the emancipation of women.

Although Ibsen holds an exceptional position in 19th-century literature, he does not stand alone. From the mid century on, many authors emerged and helped put Norway on the world literary map.

Knut Hamsun (1859–1952)

(Drawing by Olaf Gulbransson) He was critical of both earlier and contemporary Norwegian literature. In his first works the principal characters are lonely, nervous men. His disapproval of industrialisation became gradually more pronounced. And from the early 1930s he sympathised with the Nazis in Germany.

Amalie Skram (1846–1905)

To a greater extent than her male contemporaries, she wrote from personal experience. She produced harrowing descriptions of young and inexperienced women's encounters with marriage and sexuality. For this she was severely criticised. Her later works were about destitution and her experiences as a patient in a mental hospital. All the obstacles she had to face made Amalie Skram at the end of her life wish to be thought of as a Danish author.

1860s	1870–1890
 Fascination with the typically Norwegian and with Norwegian history persisted into the 1860s, and both Henrik Ibsen and Bjørnstjerne Bjørnson wrote historical plays. Two of Bjørnson's plays of the 1860s have medieval themes, *King Sverre* and *Sigurd Slembe.* Bjørnson also wrote the words of Norway's national anthem. Yet the most celebrated works of the decade are Ibsen's plays *Brand* and *Peer Gynt.* 	This period tends to be labelled «realism» in Norway. The goal of artists was to re-create reality and to provoke discussion of contemporary problems. The role of women in society, the position of the Church, and education were issues frequently treated in literature. The drawing shows Nora dancing the tarantella in *A Doll's House,* probably Henrik Ibsen's best-known play (1879). Around 1890 some authors began to draw on different subjects and write more about the emotional life of the individual than about social problems. 

Towards a New Society 1800-1850

In 1800 the population of Norway numbered nearly 900 000, and increased rapidly during the following century. By 1865 the figure had reached 1.7 million, and by 1900 a remarkable 2.2 million. Reduced infant mortality was decisive to this growth.

Historians have found several reasons for this population growth. Nutrition improved when herring and potatoes replaced barley porridge as the most common daily food. Cultivation of potatoes expanded noticeably after 1800. Harvests of potatoes were dependable, yielding almost double the nutritional value of grain on the same plot of land. After the turn of the century, increased herring fisheries led to fish becoming cheap, common, everyday food even in inland areas.

Hygiene also improved. In the 1700s fireplaces with chimneys or iron stoves were installed in most houses in eastern Norway. This led to greater cleanliness, because of less soot and smoke than from the old-fashioned open hearths. Western and northern Norway followed after and by 1850 fireplaces and iron stoves were in use all over the country. The system of district medical officers introduced in the late 1700s was also of extreme importance. Smallpox vaccination was introduced in 1801 and by the middle of the century over 80 per cent of all infants were vaccinated shortly after birth.

The period between 1814 and 1850 saw the first signs of the radical changes which would arrive full force later in the century.

Rural districts were able to absorb the growth in population. Much new land was cleared before 1850, which in turn required a larger labour force. This led to continued growth in the number of crofter families, peaking at 67,000 people around 1850. Many districts were now overcrowded. Farmers could afford better equipment such as iron ploughshares and harrows, resulting in larger harvests. Nevertheless one cannot speak of a technical revolution in Norwegian agriculture at this time.

Towns also began to grow. In Christiania, the capital city, the population increased from about 9000 in 1800 to nearly 40,000 in 1855. Christiania was changing from a sleepy provincial town to a modern capital city. The Storting voted funds for buildings which still characterize the city: the Royal Palace, the University, the National Hospital and the Bank of Norway.

Emigration to America also started up in this period, with the departure in 1825 of the sloop, *Restaurationen*, bound for New York from Stavanger. The tiny ship carried 52 passengers, all Quakers, who left Norway for religious reasons. As time passed, many Norwegian settlements were established in the Midwest, and these pioneering efforts eased the way for those who followed. Mass emigration did not really begin until the 1860s, however. And since over 800,000 Norwegian emigrated to America before 1930, there are now just as many persons of Norwegian descent in the United States as there are in Norway itself.

The textile industry, which grew up in Norway during the 1840s, differed greatly from the old mining and sawmilling works of the 1700s. Within a few years, textile mills had been built on the banks of the Aker River in Christiania and near Bergen, some of them employing over a hundred workers. After restrictions on export of British machinery had been abolished in 1843, factory owners bought machines and equipment in Britain and also acquired the necessary expertise there. The mills produced for

A. Tidemand: *Norwegian Christmas Custom*, painted in 1848. The artist was strongly influenced by the national romantic movement sweeping through the cultural life of Norway at this time.

the home market only during this first phase of Norwegian industrialization. The first engineering works were established in the 1840s due largely to the necessity for keeping textile machines in good repair and because Norwegians soon wanted to develop and produce such machines themselves.

At about this time population pressure began to be felt in rural districts. Competition for work became stiffer and it was equally difficult to get a croft. An economic crisis hit the country in 1848-49. Mine owners' and timber merchants' difficulties in selling their products resulted in lower wages and unemployment for lumbermen, carters and charcoal burners. These factors are among the reasons for the emergence of the Thranite Movement.

Marcus Thrane (1817-1890) was a young student when he founded Norway's first labour organization at the turn of the year 1848-9. Starting with an initial membership of 160, the movement grew so rapidly that two years later there were 400 such organizations around the country with about 30,000 members. The majority of the members were crofters, workers or craftsmen, but there were also some farmers among their number. Leading figures in the world of arts, such as poets Henrik Ibsen (1828-1906) and

Aasmund Olavsson Vinje (1818-1870) also supported the movement. The Thranites fought for equality. They demanded universal suffrage for men, general conscription, better primary schools and equality before the law. They also pressed for lower prices and, in partidular, for repeal of the import duty on grain. And finally, they insisted that the authorities help people own their own land by alloting uncleared land to those who had none.

Such dissatisfaction can be explained as a result of tensions in Norwegian society due to population pressure and lack of available land. Marcus Thrane did receive impulses from abroad, however. He had visited London and Paris and was familiar with the ideas that had inspired the February Revolution of 1849, while the revolution itself was of great inspiration to him. Both public officials and farmers feared the Thranites with their talk of "revolution», and in 1851 Thane and other leaders of the movement were arrested. Thrane was released in 1858 and emigrated then to America. The movement he had founded had ceased to exist. Even though this first workers' movement was crushed, it still heralded the beginning of a new age.

In 1824 Klein Pedersen Hesthammer was sent to the USA by Norwegian Quakers to investigate the possibility of emigration. In America he was given the name Cleng Peerson.

Emigration

After 1860 emigration to the USA began in earnest. The rapid increase in population in Norway meant that times were hard for many. America seemed very tempting. People had heard about fantastic wages and cheap farm land. In 1862 the American Congress passed the Homestead Act which granted new settlers up to 160 acres of land to farm. Friends and relatives wrote letters from America, praising their new country.

Emigration took place in phases. When the last great wave was over, more than 800,000 had crossed the Atlantic. Only Ireland had a higher emigration rate in relation to the total population. Mainly young people emigrated, the majority of them men. Until 1880 whole families would set off together. Later it was mainly single men and women. Most did well in their new home, though there were some who died during the sea-crossing, came to sad ends in the slums of big cities, or were killed by Indians. Nowadays there is hardly a Norwegian family without relatives in the USA.

Emigration 1876–1890

- More than 15 per 1000 inhabitants
- 10–14 per 1000
- 7–9 per 1000
- 4–6 per 1000
- 1–3 per 1000

Seen in relation to the county population figures for this period, it was from Oppland, Hedmark, Buskerud and Rogaland counties most people emigrated.

The second phase of emigration peaked in 1882. Almost 29,000 people left Norway, more than the combined populations of the cities of Trondheim and Tromsø. An important cause was the crisis in the shipping industry.

The sloop «Restaurationen» sailed from Stavanger in 1825 with 52 emigrants on board. They were Quakers and wished to practise their religion unmolested. They settled in the Fox River valley in Illinois.

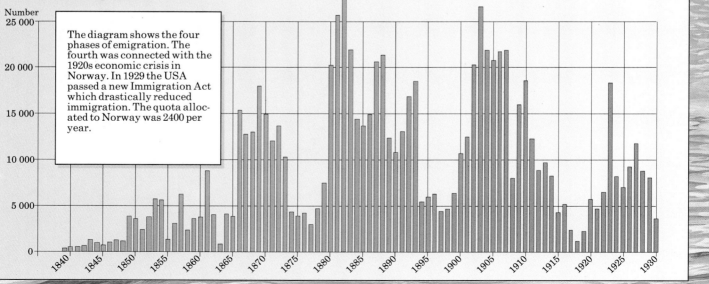

Emigration up to 1930

Number

The diagram shows the four phases of emigration. The fourth was connected with the 1920s economic crisis in Norway. In 1929 the USA passed a new Immigration Act which drastically reduced immigration. The quota allocated to Norway was 2400 per year.

25 000

20 000

15 000

10 000

5 000

0

1840 1845 1850 1855 1860 1865 1870 1875 1880 1885 1890 1895 1900 1905 1910 1915 1920 1925 1930

Farmers of Norwegian descent harvesting wheat in Koshkonong, Wisconsin, c.1875. The photographer was Andrew Dahl (1844–1923).

This map shows where most of the immigrants of Norwegian origin settled prior to 1910. The majority had been attracted to the states of the Midwest, west of the Great Lakes. Nowadays Norwegian place-names abound in these rich agricultural areas. But the states of the north west were also popular with Norwegians.
The figures on the map represent persons born in Norway or born in the USA to Norwegian parents.

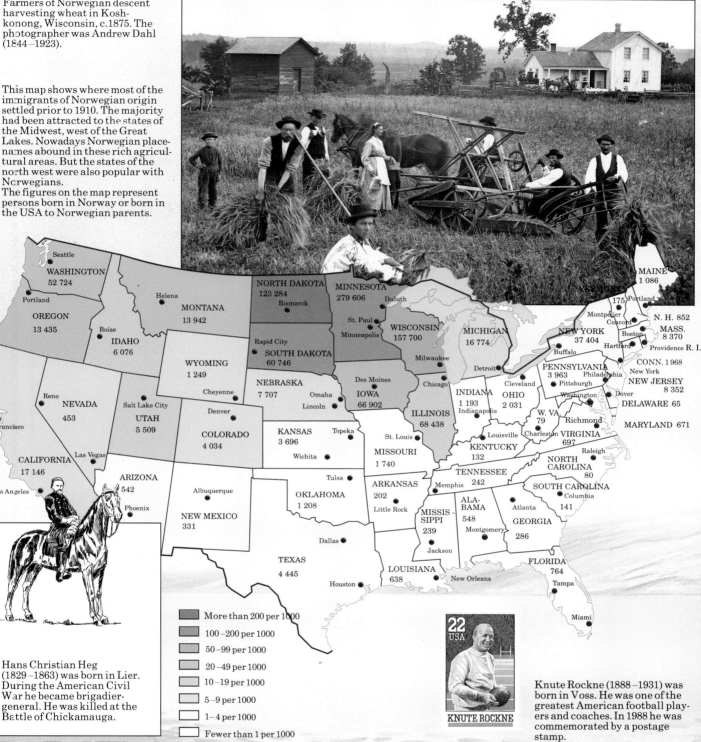

Seattle
WASHINGTON
52 724
Portland
OREGON
13 435
Helena
MONTANA
13 942
Boise
IDAHO
6 076
NORTH DAKOTA
123 284
Bismarck
MINNESOTA
279 606
Duluth
St. Paul
Minneapolis
WISCONSIN
157 700
Milwaukee
MICHIGAN
16 774
Detroit
MAINE
1 086
VERMONT
175   Portland
Montpelier
Concord   N. H. 852
Boston
Hartford   MASS.
8 370
Providence R. I.
CONN. 1968
New York
NEW JERSEY
8 352
Rapid City
SOUTH DAKOTA
60 746
WYOMING
1 249
Cheyenne
NEBRASKA
7 707
Omaha
Lincoln
Des Moines
IOWA
66 902
Chicago
ILLINOIS
68 438
St. Louis
INDIANA
1 193
Indianapolis
OHIO
2 031
Cleveland
Pittsburgh
PENNSYLVANIA
3 963
Philadelphia
Washington   Dover
DELAWARE 65
MARYLAND 671
Buffalo
NEW YORK
37 404
Reno
NEVADA
453
Salt Lake City
UTAH
5 509
Denver
COLORADO
4 034
KANSAS
3 696
Topeka
Wichita
MISSOURI
1 740
KENTUCKY
132
Louisville
W. VA.
79
Charleston
Richmond
VIRGINIA
697
Raleigh
San Francisco
CALIFORNIA
17 146
Las Vegas
ARIZONA
542
Phoenix
Los Angeles
Albuquerque
NEW MEXICO
331
OKLAHOMA
1 208
Tulsa
ARKANSAS
202
Little Rock
Memphis
TENNESSEE
242
NORTH CAROLINA
80
SOUTH CAROLINA
141
Columbia
Dallas
TEXAS
4 445
Houston
LOUISIANA
638
New Orleans
MISSIS-SIPPI
239
Jackson
ALA-BAMA
548
Montgomery
GEORGIA
286
Atlanta
FLORIDA
764
Tampa
Miami

More than 200 per 1000
100–200 per 1000
50–99 per 1000
20–49 per 1000
10–19 per 1000
5–9 per 1000
1–4 per 1000
Fewer than 1 per 1000

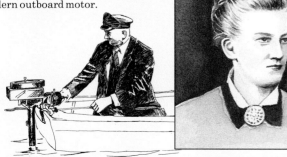

Hans Christian Heg (1829–1863) was born in Lier. During the American Civil War he became brigadier-general. He was killed at the Battle of Chickamauga.

22 USA
KNUTE ROCKNE

Knute Rockne (1888–1931) was born in Voss. He was one of the greatest American football players and coaches. In 1988 he was commemorated by a postage stamp.

Ole Evinrude (1877–1934) of Toten in Norway grew up in Wisconsin. He invented the modern outboard motor.

Agnes Wergeland (1857–1914) from Oslo was the first Norwegian woman to gain a doctorate. Though she found no employment in Norway, she became professor of history and languages at the University of Wyoming.

Walter Mondale (born 1928) has family roots in Mundal, Sogn. He was senator for Minnesota from 1964 to 1977 and US Vice-President 1977–1981. He was the Democratic Party's candidate in the presidential election of 1984, but did not win.

The Dawn of an Industrial Society

The trade carried out from the 18th century and until the Russian revolution in 1917, between the people of Finnmark and Troms counties and Russians living on the White Sea, is called the **Pomor** trade (from the Russian *pomor*, those who dwell on the coast). The Russians' principal trade item was rye flour, while the Norwegians had fish to trade. This trade was first forbidden but was legalized in the late 18th century due to more liberalistic views of commerce. The illustration shows the unloading of huge sacks of flour, so-called "flour mats», from a Pomor ship, in Hammerfest in the 1890s.

It is impossible to understand the expansive development of the latter half of the 19th century without first looking beyond Norway's boundaries. All Europe was undergoing change. Germany and Italy had been unified into populous nation-states, industrialization gathered headway and railways linked every part of the continent. This led to greater demands for goods and services, even from little Norway on the very fringe of Europe. For better or worse, Norwegian economy was more closely linked to other countries. Norway became more prosperous, but also more affected by international business cycles. Ordinary people got a taste for new products, and imports of sugar, chocolate, tropical fruits, coffee and tea soared. Large segments of the population adopted a money economy.

During the 1840s and '50s, the Storting passed several laws easing domestic trade. Anyone who wanted could now work as a craftsman in town or country, while country shopkeepers no longer had to be burghers of a town. The abolishment of sawmill monopolies meant that anyone could run his own sawmill. This kind of trade policy was in keeping with the economic liberalism now dominating Europe. The Storting also passed resolutions removing many of the country's protective import duties.

Roads were built at a rate which doubled the total length of the country's roads in fifty years' time. Steamships plied scheduled routes along the coast and on the largest inland lakes. The country's first railway opened in 1854 between Christiania and Eidsvoll. Timber from Lake Øyeren to Christiania was the main freight, but farm produce was also carried. The capital city's rapid growth increased the need for fresh foods supplies from nearby districts. This first railway had been built and partly financed by a British company, but the state participated actively in building and financing the tremendous railway construction work of the next fifty years. By 1910 three-fourths of the present railway network had been built. After the first telegraph line was opened in 1855, lines soon criss-crossed the country. In 1880 Norway's first telephone line was opened in the presence of the inventor, Alexander Graham Bell (1847-1922).

The steamship *Ganger Rolf* of Christiania was built in 1856. The reason steamships also had sails was that the steam engines were as yet unable to utilize fully the energy in the coals. Painted by W.D. Penny in 1857.

By 1900 there were 24,000 telephones in Norway. Postal services were also facilitated when postage rates were standardized country-wide.

Norwegian shipping experienced its third "golden age" between 1850 and 1880. The merchant fleet increased from 300,000 to 1,5 million net registered tons, while individual ships were larger. 60,000 seamen had signed on to Norwegian ships by 1880. The country's merchant fleet was the world's third largest after Great Britain and the United States.

There was good reason for Norwegian success. Sea transport was the natural way of transporting bulk goods. World trade increased by more than 50 per cent in each decade from 1840 to 1870. Populous Great Britain, Norway's most important trading partner, was dependent on seaborne supplies. With the repeal of the Navigation Act in 1850, ships from any nation could freely transport goods to Britain. Norwegian shipowners seized this opportunity. Norway's seafaring tradition was illustrious, and well-qualified seamen from coastal areas were ready and waiting to sign on. Wages were low, however, and many ships in wretched condition.

In 1850 Norwegian ships sailed mostly in European waters with timber as the main cargo. From 1860 on, however, long-distance trades became more important. Norwegian ships began sailing to the United States, Africa, South America, China, India and Australia, carrying varied cargoes: rice, coffee, cotton, coal, ice and tropical fruits, but timber still made up more than half the freight volume in the mid-1870s.

Joint ownership, with several people owning shares in a ship, was the most common ownership form. Merchants probably owned most shares, but farmers, timber - merchants, shipbuilders, sailmakers, captains, first mates and even ordinary seamen could own shares in a ship. It was not unusual for those who supplied materials or labour for a ship to be paid with shares instead of money. Joint ownership has been called "ownership by the people", and even if this is an exaggeration, the system did help finance a shipping boom in a country lacking a well-developed system of financial institutions.

Shipping also helped land-based employment. Shipyards lay scattered along the coast, and although small, still provided jobs for more than 5000 people in the 1870s. Rope-makers, sail-makers, and other craftsmen producing ship's equipment provided jobs for both men and women, while lumber-yards and sawmills made good money on deliveries to the yards.

Norwegian shipping declined in the late 1870s and the number of seamen dropped by 20,000 during the next decade. Historians disagree as to the reasons for the crisis. Did Norwegians lose out because of not converting from sail to steam quickly enough? Conservative Norwegian shipowners were known to have clung to their white sails.

Workers of various ages at the Mesna Works in Lillehammer in the 1890s. To the left, Børsum's famous horse-drawn rake, to the right a two-horse reaper. Manager Børsum himself in the middle, holding all the medals won by the company.

Another reason can be found in the country's lack of capital. Steamships did cost five times as much as sailing ships of the same size. Nonetheless, some shipowners bought steamships during the 1890s. One of them, Halvdan Wilhelmsen (1864-1923), built up Norway's largest shipowning company over the next few decades. The age of joint ownership and the age of sail were over. By 1907, Norway's merchant fleet had more ships under steam than under sail.

A new phase of industrialization began in Norway in the 1860s. While the textile mills of the 1840s had produced for the home market only, new industrial concerns now aimed at export. Steam engines became the source of power for sawmills, planing mills were established and in 1863 the country's first pulp mill manufacturing paper was opened at the Bentse Works at Sagene in Christiania. Pulp mills were later fitted with water-turbines to provide more power to the machines. By 1890 there were 60 pulp mills, all of which made profits even during the 1880s-depression. Norway's first cellulose factory, Hafslunds chemiske Trævare-fabrik near Sarpsborg, began operations in 1874. Planing machines and turbines were produced by the rapidly expanding engineering works. The technologically innovative

Myren's Works in Christiania sold equipment to planing mills in both Sweden and Finland. Canneries also produced for the export market. As early as in 1870, for example, canneries in Moss and Stavanger exported over 100 tons of tinned fish.

All this new industry required a great deal of capital, much of which came from abroad, especially from Great Britain. Foreign investors were interested in Norway because of its abundant natural resources and cheap labour force. Invaluable capital was also raised by the Norwegian commercial banks which had been established around 1850. By the turn of the century, industry accounted for 28 per cent of the country's gross national product and employed over a quarter of its active workforce.

People flocked in from the countryside to towns and villages in search of work. In 1870 about 20 per cent of the population lived in towns and built-up areas. By 1900 the figure had grown to well over 30 per cent. Christiania's population grew from 75,000 in 1870 to 230,000 in 1900. Bergen and Trondheim acted like regional capitals, with 72,000 and 38,000 inhabitants respectively at the turn of the century.

The industrial worker's day was long and monotonous, lasting some 10 to 12 hours.

Many worked overtime and none had annual holidays. Open cog wheels, uncovered driving belts and cold premises made work-places dangerous and unhealthy. The first laws concerning worker protection were not passed until the 1890s. Men and women were paid differently even when doing the same job. Women, not being family bread-winners, got half a man's wages. Child labour was widespread. It was cheap and many families needed their children's earnings desparately. Children down to the age of six were given into the care of factory foremen, a practice which could be just short of negli-gence. "If a child appears ill, it must not be forced to work too hard," as the regulations for a tobacco factory stated. It was in just such tobacco and match factories that half the workers were under the age of 15. In 1875, this was true of nearly 10 per cent of the total industrial work force. It was not until 1892 that legislation sett the age limit for child workers to 12. Young people under 18 years of age were permitted to work "only" 10 hours a day.

Slum areas grew up around the factory buildings in these early years. Large tene-ment blocks with tiny flats for working families later made huge profits for the owners, but the spirit of community in such crowded quarters led to worker solidarity.

The well-to-do lived far from the noise and smoke of the factories, in detached villas or huge apartments, with servants to do the housework and take care of the children. Class distinction was clearly noticeable in towns, and even though industrial workers had as high a standard of living as did crofters or servants, they still felt they ought to receive a larger share of the wealth created by their efforts in industry.

Old tavern along Maridalsveien near Oslo. Painted by J. Flintoe about 1830.

Industrialisation

New manufacturing industries arrived from Great Britain in the 1840s. The first textile mills were built in Christiania and near Bergen and Trondheim. Engineering workshops made their appearance at about the same date. In the 1860s and 70s came pulp mills and cellulose factories.

A third phase of industrialisation opened after 1900. The power of waterfalls was harnessed, and the factories began using electricity. New roads were built, and railway, steamer, postal and telegraphic services linked the different parts of the country. Between 1865 and 1900 the urban population increased from 15 % to 30 % of the total population. In 1900 manufacturing industry accounted for 28 % of the gross national product and employed over a quarter of the country's active labour force.

Røros copper works exemplifies the old type of industry in Norway. This 18th-century painting by Mathias Dalager shows the smelting works with Røros church in the background.

The engineering works Trondhjems Mekaniske Verksted A/S dates from 1843. It produced the first Norwegian-built locomotive «Thrønderen» in 1861.
▼

The textile factory Hjula Veveri on the river Aker in Christiania was established in 1849. On this 1866 view by Carl Baagøe it is seen to the left of the waterfall. To the right is the paper mill Nedre Papirmølle. The weaver (right) at the Hjula mill was painted in 1887–8 by Wilhelm Peters; the picture was commissioned by the factory owner. Most of the workers in the textile industry were women.

Norway's first railway went from Christiania to Eidsvoll and was opened in 1854.

Norway's first telegraph line, between Christiania and Drammen, came into operation in 1855. By 1871 telegraph wires extended as far as Kirkenes in Finnmark county. The first Norwegian postage stamp was issued in 1854, when the same postal rates were applied to the entire country. The postal and telegraphic services provided employment for many women.

Borregaard fabriker, Sarpsborg

The cellulose and paper factories at Borregaard near Sarpsborg were built for a British company in the 1890s. In 1905 this enterprise was Norway's largest with about 1000 employees.

The turn-of-the-century photograph below shows women workers in a canning factory in Stavanger. The «Man with the Fish» sardine-tin label was designed by Theodor Kittelsen in 1905.
▼

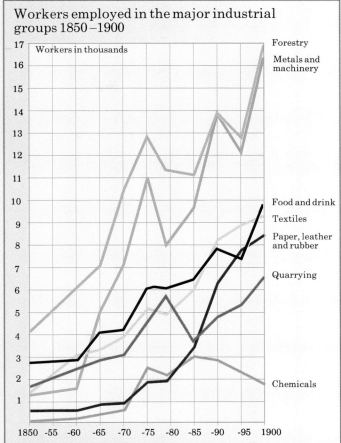

Workers employed in the major industrial groups 1850–1900

Workers in thousands

17
16
15
14
13
12
11
10
9
8
7
6
5
4
3
2
1

1850 -55 -60 -65 -70 -75 -80 -85 -90 -95 1900

Forestry

Metals and machinery

Food and drink

Textiles

Paper, leather and rubber

Quarrying

Chemicals

FINEST NORWEGIAN
Sardines
in OLIVE OIL
CHR. BJELLAND & CO.
STAVANGER.
Net weight
3½ oz.
7 GRAND PRIX 6 DIPLOMAS OF HONOR 20 GOLD MEDALS

In 1899 several trade unions wishing to unite in the struggle for better pay and working conditions formed what today is the Norwegian Federation of Trade Unions. In response, the Norwegian Employers' Confederation was founded the following year. Not until 1935 did the two bodies sign an agreement which regulated relations between employers and employees.

8
Timers
arbeidsdag

Many of the navvies who built the railways moved from one construction site to another. A good number of them were Swedes. The illustration shows a Mayday demonstration for shorter working hours. The claim for an eight hour working day in industry was not met until 1919.

Revolutionary Changes in Agriculture

Agriculture also changed profoundly during the latter half of the 19th century. Author Inge Krokann (1893-1962) gave this upheaval the name *Det store hamskifte*t ("the great sloughing-off") because rural communities changed so greatly, both economically, socially and culturally.

Around 1850 most farms were self-sufficient, even though farmers all over the country often took work also as lumbermen, log drivers, charcoal burners or fishermen. Spinning wheels and looms were in constant use, while farmers forged their own implements in the farm smithies. Only fifty years later, however, cash-crop farming was common in most areas of the country. New equipment had made farming more efficient and lessened the need for crofters and servants. Thousands had moved to towns or emigrated to America. Nonetheless, it must be emphasized that the greatest changes did not occur simultaneously all over the country.

The growth of cities had created larger markets for farmers' produce, a development that was greatly influenced by the new forms of transportation and industry. The growth of foreign competition and the authorities' policies on free trade also affected matters. The grain crisis of the 1860s is a good example of this.

After the close of the Crimean War in 1856, cheap grain flowed into the country, hitting farmers in eastern Norway especially hard. Bad harvests and floods reinforced the crisis, and many farmers were forced to reorganize their production from grain to cattle farming, sowing hay on former wheat fields to get enough fodder for their cattle. The imported wheat was not only cheap, it was of such high quality that many farmers saw an advantage in not having to grow wheat themselves. Wheat cultivation was often a gamble in many districts with their short summers and cold and rainy weather. Fresh produce, such as milk, eggs and meat, was an area where foreigners couldn't compete.

Emigration to the United States and moving to towns sapped country districts of their labour force. Many farmers therefore became interested in using labour-saving machines. Some even began to rotate their crops and to use artificial fertilizers. Strong iron ploughs meant larger crops, while horse rakes, horse drills, reaping and threshing machines needed fewer hands. Use of such equipment increased greatly towards the turn of the century. In 1875 there were 1300 reaping machines in the whole of Norway, while the figure twenty-five years later had leaped to 30,000! Cattle were better fed and cared for, giving more milk. In areas of the country where strip cultivation was common, exchanges of land were arranged by the authorities to collect farmlands into larger units for more efficient operations.

Farmers needed capital in order to reorganize their operations, however, and the authorities met this need in various ways, among them the establishment of a Royal Norwegian Mortgage Bank in 1851. The bank was a state institution which attracted foreign capital to Norway and then loaned this as cheap, long-term mortgages in rural districts. In time local savings banks also were able to give farmers loans. Farmers could learn new methods at the state agricultural schools that grew up all across the country. In 1859 the Agricultural College at Ås, not far from Oslo, was founded.

Starting in the 1870s, farmers cooperated in building dairies, after butter- and cheese-making on individual farms no longer was profitable. By 1875 there were 100 such dairies in Norway, mostly in the eastern districts, but their production still was only a small part of the national total. Many farmers furthered their economic security through membership in purchasing cooperatives and local savings associations. In 1896 farmers in eastern Norway founded the first professional agricultural organization, the Norwegian Farmers' Union, to work for the interests of the farming community and to influence politicians so that agriculture could receive "that support to which it is entitled". In 1922 the name was changed to the Norwegian Farmers' Association.

Although farmers organized themselves and sent demands to the central authorities, few thought of using the power of the state to their own advantage. They were more interested in lowering taxes and state expenditures, and transfering power to local councils and boards of aldermen. But in order to accomplish such decentralization, farmers and their supporters had to take control of the seat of power. Which social forces could challenge king and public officialdom?

COUNTER-CULTURES

"Counter-cultures" is a term designating groups in Norwegian society who opposed the public officials, urban culture and the union with Sweden. They were instrumental in the political struggles of the 1870s and '80s and in the dissolution of the union in 1905.

The first folk high school was founded in 1864, inspired by the work of Danish bishop Nicolai Grundtvig (1783-1872). *The folk high school movement* opposed the cramming and passive learning of the cathedral schools and the university. Teachers at the folk high schools tried instead to inspire to national, cultural, religious and human values. People active in the folk high school movement were often leaders in *the liberal youth movement.* They joined together in the nationwide Norwegian Youth League in 1896, whose more than 20,000 members acted to further "popular knowledge on a wholly Norwegian basis". Both folk high schools and liberal youth movements were strongly influenced by *the New-Norwegian language movement.* They fought for official recognition of Ivar Aasen's *landsmål,* or New-Norwegian, based on Norwegian dialects, as being equal to *riksmål,* the Danish-influenced language spoken by most townspeople. This occurred in 1885. The Christian *laymen's movement* was, however, the strongest of them all. Deeply influenced by Hans Nielsen Hauge's 18th-century evangelistic movement, charismatic lay preachers emerged to support personal Christian engagement. Enthusiasm for missionary work was equally great. This work was carried out outside the Norwegian Church, even though missionary organizations cooperated with Church and clergy. The Norwegian Missionary Society, founded in 1842 as the first of such groups in Norway, established missions in Madagascar. Work with an inner mission began in the 1850s, while the Norwegian Lutheran Foundation was founded in 1868. Its aim was the furthering of pietistic, true Christianity in Norway. This foundation had great influence in the Church and in Norwegian society as a whole. The *temperance movement* is also considered counter-cultural. The growing misuse of alcohol, especially among labourers in the cities, was a matter of great concern. Total abstinence was a goal of such obvious simplicity that it could be understood by everyone. By the turn of the century 150,000 people had taken the pledge of total abstinence. The upper and middle classes were on the whole hostile to the temperance movement. Wines and spirits were a natural part of their daily lives, illustrating one more example of cultural contrasts.

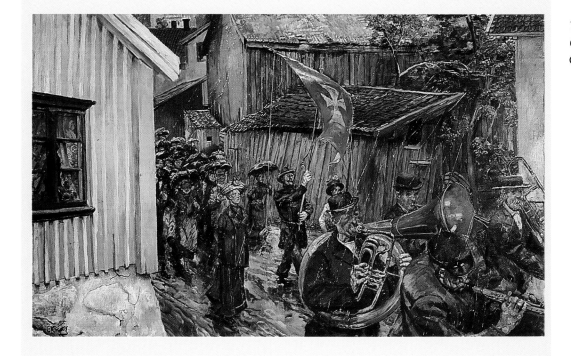

The Total Abstainers' Sunday Outing, painted by Christian Krohg in 1913.

The Collapse of State Officialdom. A Change of Political System.

In the 1860s, an organization called *Bonde-vennene* (Friends of the Farmer) was founded by Søren Jaabæk (1814-1894), a farmer and representative to the Storting. The 25,000 members of this first voters' association came from every part of the country except Finnmark county. It was instrumental in the election of even more farmers to the Storting, who held the majority from 1868. The Friends worked for the growth of local self-government. They disliked the use of public funds to assist trade and business, feeling that taxation hit farmers too hard. By 1870, the level of municipal taxes had risen to twice that of in 1850, in itself an excellent argument for frugality in local and state governments. The group was loosely organized and died out in the 1870s. By that time the grain crisis in eastern Norway had passed, emigration to America provided a safety valve for discontents, while Jaabæk himself had challenged the counter-cultures by declaring himself a republican, an atheist and a supporter of universal suffrage. If government by officialdom was to be defeated, firm leadership was needed. This came about when Søren Jaabæk and his supporters in the Storting were allied with Johan Sverdrup (1816-1892), a lawyer and member of the Storting, and leader of a group of radical academics. Sverdrup was first elected to the Storting in 1851, and during the constitutional disputes of the 1870s and '80s, proved himself to be one of the foremost political leaders in Norwegian history.

The opposition saw the government as its principal opponent. Public officials still dominated politics and the king still appointed only officials as ministers. The Storting increased its power in 1869, however, when annual parliamentary sessions were adopted. Sverdrup and his supporters could now carry out continuous opposition tactics. The struggle for power could now begin in earnest.

In 1872, the Storting discussed a constitutional amendment concerning the duty of ministers to participate in parliamentary meetings in order to defend the policy they conducted. Sverdrup argued that "[...] at that Instant when all Power and Might is gathered in this Chamber to determine the Greatest and most Important of Society's Affairs, a mighty Revival will sweep this Nation [...]". The Storting adopted the amendment, so that ministers might be "forced from the gloom of their offices".

The king refused to approve the amendment, however, pointing to the separation of powers as the foundation of the Constitution. In addition he and the government maintained that the king had an absolute veto in matters concerning the Constitution, even though the document contained no mention of this. Sverdrup and the farmers insisted that the king had no such power.

King Oscar, the coachman in this cartoon, is having problems controlling his team, labelled "Right" (Conservative) and "Left", who are pulling a sledge with a very worried "Mother Norway" on board.

The amendment proposition was passed by three consecutive sessions of the Storting. The government continued to advise the king that he ought not give sanction. The situation was at a stalemate.

The farmers' opposition in the Storting decided to use its last resource: to impeach the government before the *riksrett*, a special court where members of the *Lagting* chamber sit in judgement together with the High Court justices, while the *Odelsting* prosecutes. In the elections of 1882 Sverdrup's supporters, who were now known as *Venstre* (the Left), won 83 of 114 seats. Several ministers, headed by Prime Minister Christian August Selmer (1816-1889) were sentenced to loss of office, while others were fined. The majority of the court, all members of the Lagting, determined that the government should not have advised the king to refuse sanction in the matter of ministers' prescence in the Storting.

King Oscar II had in deepest secrecy made plans for a coup, but the plans were abandoned. In June of 1884, he asked the leader of the majority in the Storting, Johan Sverdrup, to form a government. This was the first time a politician had become prime minister due to the support of a majority of the members. State officialdom had been defeated and parliamentarism had been introduced in Norway. Hereafter, governments would alternate acccording to the strength of the various factions in the Storting.

This ministerial matter and the dispute about the king's veto rights led to the founding of two political groups, Liberal (*Venstre* or "Left") and Conservative (*Høyre* or "Right"), first as distinct groups in the Storting and thereafter as country-wide political parties. The Liberals were supported by farmers, teachers and white-collar workers. In the 1880s many of the party's leading issues were adopted. Among these was a new electoral law giving about half the male electorate the vote, although universal suffrage for men was not introduced until 1898. *Landsmål*, or New-Norwegian, was put on an equal footing with the Dano-Norwegian language used by many townspeople, giving the country two official written languages. A Criminal Procedures Act stipulated that a jury of laymen were to determine the question of guilt in criminal cases. The Education Acts introduced seven years' compulsory schooling for all children. Sverdrup did experience problems, however, and the Conservatives, who were supported by public officials and the bourgeoisie, took over the government in 1889.

Ordinary people outside the Storting also organized themselves. During the 1880s and 1890s, it became increasingly customary for both men and women workers to organize in trade unions. Conflicts with employers had shown the need for solidarity in the struggle for improved working conditions and higher wages. Local unions in the

This drawing is of a session of the impeachment trial in February 1884, with the principal defendent, Prime Minister Selmer, seated alone in the background to the left.

Th. Kittelsen's *Strike* is the first Norwegian painting with a clear social message. The first sketch for the painting was done in 1877.

Prostitution was widespread in the larger cities in the 1800s. Christian Krohg attacked society's double standard of morals concerning prostitution in his novel *Albertine* published in 1886, the same year he painted *Albertine in the Police Doctor's Waiting Room*. Bordelles were closed down in the late 1880s and examinations by the police doctor also ceased. Local health boards then took over responsibility for the control of venereal diseases.

same trade formed nationwide federations, which in 1899 joined together in the *Landsorganisasjon i Norge*, the Norwegian Federation of Trade Unions. One of its purposes was to advise members on all matters affecting trade unions. This growing threat from organized labour was met the following year by the founding of *Norsk Arbeidsgiver-forening*, the Norwegian Employers Confederation. 1887 saw the founding of the Norwegian Labour Party. It soon adopted socialism, demanding shorter working hours and universal suffrage. Few workers voted for the party at first, most of them preferring to support the Liberals, but in 1903 the Party won four seats in the Storting. Three

of these members came from Troms county in the far north, where fisheries were of vital importance. It appeared that not only industrial workers but country folk as well could consider voting Labour.

Equality of the sexes was another important issue in the final decades of the 1800s. New opportunities opened up for women, particularly middle class women. Primary schools, the postal and telegraph services being in need of qualified labour, women now gained the right to attend secondary schools. In 1884 women won the right to sit all final examinations at the University, although some time elapsed before appreciable numbers applied. Opportunities for academic employment were also few. Leading figures began speaking out in behalf of women, while the dramas of both Henrik Ibsen and Bjørnstjerne Bjørnson also provoked debate on the issue. Men and women alike joined the *Norsk Kvinnesaksforbund*, the Norwegian League of Feminists, founded in 1884. Women founded a suffrage union the following year, but their demands met opposition both within and outside the Storting. Women's place was in the home, it was said, their instability making them unfit for positions of responsibility. But women captured one position after another. While the right to vote was first granted only to women above a certain level of income, the Storting adopted suffrage for all women in 1913. In 1924, the first woman was elected a member of the Storting.

FRIDTJOF NANSEN AND THE BUILDERS OF NATIONAL UNITY

As the 20th century dawned, Fridtjof Nansen (1861-1930), biologist, polar scientist and politician, was one of Norway's most well-known and respected men. His crossing of Greenland on skis in 1889 had won him nation-wide recognition. Between 1893 and '96, he led North Pole expeditions. He sailed to the extreme North on board the "Fram", a ship especially reinforced to withstand arctic ice. After the ship was stopped by ice, he and lieutenant Hjalmar Johansen proceeded on foot and on 7 April 1895, they reached 86° 14' north – farther north than any previous expedition. In his scientific reports, Nansen often emphasized the special character of the Norwegian:

"[...] Norwegians are indubitably members of that nation best suited to conducting polar science. We are conditioned to better tolerance of the climate, and in our skiers we possess a superiority of the first importance". (Letter to the national government, 1888)

Fridtjof Nansen's interests extended to far more than science. He was a central figure in the so-called *Lysakerkrets*, or Lysaker Group, a cultural-political circle of artists and scientists who lived at Lysaker just outside Christiania. Members of the circle included artists Erik Werenskiold (1855-1938), Gerhard Munthe (1849-1929), and Eilif Petersen (1852-1928) as well as professors Gerhard Gran (1856–1925) in litterature, and Moltke Moe (1859-1913) in folklore. Historian and Liberal Party member Ernst Sars (1835-1917) did not belong to the group, but because he was Nansen's brother-in-law, his opinions and historical vision carried great weight.

The Lysaker Group had roots reaching back to the bourgeois nationalism of the early 19th century. Its aim was the transformation of Norway into a modern, European cultural nation. The group's ideology of national cohesion attempted to reconcile the gap between rural and urban culture and to combine the traditional with the modern, making Norwegians more aware of their national character. The Lysaker Group would build a *Norwegian nation.*

This theme of reconciliation was evident in the famous speech Fridtjof Nansen held on 17 mai 1905 – a few short weeks before the Union was dissolved:

"[...] unity has never distinguished Norwegians at any time in history. The distance in our country between one farm and the next or between districts was so great that neighbour could not consult with neighbour over every trifling matter; each made up his own mind, self-sufficient and confident of his own abilities. [...] This self-willed inclination has no doubt flourished most wonderfully in an Ibsen, who formed the maxim that that man is strongest who stands most alone. [...] Therefore let us not accuse one another too strongly for having difficulties in reaching agreement. But let us believe that once we do reach agreement, then that will which ties us together can become an invincible force; *one* will uniting us all, promising that those goals which we have set will also be achieved."

Fridtjof Nansen, 1900

The Severance of the Union in 1905

Ever since 1814 Norway had been the junior partner in the union with Sweden. Conflict about the union arose again in the late 1800s. Most people believed that the union had less and less economic significance for Norway. The best example of this was when Sweden terminated the free trade agreement, *Mellomriksloven*, between the two kingdoms in 1897. Swedish foreign policy was another matter that alarmed Norwegians, who had strong ties to Great Britain. In the 1880s, King Oscar II had declared that "Germany is and should be our closest and most natural ally». Norwegians also objected to having a Swede as joint foreign minister and to joint consular representation abroad. The best interests of Norwegian business would be looked after only when Norway had its own consulates.

In the 1890s, the Liberal Party took the initiative in an attempt to solve the foreign affairs dispute. The party strongly advocated that Norway have its own foreign minister, with a minimum requirement being the establishment of a separate consular service. The Conservative Party supported this last demand but insisted that any such innovations must be the result of negotiations with the Swedes. In 1895 the Liberal Party was forced to assent to negotiations when Sweden threatened war. In the years that followed, the two parties alternated in having power, and eventually the negotiations were postponed indefinitely. During this period, how-ever, the Storting allocated more funds to defence. Fortifications were built along the border between southern Norway and Sweden. These were earthworks with fortified command rooms and trenches. Norway ordered four new ironclad ships from Great Britain as well as 140 German rapid-firing guns.

Sweden took the initiative for new negotiations on consular representation in 1902. Agreement was reached that Norway should have her own consuls and that Sweden should propose the necessary legislation. This agreement split the Liberal Party once again. Radical members of the party felt that the agreement would prevent Norway from acquiring her own foreign service. The more moderate members, led by shipowner and Storting member Christian Michelsen (1857-1925), broke away and fought the ensuing election together with the Conservatives, as the Unity Party. Dramatist Bjørnstjerne Bjørnson devised the party's motto as, "We know of no other course save negotiation!"

The Unity Party won the election. Sweden now proposed legislation on consular representation. Norway was to have her own consuls, but the foreign minister would continue to be Swedish and the Norwegian consuls would be subordinate to him. The Norwegians could not accept this and the political parties prepared for battle under the warcry "Out of the Union!" Christian Michelsen became prime minister in a broad coalition government where only the Labour Party was not represented.

In the spring of 1905, the Storting passed legislation on a separate Norwegian consu-

Norwegian soldiers sharpening their sabres in connection with the severance of the union in 1905.

lar service. When the king refused sanction, the government resigned. On the 7th of June the Storting carried a resolution to the effect that "the union with Sweden under a single Monarch has ceased to exist, as a consequence of that Monarch having ceased to function as King of Norway". The chief argument was that he had failed to give the country a new government.

The resolution of 7 June caused consternation in Sweden where the Conservatives advised going to war. Norwegian soldiers were ordered to patrol the borders, but more moderate forces prevailed in Sweden and new negotiations were started. The Storting attempted to reassure the Swedes by offering the Norwegian throne to a prince of the royal family, but the offer was rejected. A plebiscite on the union was held in August. Only 184 men voted in favour of continued union while women collected 250,000 signatures in support of severance. After difficult negotiations, Norway agreed to destroy most of the border fortifications. The threat of war was over.

Now only one problem remained. Should Norway continue to be a monarchy? The Government decided in favour of this, offering the throne to Prince Carl of Denmark. He was married to Princess Maud, daughter of the British King, and they were the par-ents of a two-year-old son. The prince insisted on a referendum. 80 % of the electorate voted in favour of monarchy.

On a snowy November day, the new royal family landed in Christiania. The king adopted the name Håkon VII and gave his son the name Olav. Norway had made a wise choice by binding Denmark and Britain to the royal family. After centuries of union, Norway could finally take her place as one of the independent nations of Europe.

Edvard Grieg (1843-1907) is unchallenged as Norway's greatest composer. Grieg's compostitions contain many elements of Norwegian folk music, and have won acclaim in the international world of music.

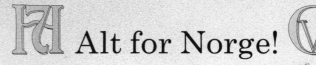

Alt for Norge!

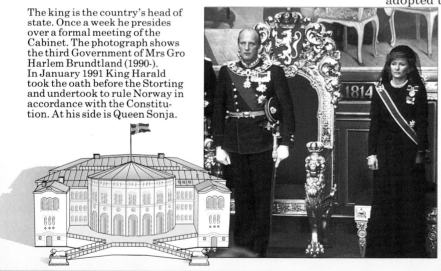

King Haakon VII with Crown Prince Olav on his arm is welcomed by Prime Minister Christian Michelsen in 1905.

The Royal Palace in Oslo is at the western end of Karl Johans gate, the main street of the capital.

In 1905 the people of Norway chose Prince Carl of Denmark as their king. He was married to Princess Maud of England and they had a two-year-old son. Prince Carl took the style Haakon VII and the Crown Prince was given the name Olav. In 1929 Crown Prince Olav married Princess Märtha of Sweden. They had three children, Ragnhild, Astrid and Harald. King Haakon died in 1957 and the Crown Prince came to the throne as King Olav V. On the death of King Olav in 1991 the Crown Prince became King Harald V. In 1968 he had married Sonja Haraldsen of Oslo, and she now became Queen. The King and Queen have two children, Märtha Louise and Haakon Magnus. All three kings adopted the motto «All for Norway».

The king is the country's head of state. Once a week he presides over a formal meeting of the Cabinet. The photograph shows the third Government of Mrs Gro Harlem Brundtland (1990-). In January 1991 King Harald took the oath before the Storting and undertook to rule Norway in accordance with the Constitution. At his side is Queen Sonja.

King Olav on a 1975 state visit in the USA.

King Haakon's coronation in Trondheim, 1906

Queen Maud (1869–1938)

Crown Prince Olav ski jumping, 1923

Crown Prince Olav during the Liberation, 1945

The Norwegian royal family have always been keen on outdoor life and sport. The illustration shows King Haakon, Queen Maud and Crown Prince Olav skiing, c. 1910.

Crown Princess Sonja with Queen Margrethe of Denmark skiing in the Rondane Mountains, 1990.

There have been very enthusiastic yachtsmen in the royal family. At the 1928 Summer Olympics Crown Prince Olav won a gold medal in the 6-meter class. On several occasions Crown Prince Harald represented Norway in the Olympics and in World Championships with considerable success. In 1988 in «Fram X» he won the one-ton class World Championship. From 1965 to 1969 he was Commodore of the Royal Norwegian Yacht Club.

King Olav soon became a very popular king. He travelled about the country to gain first-hand experience of his people.
During the oil crisis of the mid-1970s there was petrol rationing and even the King used public transport. The photograph shows King Olav in a tram on his way to ski in Oslo's Nordmarka forest.

The royal family on the balcony of the Royal Palace on 17 May, Constitution Day, in 1989. Left to right: Prince Haakon Magnus, Crown Princess Sonja, King Olav, Princess Märtha Louise and Crown Prince Harald.

The National Aid Fund for War Victims

Crown Princess Märtha (1901–1954)

King Olav's consecration in 1958

King Olav sailing

King Olav in dress uniform

King Olav judging ski jumping

Norway an Independent Country 1905–1940

The New Working Day 1905-1914

In a speech held after the severance of the union, Prime Minister Michelsen spoke of the beginning of "a new working day" in Norway. In this he was far-seeing. Ample water power gave the country an advantage, and led to decisive growth in industry in the post-1905 period. Towns continued to grow, giving farmers larger markets and better prices. Change in agriculture continued at an ever-increasing pace, as again indicated by the growing number of reapers: between 1907 and 1917 their number increased from 50,000 to 90,000. Communications systems developed, water power allowed for the installation of electric power in more private homes, and electric tramcars were introduced in the largest cities. Motor-powered vessels pointed to imminent change in the fishing and merchant fleets, while motor cars appeared on Norwegian roads. At the centennial celebration of the Constitution in 1914, the Jubilee Exhibition in Christiania was proof of material, artistic and scientific achievements. The thousands of electric lights reflected in the exhibition's artificial pond were an impressive sight. As reported in the daily paper, *Morgenbladet*, the exhibition was a manifestation of "[...] joy in labour, in invention, in talent, in the wish to benefit mankind [...]".

While the common struggle over the union with Sweden had united politicians, this concord soon disappeared after 1905. The Unity Party having withered when Christian Michelsen resigned as prime minister in 1907, the Right and Left rebuilt their party organizations. Michelsen's ideals did live on in the Liberal Right (Frisinnede Venstre) Party, founded in 1909, which co-operated closely with the Right. These three non-socialist parties competed with the Labour Party for favour of the electorate.

Around the turn of the century, foreign and Norwegian interests had begun large-scale purchase of waterfalls. Farmers owning the falls were often more than eager to sell, because they wanted capital to invest in their farms or for emigrating to America. And offers could be appallingly low. The rights to one-half of the Rjukan Falls were sold for 600 *kroner*, the original offer having been only 50! By 1906 three-fourths of the developed waterfalls were owned by foreigners, raising fears of a threat to national sovereignty.

General opinion held that the state should indeed make demands on industry. Towns in which hydroelectric plants were located ought to be provided with cheap electricity. Workers were to be offered decent housing. The state ought to ensure its receiving tax revenues, while developers ought to use Norwegian goods and services. Such radical proposals led to dissent in the Storting, but resulted in both Norwegian and foreign investors having to apply for permission (concessions) before starting up. This again made it possible for the state to impose con

Opposite:
The harnessing of the waterfalls inspired many artists. This painting is from Th. Kittelsen's *Rjukan series*, 1908-09. Optimism for the future radiates out of the picture. Man has succeeded in taming the forces of nature!

The first motor-cars aroused great interest. Here two young people from Setesdal have dressed up in their best clothes to be photographed by the famous A.B. Wilse.

NORSK HYDRO

About 350 people lived in Dal in mountainous Tinn in Telemark county at the turn of the century. A few tourists visited to view the magnificent Rjukan Falls, but mostly the place was left in peace. The next 20 years witnessed a revolution. By 1920 the Rjukan Falls had been tamed, its waters forced into conduits and an industrial town of 9,000 inhabitants built.

Industry was attracted to the mountain village by the power of the falls. In 1905 Norwegian industrialist Sam Eyde (1866-1940) had founded Norsk Hydro, with Swedish, French, German and Norwegian backing, to utilize Professor Kristian Birkeland's electric arc method. Birkeland's electric arc furnace utilized nitrogen in the air to produce nitrates (saltpetre). The first factory for producing this fertilizer was established in Notodden. Because the process required enormous amounts of electric power, the company built power plants at several waterfalls in Telemark. A new fertilizer factory was opened in Rjukan in 1911 and the little community grew up around it. The photograph shows the saltpetre factory at Såheim in 1911.

After World War II, Norsk Hydro began producing other products. Factories in Porsgrunn opened in the early 1950s for producing magnesium and PVC, a raw material for plastics. Ten years later an aluminium smelting works was established at Karmøy. The company was now involved in petroleum exploration in the North Sea. During the '70s and '80s, the company purchased fertilizer factories and aluminium plants abroad and built the petrochemical plant at Rafnes in Bamble. The company was also active in the pharmaceutical industry and in aquaculture. Norsk Hydro employ 32,000 people in 1995, about half of whom work in Norway. 51% of the shares are owned by the Norwegian State.

ditions. The law also stated that all developed waterfalls were to resort to the state after 60 to 80 years, and refused all foreign purchase of forests. These concession laws may have slowed the growth rate of Norwegian economy, but they also allowed for public control of the nation's natural resources. Another result was that the Norwegian government's heavy investments made it northern Europe's largest owner of water power.

Industrialization did not lead to general prosperity. Many town dwellers felt insecure without the old community spirit of rural areas. Unemployment, alcoholism, prostitution and poor housing raged in working-class districts. Demands for a more just division of wealth were raised by the Labour Party and the trade unions. Many of the bourgeoisie, especially those belonging to the Liberal Party, felt that the state was responsible for protecting the weak and for improving workers' conditions. The Storting therefore passed much reform legislation in the years preceeding World War I, such as provisions for sick pay and factory inspection, a Workers' Protection Act, and the ten-hour day. The eight-hour day was introduced in 1919. That same year, 115,000 industrial workers gained a legal right to one week's annual paid holiday.

Children born out of wedlock also gained rights, even though the Right warned of the effect such legislation had on public morals, marriage and the family. The Storting passed laws assuring "illegitimate" children of a fair share of their paternal inheritance and to the use of their mothers' or fathers' family names. Unmarried mothers received economic support during pregnancy, while requirements for fathers' economic contributions were tightened.

Norway during World War I

In 1905 the Storting and the government wished to keep the country out of international conflicts, and followed the example of Denmark and Sweden in adopting a policy of neutrality. With the outbreak of World War I in August 1914, however, Norway's position was threatened. Despite official neutrality, many Norwegians sympathized with the British, while the country's economy depended on good relations with Britain. Great Britain supplied vital products such as oil and coal, so that a British blockade of the merchant fleet was to be avoided at all costs. And the British applied pressure in this matter. In 1915, for example, they forced Norway to stop exports of fish to Germany. The merchant fleet also gave Great Britain and its allies valuable support. Norway was therefore spoken of as "the neutral ally".

This led to tense relations with Germany. German submarines caused great damage to the Norwegian merchant fleet by sinking half its ships, and over 2000 seamen lost their lives. Norwegian vessels often sailed in the most dangerous waters.

There were several reasons why Norway did not become directly involved in the War. Neither the Triple Alliance, led by Germany, nor the Triple Entente between Great Britain, France and Russia were interested in Norway's participating. Both blocks profitted by Norwegian neutrality and because Norway was a comparatively weak military power, alliance with her could be risky. Neither side wished to tie up troops on Norwegian soil.

Some Norwegians experienced the first war years as a time when money simply flowed in. The stock market boomed due to a demand for Norwegian goods and services. This was particularly true of shipping stocks, but trading in industrial stocks also increased and the number of corporations and commercial banks rose sharply. Some made enormous profits speculating on the exchange, but later most of these newly-rich went bankrupt.

The last two war years brought increasing difficulties to most people. Shortages of goods and rising prices hit the poorly-off. The authorities tried to lessen the effects of these hard times, but introduced their measures too late. Municipal supply committees were set up so that the state could control sales of foodstuffs. Monopolies on sugar and grain were introduced, while the use of potatoes and grain for distilling spirits was prohibited. Import of distilled spirits was forbidden in 1916, as were fortified wines the next year. Grain, flour, sugar, bread, coffee and tea were rationed during the last year of the war, with every family having a ration card to deliver to their shopkeeper. Rents were also controlled because they had risen sharply. The

National Price Directorate, established in 1917 to implement government price policies, exists to this very day. Such state intervention in the daily lives of ordinary people had hitherto been quite unknown.

Hard times and shortages, black marketeering and extravagances by the newly-rich irritated ordinary people, leading to an intensification of class antagonism in Norway during the war years.

This drawing from the Corsar Magazine shows Norway under pressure from the Great Powers during World War I.

Finance, Business and Industry during the Inter-war Years

A typical feature of financial development in the years between World Wars I and II is the lack of stability. Following a short period of expansion from 1918 to 1920, Norway was hit by falling prices and marketing difficulties. Later in the 1920s, both prices and monetary values fluctuated. This in turn led to wage disputes. Workers went out on strike while employers answered with lockouts.

The fiscal policy followed by the Bank of Norway during the 1920s intensified the problems. The Bank had issued far too many banknotes during the war, leading to strong inflation and a fall in the value of the *krone* when peace was declared. Measures, such as reducing the supply of money and increasing interest rates, were introduced to strengthen the *krone* in relation to the pound sterling and the gold standard, but it was not until 1928 that the value of the *krone* had reached a level acceptable to the central bank.

Edvard Munch (1863-1944) is Norway's most famous artist. In the inter-war years, he became engrossed by the advances made by the working class. This painting is entitled *Workers in snow*. In a letter from 1929, Munch wrote: «This is the age of the workers. Will art once again belong to everyone?»

The rising value of the *krone* created new problems. Investment in business and industry sank when it became more difficult to raise loans and repay debts. Those who had already borrowed money also had problems. Interest and instalments had to be paid in *krone* that were worth far more than when loans had been raised. Thousands of farmers who were hit by this increased burden of debt lost their farms by forced sale, and joined the army of the unemployed to find other work.

Most farmers who went bankrupt did not lose their farms, however, as their neighbours banded together to boycott the forced sales. They also threatened potential buyers against bidding on the properties. With no buyers, the banks usually reduced the debt and allowed the original owner to take over the farm again.

Many farmers tried to reduce indebtedness through increased production. This led to a surplus of farm produce because consumers in towns had less money with which to buy food. Competition between farmers increased and prices fell. Some solution had to be found, and in 1930 the Storting passed a sales law. Sales cooperatives were established by farmers in cooperation with the government to regulate sales of agricultural products. Dairy cooperatives, for example, determined how much milk was to be sold to consumers and how much was to be used in the production of cheese and butter. The cooperatives set prices, organized exports, and had the authority to excise products. Excise revenues were used to stabilize prices.

The fishing industry was especially hard hit by the crisis in the inter-war years. Fishermen had also borrowed money for new equipment in the post-1905 boom year. As export prices fell and loans grew more expensive in the 1920s, many fishing families experienced real poverty. About half the adult male population of the northernmost counties had fishing as a main or secondary source of income. Many of them could no longer afford to own motorized decked boats with modern equipment, but had to fish from open boats with hand-held lines.

The fishery crisis forced politicians to take action. The National Fishery Bank of Norway was established in 1919 to provide cheap loans. The government also encouraged fishermen to organize themselves, and the Norwegian Fishing Association was founded in 1926. Several laws regulating sales of fish were passed by the Storting in the late 1920s.

Many industrial concerns tried to survive the crisis by cooperating with other firms, entering into price agreements, dividing markets or setting production quotas. Such cartel activities were encouraged by the authorities. A new trust law in 1926 gave the Trust Control the power to control terms of competition and to regulate business markets. The world depression that started in the USA in 1929, reached Norway one year later. Recent research has shown that unemployment reached about 10 % from 1931 to 1933. During the whole of the 1930s, about one-tenth of the population was dependent on poor relief.

Unemployment in Norway was not espe-cially high during the inter-war years compared to other countries, except for that in the late 1920s due to the fiscal policies of the Bank of Norway. Poor statistical material makes accurate estimations of the number of unemployed difficult. There is, however, general agreement that unemployment was greater among men than women, and hit built-up areas harder than rural districts. Job opportunities in agriculture actually increased during the inter-war years, in contrast to the period between the 1860s and 1914, which saw a reduction. Development in real income for both agriculture and forestry was negative, however. Purchasing power decreased by about 40% between 1920 and 1935.

The depression was not the only reason for the rise in unemployment during the 1930s. The number of young people reaching working age rose sharply, mass immigration to the USA had been restricted, and more women delayed marriage and sought employment.

Many companies went bankrupt when prices fell and wages and interest rates rose. This led to banks losing large sums on unredeemed debts. Ordinary people, afraid of losing their savings, rushed to their banks to withdraw their money. The government reacted by supporting banks with sizable amounts, but this was unsuccessful. Many banks went out of business, and many depositors lost their money.

Towns and cities also felt the crisis. Un-

A forced sale at Skullerud farm in Oslo in 1934, with police present to prevent disturbances. The Rural Crisis Assistance was founded in 1931 to boycott fixed sales of farms. The organization had 10,000 members at its peak, but broke up in 1933 after several leaders had begun cooperating closely with the NS.

The Unemployeds' Café was run by the trade union movement in Oslo from 1929 to 1939. Here the unemployed received a free meal every day.

Advertizing became a separate profession in the 1920s. Many companies soon used this new medium. Tobacco companies made great efforts to get women to begin smoking.

employment and business failures lowered tax revenues, while costs of poor relief and relief work soared. Towns that were especially hard hit had to renounce local self-government and let the state take control of their economy. Many towns were given loans from the National Bank for Municipalities established by the Storting in 1927.

Government initiatives of this kind show that the non-socialist majority in the Storting was not paralysed by the economic problems. Public responsibility and authority increased between 1918 and 1935, while election promises of cuts in public spending were not realised.

The inter-war years were not only a time of crisis. Statistics show that the gross national product doubled and that industrial production increased by about 80 %, despite there being no more industrials jobs than

in 1915. One important reason was that companies began using new, electric-powered machines and rationalized production methods of American model.

Those who were fortunate enough to keep their jobs in industry or the public sector received more for their wages than before. They bought electric cookers, irons and water heaters, and installed lavatories and bathrooms. Many of them could afford to buy radios and the most prosperous bought cars. People used more money on leisure-time activities, clothing and equipment.

Most of the consumer goods made available in the inter-war years were produced in newly established small companies, often in rural districts. Many such companies were started up by the unemployed who found no other work. They had an advantage in that Norway, like most other countries, increased import duties to protect domestic industry. The authorities and business concerns cooperated on advertizing campaigns encouraging consumers to buy Norwegian goods. Both export and import portions of the GNP were reduced during the inter-war years.

Although many ships were laid up during the worst depression years, the inter-war years were on the whole a period of growth in shipping. During the 1930s, only Great Britain and the USA had larger merchant fleets than Norway. Norwegian shipowners were among the first to replace steamships with motor vessels. By 1939 Norway had the most modern merchant fleet in the world, including specialized vessels such as oil tankers and refrigerator ships. Many shipowners also withdrew from the tramp trade, directing their efforts towards liner shipping with fixed routes across the world's oceans. Long-term freight contracts, such as those with petroleum companies, also became more common. Norwegian shipowners no longer attracted customers by offering cheap freights on old ships whose crews had starvation wages. They now won new market shares under the motto "Speed and service".

Shipping companies ordered most of their new ships from British and Swedish yards, with most financing being arranged abroad. Towards the end of the 1930s, shipping played a key role for foreign trade. Freight incomes accounted for nearly 40% of the country's export incomes.

WHALING

A whale being flensed in front of the whaling station at Grytviken in South Georgia. The station started operations at the turn of the year 1904-05. It lost most of its importance after the mid-1920s, when floating factory ships were set in on the whaling grounds.

Norwegians have hunted whales ever since the Stone Age, but it was not until Svend Foyn invented the harpoon-gun in the 1860s that whaling became an important industry in many coastal districts. Until the turn of the century, whaling was carried out along the coast of Norway and in the north Atlantic. As northern stocks of whales became seriously depleted, new hunting grounds were necessary and the Antartic Ocean became the most important whaling area. Blue whales were processed in plants built up on several of the British islands in the Antarctic, of which South Georgia was the most important.

The industry's profitability increased greatly when the fat industry began using a new process for hardening fats, enabling use of whale oils in margarine production. Norwegian whalers faced another problem, however, when the British increased taxes on catches and prohibited the building of new land-based factories. Faced with exclusion from a growing market, the Norwegians reacted by building huge factory-ships, where blue whales were processed on the open sea. The hauling slips on board the factory ships were an especially important innovation, enabling carcasses to be hauled up on the deck where they were cut up and rendered in huge vats.

Profits were enormous. In the record year 1930, whalers enjoyed an average wage twenty times that of a fisherman. 6000 men on 21 factory-ships and 166 whale-boats participated in whaling expeditions. Most of the men came from Vestfold county whose largest town, Sandefjord, was the country's undisputed Whaling Capital.

The boom did not last long. Before the decade was over, the price of whale oil had sunk drastically, partly because the Depression led to falling demands. Whaling capacity increased at the same time with whalers from Japan and Germany taking part. The Norwegian share of the world production of whale oil sank from 65 to 30 percent from 1927 to 1938.

Whaling in the Antarctic resumed after 1945. Overtaxing led to stocks of whales being seriously threatened. Since 1967, no Norwegian whaling expeditions have been sent to the Antarctic.

Whaling for minke whales along the Norwegian coast has continued until the present. Even though this whaling activity has been moderate and does not threaten the stock of minke whales in the opinion of Norwegian marine scientists, Norway has been sharply criticised by animal and nature conservation organizations in many countries.

Opposite:
The first radio broadcasts were started in 1925 by a private company in Oslo. When the state took over the company in 1933, the number of licenses increased rapidly. By 1940 over 400,000 licenses had been sold. This advertising poster shows how town and country are linked by radio waves.

Fishing, Whaling and Sealing

Exports of clipfish (dried cod) became increasingly important from the mid-eighteenth century onwards. The herring fisheries provided a good livelihood for the coastal population, but the herring stocks disappeared at certain periods. Cod never disappeared completely, but catches varied consideraby from one season to the next. Great progress was made in the fishing industry around 1900. Fishing boats were built with decks and engines, so the fishermen were able to go out to the fishing banks. New equipment, such as drift nets and purse seine nets, led to increasingly large catches. After the Second World War the catches were even bigger, as the fishing boats had trawl gallows and ring nets while sonar and echo-sounders made it easier to find the fish. Factories were built on land for the production of frozen fish, fish fillets, fishmeal and fish oil.

Coastal whaling has long traditions in Norway and has no connection with the pelagic whaling carried out by Vestfold shipowners. Seal hunting began round Svalbard in the 1790s and later spread to the Barents Sea, Greenland and Newfoundland.

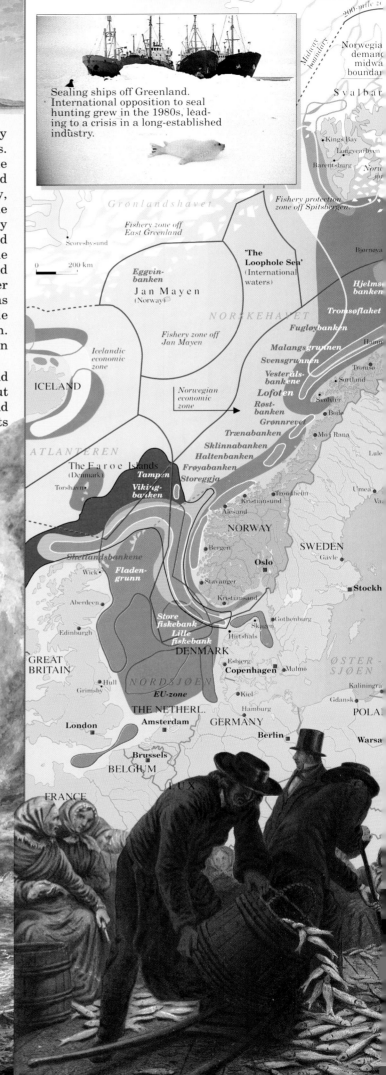

Sealing ships off Greenland. International opposition to seal hunting grew in the 1980s, leading to a crisis in a long-established industry.

Important fisheries

- Shrimp
- Cod
- Coalfish
- Mackerel
- North Sea Herring
- Blue whiting
- Sand eel
- Capelin

— Zone bounderies

--- Median lines under negotiation

During the 1990s a conflict arose between Norway and Iceland when Icelandic fishermen began fishing in the fishery protection zone off Spitsbergen and in the "Loophole" Sea. The government claimed that the Icelanders did not have historic fishing rights in the Barents Sea, and that their un-controlled fishing in the Loophole Sea threatened arctic fishery resources. Several Icelandic trawlers were boarded by the Norwegian Coast Guard for fishing in the Spitsbergen zone, several of these were fined. Norway was met with minimal international understanding when the country resumed whaling for the mike whale in the 1990s.

The best cod fishing in the country takes place each year in Lofoten in Nordland county. In 1896, the record year, over 32,000 fishermen took part in the Lofoten fishery.

The number of fishermen has declined sharply since the Second World War. There were approximately 85,000 fishermen in 1948 and only about 28,000 in 1989. In that year about 12,000 people were employed in the fish processing industry. Fishing and fish processing are extremely important for the population along large sections of the Norwegian coast, particularly in northern Norway. At the end of the 1980s almost 15 percent of the employed population was involved in the fishing industry. The illustration shows a modern trawler.

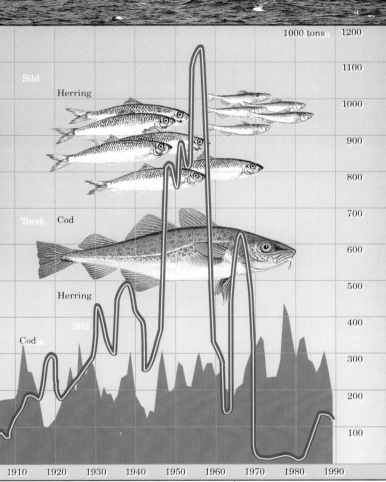

The *sjark* is a typical Norwegian fishing boat used in modern coastal fishing.

This painting by Knut Bergslien shows people in a wharfside shed in Bergen in about 1850. When a herring catch was brought ashore, men, women and children took part in the work. The merchant in the background is following their work closely.

Bottom left: "Nordland boat at Sea", painted by Karl Erik Harr.

Aquaculture

Aquaculture in sea water emerged as a separate industry in the early 1970s. Floating nets (*merder*) made it easier to hold and feed fish in ocean waters.
Most early efforts concentrated on rainbow trout, but by 1976, salmon was the most common fish raised in captivity. Norway exported fish and fish products valued at 15.7 billion *kroner* in 1993. Aquaculture's share was nearly 5 billion.
Aquaculture has been a contributing factor in maintaining a stable population in many coastal communities.

Non-socialist Politics in the Inter-war Years

The non-socialist parties won majorities in all elections held in the inter-war years, but proved unable to establish stable governments. Between 1918 and 1935, Norway had nine different governments. Nearly all were minority governments and most originated with the Liberal Party – the Left (Venstre).

Although the labour movement grew in strength, with some segments speaking of revolution and class struggle, the Liberal Party refused to take part in a broad, anti-socialist, non-socialist block. They hoped to rise above class differences and to use the full resources of the nation to help the weak. The Liberals believed that social reform, price control and laws limiting capitalist power would remove much of the basis for dissatisfaction among the working classes.

The Liberal Party had its strongest support in the southern and western regions of the country, regions with a strong interest in the New Norwegian language, the tempe-

rance movement and the Chistian lay movement. The party also advocated a reduction of duties on agricultural products to bring down food prices. This policy led to conflict with farmers. They founded their own Agrarian Party in 1920 and, with the Labour Party, made inroads into the Liberal Party supporters.

Until the 1930s, the Agrarian Party had believed that the Liberals were too tolerant of the labour movement, too sympathetic to government intervention in business, and too little concerned with limiting costs in national and local government. For their part, they favoured state subsidies for clearing new land and for producing wheat, to better both the country's self-sufficiency and the condition of freeholding farmers. The party was firmly convinced that a strong farm society afforded the best possible defence against revolutionary socialists.

The Conservative Party had great success in the elections held just after World War I. Due to concern over revolutionary tendencies, the party proposed several social reform measures, such as old-age pensions and rent control, but resumed its more con-

In this painting artist Erik Werenskiold indicated the mixed feelings of the upper class when confronted with the poverty of the inter-war years.

servative bearing when the Labour Party became weakened by dissent. During the 1930s, the Conservatives emerged more clearly as the party of business and industry with the firm support of middle-class towns-people, especially in eastern Norway. Even though the party lost some voter support, they emerged the largest non-socialist party in all inter-war elections. Of the non-socialist parties, it was the Conservatives who viewed increased state intervention and expenditures with the greatest alarm. They meant that taxes and public expenditure should be greatly reduced in time of crisis to encourage so that business concerns to invest in new enterprise. The party won support among all opponents of socialism. They emphasized the importance of "law and order", promising strong reactions if the socialists made good their threats against middle class society. The Conservatives were sceptical to New Norwegian and held liberal views in matters concerning religion, alcohol and morality.

Because of widespread strikes and threats of revolution from the labour movement, several laws were passed by the Storting to protect middle class society. Terms of imprisonment were introduced for anyone preventing strike-breakers from working. The same punishment awaited those who supported illegal strikes, refused military service or agitated against the military system. Several Labour party leaders were imprisoned for anti-militaristic activities.

Non-socialist governments did not hesitate to use police or military force to protect strike-breakers, but such confrontations did not lead to appreciable bloodshed. Only one person was killed due to labour conflicts in the years betweeen 1900 and 1939. Important employers' associations, such as the Association of Banks, the Federation of Norwegian Industries and the Farmers' Association supported the building up of "Norway's Social Aid" to supply industry with new workers during labour disputes. A secret stand-by force, made up of "reliable" troops, was also set up in the army. Political authorities also agreed to establish a civil defence force trained by military officers. This "Public Defence Force" had about 10,000 members.

The most important anti-socialist organization was the *Fedrelandslag* (Norwegian

PROHIBITION

During the 1920s, disagreement over alcohol policies embittered cooperation between the Conservatives and the Liberals. This question also led to internal conflict in most of the other parties. The Liberals had introduced a temporary ban on production and sales of distilled spirits during the war in order to use as much as possible of the grain and potato harvests as food. This decision had the support of the the temperance movement, which had grown in strength since the early 1800s.

The temperance movement worked for the ban being made permanent after the war, and to expand it to include fortified wines. In a referendum held in 1919, a majority of the electorate approved these measures. Soon afterwards the Storting passed a law forbidding the sale of beverages having an alcohol content of more than 12 per cent.

This change had several unfortunate effects, however. Smuggling, illicit distilling and illegal trade in spirits flourished. Such criminality was not the most serious threat to prohibition. Far more important were the sharp protests issued by France, Spain and Portugal due to the loss of traditional export markets for their wines and spirits. The two southernmost countries also reacted by increasing the import duty on Norwegian fish. Several governments negotiated agreements with the wine-producing countries, who set hard conditions for the easing of trade barriers: Norway had to consent to the import of large quantities of wines and spirits for warehousing. These agreements were successively rejected by the Storting, with the result that three governments resigned.

By 1923 the problems for fish exporters had become so serious that the Storting resolved to repeal the ban on fortified wines. A new referendum held three years later showed that a majority of the population also desired repeal of the ban on spirits. The Storting complied with this while ensuring considerable state influence on sales of alcohol. A separate company, *A/S Vinmonopolet*, was established to control sales of wines and spirits.

League), established in 1925. The League recommended using force against the revolutionary labour movement while encouraging non-socialist coalition, public economizing and the protection of national values. The organization had over 100,000 members at its height, with such men as Christian Michelsen, Roald Amundsen and Fridtjof Nansen among its supporters. While the League had much of the credit for the non-socialist election victory in 1930, it lost support in later years. Its remnants demonstrated clearly Fascistic features.

Norway also experienced its own brand of European Fascism. *Nasjonal Samling* (National Unity) or NS was founded in 1933 under the leadership of Vidkun Quisling. The party was inspired by Mussolini's Italy, German Nazism and the Finnish Lappo movement. NS appealed to those who were dissatisfied with a non-socialist democracy and wanted to combat the labour movement. The party utilized some of the frustration that had grown up during the worst years of the depression. In rural districts the NS gained support among farmers and forestry workers who felt the stability of traditional farm society threatened from without. In their opinion, rural crisis was caused by the problems of an industrialized society, while the labour movement, with the support of foreign interests, stirred up unecessary conflict in rural areas.

The NS went in for an end to all class struggle and for uniting the entire nation in one party led by single leader. The Nordic race was proclaimed superior to all others and its members urged to overwin Jews, Bolcheviks and other "inferior" foreigners. The NS glorified Norway's mediaeval history, using the sun cross as the party symbol. The most important party meetings were called "ting" and were often held at historic places, such as Stiklestad and Hafrsfjord. The NS also had its own uniformed elite troops, called the "Hird" after the Old Norse and organized on Italian and German models.

The NS won only a few per cent of the votes in elections held during the 1930s, and no representatives in the Storting. The party was also troubled by inner conflict and by defection of members. By 1939 the NS was reduced to a tiny, isolated sect. No one suspected that this party would have an historic chance the very next year with the help of German bayonets.

Discord and Concurrence in the Labour Movement

On 1 May 1919, one of the leaders of the Labour Party held a speech at Bragernes Square in Drammen, saying among other things:

"Everywhere the tide of world revolution can be seen rising higher and higher. From Dublin to Calcutta, from Cairo to Buenos Aires – everywhere capitalism and imperialism are collapsing when confronted by the coming world socialism. We are witness to a spring flood in our time. This we shall be a part of, even though we stand here in Bragernes Square at the outskirts of the world [...]. If the middle class will not give us our due, then we will seize it [...]. We now have the strength to take over power. [...]"

This statement shows clearly that the Labour Party had deserted the social democratic course it had followed since its founding in 1887. A revolutionary faction had taken control of the party near the end of World War I. They had lost faith in improvements in the labouring classes' condition taking place under the old social order. Negotiations with employers and participation in parliamentary activity were no longer sufficient. A resolution of March 1918 stated that the party had become a "revolutionary party of class struggle" with the right to use "revo-lutionary mass action in the fight for the economic liberation of the working classes".

The radicalization of the labour movement must be seen in the light of deteriorating living conditions for ordinary people. Prices rose sharply in 1917, and shortages, black-marketeering and speculation became facts of everyday life. Newly-rich stock-jobbers wallowed in luxury, while most people had trouble making ends meet. That same autumn news from Russia reported that the Bolsheviks had overthrown the czar and established a new workers' state. Following the pattern of the Russian soviets, workers' and soldiers' councils were established in many areas and at the Labour Party conference in the spring of 1918, the revolutionary faction won the majority. The Norwegian Labour Party was the only social democratic party in Europe that chose to join the Communist International, Comintern, based in Moscow.

Giv Akt!

"Se Revolutionen LYSER OVER VERDEN!

This banner from the Rjukan workers' association expresses the revolutionary fervour characteristic of the labour movement in the 1920s.

Historians have searched for specific reasons for the radicalization of the Norwegian Labour Party. One important explanation is that the rapidity of the industrialization process after 1905 created a rootless working class only too open for revolutionary solutions. Another shows that because the struggle for parliamentarism and universal suffrage was completed before the turn of the century, no room existed for an alliance between social democrats and radical non-socialists that might have moderated the labour movement as was the case in neighboring countries. Still another may lie in the Norwegian electoral system, with majority election in one-man constituencies having led to labour movement distrust in parliamentary democracy, since the Labour Party was seriously underrepresented in the Storting.

Several historians emphasize a weak centralized Labour Party leadership unable to maintain effective control of the party organization. As a result, small and radical party groups from rural districts were able to dominate the conference in 1918. Such rural socialists were characterized by a traditional scepticism to the moderate leadership in the capital city. There is broad agreement as to the vital role played by radical leader Martin Tranmæl in the party's ideological left-wing ideology. While in the United States, he had been greatly inspired by the revolutionary labour union, the Industrial Workers of the World. With his charismatic personality and abilities, he had great influence on union and party meetings.

Conflicts soon arose between the Labour Party and the Comintern. There was growing concern in Norway over Soviet Communist demands that all member parties follow orders from Moscow without question. In 1921 the party's right wing broke out and established a new social democratic party. Two years later a majority in the Labour Party voted to break with the Communist International. The minority founded the Norwegian Communist Party (NKP), which was admitted to membership in the Comintern. In the remaining years of the decade, the NKP lost both members and voters to the Labour Party.

Both before and after the withdrawal from the Comintern, there were signs that the labour movement's revolutionary fervour was cooling down. In 1921 the Norwegian Federation of Trade Unions had taken some 150,000 men out on strike when employers attempted to lower seamen's wages by one-third. The action was a complete failure. The trade union movement did not have the means with which to support strikers in a lengthy conflict.

During the 1920s, labour movement frustration over the existing social order increased. This was clearly indicated by Labour Party antagonism towards celebrating Constitution Day on 17 May, towards the Norwegian flag and the national anthemn. The party celebrated 1 May, raised the red flag of communism and sang

the "International" instead. Even though the Labour Party had broken with the Comintern, considerable sympathy existed on behalf of the Soviet Union during all the inter-war years. Separate assembly halls, or "Peoples' Houses", were built in many towns, becoming centres for the political and cultural activities of the labour movement.

The bitter struggle between the Labour Party, the Social Democrats and the NKP exhausted the strength of the labour movement. Membership in the Trade Union Federation fell drastically. It is not surprising, therefore, that it was the trade union movement that pressed for an end to the party split. Their efforts were successful. In 1927 the Labour Party and the Social Democrats joined forces, standing for election on a platform emphasizing traditional social democratic values. The party now intended to win a majority through peaceful reforms passed by legally elected bodies. The election was a success. The Labour Party emerged the largest political party in the country and has remained so ever since.

Although the non-socialist coalition kept a majority in the Storting, negotiations among them soon reached a standstill. Amid general surprise King Håkon intervened and gave the republican Labour Party the task of forming a government,

Reidar Aulie (1904-1977) painted this fresco in Oslo's City Hall, showing workers' fight for a better society.

the same party that each year voted against allocating funds to the royal family.

The country's first Labour government took office in January of 1928. It presented a most challenging programme, advocating "a transistion to a socialistic society". Industrialists and bankers immediately transferred huge sums of money to foreign countries, and the government was defeated after only two weeks. The non-socialist parties quickly agreed on a new government now that economic stability was threatened.

These events led to a strengthening of the the Labour Party's radical elements. At the national conference in 1930, the party adopted a programme again using many of old revolutionary terms. The programme caused concern among the non-socialists, who began a strong counter-offensive in advance of the general election of 1933. During the election campaign itself, they stressed a defence of national, Christian values in contrast to the Labour Party's atheism and policy of class conflict. This proved so effective, that the election resulted in defeat for the Labour Party.

The poor election resulted in a loss of support for the revolutionary wing of the Labour Party. Unemployment and social crisis were other factors setting the party back on a more moderate course. A growing opinion insisted that the party formulate a new policy to put the country back on its feet. In 1933, the Labour Party launched a crisis programme under the motto, "Work for all". Many of the proposals were based on the teachings of British economist John Maynard Keynes, and on experience gained in Soviet planned economy. The programme broke with the well-established principle that the state should economize in times of depression. Proposals were now made that large state loans be taken up to finance activities to reduce unemployment. A Labour Party "Norwegian Three-year Plan", in the autumn of 1933, proposed large state investments in land clearance, industrial development, hydroelectric power stations, roads and railways. The means of production would not be nationalized, but the state was to have greater power to regulate and control the economy.

This new crisis policy was the main reason for the Labour Party's decisive victory in the general elections of 1933. The growth of fascism elsewhere in Europe led the party to regard non-socialist democracy more positively. This was clearly shown in 1935 when the Trade Union Federation and the Norwegian Employers' Confederation negotiated a general wage agreement for business and industry. The agreement set up rules for wage negotiations and collective agreements, and ensured workers the right to form trade unions and to elect shop stewards.

After the election of 1933, unrest increased in the Agrarian Party as a result of forced sales and unemployment in rural areas. The party presented several proposals for greater appropriations to agriculture, but these were rejected by the Liberal government. This led to closer contact between the Agrarian and the Labour Party. In 1935 they agreed on a compromize: Labour would form a government in return for a promise to increase funds to the rural economy.

The Labour Party government headed by Johan Nygaardsvold remained in power until 1945. It followed a moderate reform policy in the last pre-war years, making the Labour Party an accepted participant in parliamentary democracy. The party became more concerned with an increase in production and with social welfare than with class struggle. It even supported celebration of Constitution Day and all the national values this expressed.

This government created optimism in politics and business. It also benefitted from the improvement in international economy which led to a greater demand for Norwegian products.

The non-socialist majority in the Storting rejected the taking up of large state loans and deficiency budgeting as means for stimulating the economy. The Labour Party received the support of the Agrarian and the Liberal Parties, however, to increase taxes and excises. These increased revenues were used for work schemes for the unemployed and for social reforms. The government had a new workers' protection law adopted, ensuring all employees an eight-hour-day and nine days' annual holiday. The health insurance system was extended to cover new groups of workers, while old age and unemployment benefits were introduced. These reforms enlarged the scope of government responsibilities, while strengthening a feeling of national unity.

Outdoor Life

Many of the outdoor leisure activities in Norway today are rooted in the everyday life of country people. Early in the 19th century, well-to-do town dwellers discovered the joys of the open air and the recreational opportunities offered by the countryside. The trend was set by British anglers, huntsmen, mountaineers and hikers who came to Norway.

In 1868 the Norwegian Mountain Touring Association (DNT) was founded. For 100 years the association has built cabins providing overnight accommodation and marked and signposted paths and tracks.

Nowadays outdoor life is an important part of the Norwegian life style. Many Norwegians walk – or ski – in the forests on Sundays and many spend weekends and holidays at cabins in the mountains or by the sea.

Gjendebu in the Jotunheimen Mountains was the first of DNT's cabins. It opened in 1871.

The writer Aasmund Olavsson Vinje (1818–1870) was one of the founders of DNT. In the columns of his newspaper he encouraged people in the towns to go to the mountains.

Polar explorer and scientist Fridtjof Nansen (1861–1930) and his wife Eva (1858–1907) on skis. The couple became the ideal of young people who wanted to lead an outdoor life. Eva Nansen was the first well-known townswoman to ski in the mountains. She had a special skiing outfit, designed by her husband.

Therese Bertheau (1861–1936) was the first woman mountaineer in Norway. She is photographed here before a climb in Sogn at the turn of the century.

In the 1820s the first anglers came to Norway from Great Britain. This illustration shows fly fishing at Tana i Finnmark county. It was customary i northern Norway for Sami to help foreigners with their fishing.

In 1973 three national parks were designated in the archipelago of Svalbard which is sometimes known as Spitsbergen. These wild places are rich in bird colonies and rare species of plants. The Svalbard reindeer, polar bear and arctic fox all live there. The plant and animal life of Svalbard is very vulnerable, and Norwegian authorities have therefore not encouraged mass tourism.

Svalbard became a part of Norway in 1925. States party to the Spitsbergen Treaty may exploit the resources of the islands. All military activity is forbidden there.

National park

Protected landscape area

Area with protected watercourses

Special coastal area

Flora conservation area

Everyone has access to the countryside in Norway. Anyone may walk or ski without hindrance, camp out in the forests and mountains and swim in the sea, the lakes or the rivers.

It is important to protect the countryside. According to the Open Air Recreation Act, everyone who uses the countryside is obliged to show due consideration. It is forbidden to walk on cultivated land, damage plants and trees or disturb animals and birds. Everyone has a duty to clear up after himself.

Rondane became Norway's first National Park in 1962. The purpose of establishing national parks was to safeguard large areas of untouched countryside. In 1991 there were twenty national parks in Norway. In these areas there are strict rules for what people are allowed to do.

Map labels: Nordkapp, Tanafj., Vardø, Varangerfjorden, Hammerfest, Porsangen, Lakselv, Tanaelva, Kirkenes, Pasvikelva, **Stabbursdalen**, FINNMARK, Jiešjávri, Altaelva, **Øvre Pasvik**, Tromsø, Lyngsalpene, Reisaelva, **Reisa**, **Øvre Anarjohka**, TROMS, **Ånderdalen**, Andenes, **Øvre Dividal**, Harstad, Altevatn, Vesterålen, Narvik, Svolvær, *LOFOTEN*, Vestfjorden, **Rago**, Bodø, **Saltfjellet-Svartisen nasjonalpark**, Junkerdalen, Balvatnet, Mo i Rana, NORDLAND, Røssvatnet, Sandnessjøen, **Børgefjell**, Brønnøysund, Rørvik, NORD-TRØNDELAG, Tunnsjøen, Namsos, Snåsavatnet, **Gresså-moen**, Froan, Trondheim, Selbusjøen, MØRE OG ROMSDAL, SØR-TRØNDELAG, Kristiansund, Røros, Aursunden, Molde, Sunndalsøra, **Femundsmarka**, Ålesund, **Dovrefjell**, Femunden, **Gutulia**, Nordfjorden, **Rondane**, HEDMARK, OPPLAND, SOGN OG FJORDANE, **Jotunheimen**, Gudbrandsdalen, Sognefjorden, **Ormtjern-kampen**, Lillehammer, Hamar, Hallingdal, Mjøsa, Randsfj., Glomma, BUSKERUD, Tyrifj., AKERSHUS, HORDALAND, Hardangerfj., Drammen, Oslo, Bergen, Kongsberg, Horten, ØSTFOLD, **Hardangervidda**, TELEMARK, Fredrikstad, VESTFOLD, Porsgrunn, Larvik, ROGALAND, Bøkfj., Skjærgårdsparken, Stavanger, Nidelva, Arendal, Jærstrendene, Lygna, Otra, AUST-AGDER, VEST-AGDER, Kristiansand

Easter vacation at a cabin in Hallingdal.

Mountaineering in the Lyng Alps, Troms county

Glacier climbing on Svartisen, Nordland county

Skiers in the Jotunheimen Mountains

Reindeer hunting in the Dovre Mountains

Boating holiday off the south coast

Sunday walk outside Bergen

Fridtjof Nansen (1861-1930) fotographed together with some of his associates during a relief action for refugees in the Soviet Union in the early 1920s. Nansen stands in the door of the coach.

Foreign and Defence Policies

When World War I ended, the victorious allied powers agreed to found a world organization to safeguard the peace. The charter of the League of Nations imposed on member states the obligation to intervene with sanctions on any aggressor country. Norway's decision to join meant that the country could have to choose sides in future conflicts between the Great Powers. This was an important reason for many politicians' reluctant relinquishing of neutrality, but when the question of membership in the new peace organization came up in the Storting, it won the support of a solid majority. The chances for war seemed small, and maintaining good relations with the western powers, upon whom Norway was dependent both politically and economically, was of great importance. It would not be easy to break away from "polite society", particularly now that Great Britain had joined.

In the early 1920s, Norway became involved in League of Nations humanitarian work. Fridtjof Nansen did an excellent job as High Commissioner for Refugees in Russia, Greece and Turkey, also leading relief work during the famine in the Ukraine in 1921. The following year he was awarded the Nobel Peace Prize.

Norway participated actively in disarmament work, also hoping to set an example in international cooperation. Arbitration agreements were signed with the other Nordic countries as well as with other states, in which signatory states agreed to solve conflicts by means of negotiation, mediation and arbitration. Such agreements proved of little worth, however, since most of the Great Powers refused to sign.

As the international situation deteriorated in the late '30s, Norway and the other Scandinavian countries announced that they no longer felt obligated to participate in League of Nations sanctions. The country would again rely on the time-tested policy of neutrality.

Like many other European countries, Norway also attempted to win sovereignty over new areas of land in the inter-war years. Since Norwegians had a tradition of hunting, whaling and exploration in the Arctic region, it seemed reasonable to concentrate interest in such areas.

POLAR SCIENTIST ROALD AMUNDSEN

Along with Fridtjof Nansen, Roald Amundsen (1872-1928) was the country's foremost explorer in the years before World War II. At age 21 he resolved to become a polar scientist. After completing the examination for a master's certificate, he signed on a sealing vessel. He was also first mate on board the vessel carrying the Belgian Antarctic Expedition led by Adrien de Gerlache de Gomery (1866-1934). Amundsen acquired much valuable experience when the expedition was forced to winter in the polar ice in 1899.

After 1900 Amundsen's aim was to find the North-west Passage - the waterway between Europe and Asia north of the North American continent. He and his crew set out from Christiania on board the sloop *Gjøa* in 1903. The expedition first spent two years in Gjøa Harbour on King William Island off the coast of Canada. The island lay near the magnetic north pole, enabling Amundsen to make valuable observations concerning earth magnetism. In the spring of 1905 the expedition continued and in 1906 *Gjøa* arrived in the Bering Straits after having spent one more winter ice-bound. Amundsen left the expedition in the autumn of 1905. With one companion, an American, he covered 800 kilometres by dog sledge across polar ice. Amundsen reached the telegraph station at Eagle City on 5 December and the world received news of the successful expedition.

His fame and thorough scientific results enabled Amundsen to finance new expeditions. He had hoped to reach the North Pole, but changed his plans when an American, Robert Peary (1856-1920), accomplished that in 1909. He set out on Fridtjof Nansen's ship *Fram* for the South Pole and the famous race with Robert F. Scott (1868-1912) of Great Britain. With four of his men, Amundsen reached the pole on 14 December 1911. Five weeks later Scott found Amundsen's tent and flag, but on the return journey he and his men lost their lives.

After World War I, Amundsen led new expeditions. The most famous may be the journey over the North Pole on board the airship *Norge* in 1926, known as the Amundsen-Ellsworth-Nobile Transpolar Flight. Umberto Nobile (1885-1978) of Italy both constructed and captained the airship. The American polar scientist, Lincoln Ellsworth (1880-1951), contributed funds and took part in leading the expedition. They left Spitsbergen on 11 May and after 16 hours of flight, dropped the flags of the three participating nations over the Pole. *Norge* landed in Alaska on 14 May, after having completed the first air voyage between Europe and America.

Roald Amundsen lost his life on a rescue operation after Nobile's airship *Italia* had been wrecked in the Arctic in 1928.

During the post-World War I peace negotiations, Norway claimed control over Svalbard. A treaty was set up securing Norway's sovereignity over the group of islands, with all signatory countries having equal rights to engage in commercial activities there. Towards the end of the 1920s, Norway also gained control of Jan Mayen, Bouvet Island and Peter I Island. These two last-named islands were of particular interest for whaling operations in the Antarctic Ocean. Norway's claims to large areas on mainland Antarctica resulted in Queen Maud Land coming under Norwegian hegemony in 1939.

A conflict arose in the 1920s between sealers from western Norway and Danish authorities, as to sealing and fishing rights in East Greenland. A nationalistic folk movement, the "Greenland Association", grew up at different places in the country, agitating for Norway's annexation of the disputed area. The association rejoiced when a few activists occupied East Greenland in 1932, with support from the Agrarian Party government. In keeping with the arbitration agreement between Denmark and Norway, the case was brought before the International Court of Justice in the Hague, which awarded full sovereignty over all of Greenland to Denmark.

Norway's view of Finland was permeated with suspicion. Widespread anxiety arose over Finnish nationalist groups' claims for a Greater Finland, also including Finnish-speaking districts of Troms and Finnmark counties. Police authorities started an extensive surveillance of Finnish-Norwegians, while the general staff halted the building of roads between Norway and Finland, fearing that the Finns might use these roads to invade Norway. The authorities subsidized new Norwegian settlement in border areas, such as Pasvikdalen, and also built a folk high school and a radio broadcasting station here to further Norwegian culture in the north. It was only after war broke out between Finland and the Soviet Union in the winter of 1939-40 that fear of Finnish agression disappeared in Norway.

Optimistic prospects for peace in the 1920s had led to reductions in defence expenditures. In 1932 the Storting passed a new defence plan setting up a small border defence group to be supported by mobilized troops if war appeared imminent. The Ministry of Foreign Affairs was to notify the government if and when these extra forces were to be called up.

Despite increasing international tension in the following years, there was no build-up of the defence forces conceived of in these plans. The conviction that Norway would be able to keep out of any new wars was strong. The country had lived in peace since 1814, with good experience in using negotiation when war threatened. There was general belief that the peaceful outcome of the conflict with Sweden over the union had been due to skilful Norwegian diplomacy. Few attached any importance to the fact that rearmament and mobilization had strengthened the Norwegian negotiating position. Most people also believed that it was the government's wise foreign policy - not the country's military strength – that had kept Norway out of World War I.

The possibility that any foreign country would wish to occupy Norway was considered minute. Great Britain was considered to be the nation most interested in controlling Norwegian territory in a crisis, but that opinion did not assign enemy status to the British. It was generally believed that the British fleet would prevent invasion by other countries. If Norway, contrary to all belief, were forced to choose sides in a new worldwide war, most Norwegians were prepared to support Great Britain.

The majority of politicians were convinced that Norway would be unable to repel an attack by any of the Great Powers, no matter how much the country armed itself. They believed that a strong defence might seem provocative and were not willing to risk material loss or human lives. The depression also made it difficult to increase the defence budget. Nor were defence plans based on the assumption that Norwegian forces were to be involved in lengthy warfare. Their main purpose was to indicate that Norway would not accept being occupied.

When the Labour Party took over power in 1935, many feared that they would continue their anti-militarist policies. This was not the case. The party continued the defence policy drawn up by the Liberals, supporting the main principles of the defence plan laid out in the early 1930s. In the years that followed and up until 1940, the Labour Party, the Liberals and the Agrarian Party concurred on defence policy. The Conservatives protested that allocations were too small, but with little success.

Great Power Rivalry over Norway

In September of 1938 Germany carried out a surprise attack on Poland. Great Britain and France, in solidarity with Poland, declared war on Hitler Germany. This was the beginning of World War II.

The government, declaring that Norway would maintain strict neurality, set up a border defence force as had been the case in 1914. Naval, air force and anti-aircraft units were called up, but only some few of the coastal forts and army divisions were put on war alert. The Minstry of Foreign Affairs saw no reason for recommending the extensive mobilization called for by the defence plans. Most people thought that chances of a German attack were slight. Any British and French operations would be met with symbolic resistance. Considered

in this light, there seemed to be no need for an extensive army mobilization.

After war had broken out, the French government proposed starting up military operations in Scandinavia. They wished to engage Hitler in more distant countries to relieve the pressure on France. A Franco-British campaign in the north would also satisfy opposition demands in the French National Assembly for a more active military strategy. The French were also intensely interested in stopping Swedish iron ore exports to the German armaments industry. Most of this ore was shipped via Narvik in northern Norway.

With the exception of the First Lord of the Admiralty, Winston Churchill, the British government was at first uninterested in the French proposals. During the winter of 1939-40 the British also inclined towards taking action. They observed with increasing unease how German ships avoided the British North Sea blockade by sailing in neutral waters along the Norwegian coast. London's dissatisfaction with the Norwegian neutrality policy increased sharply in December of 1939, when three British merchant vessels were torpedoed within the Norwegian three-mile limit. After this episode the British made it clear to the

Adolf Hitler visited the Norwegian fjords in 1934, accompanied by some of his senior officers.

The coffins of Germans killed during the British attack on the *Altmark* being put ashore in the Jøssing Fjord in February 1940.

set up a larger force that was to land in Trondheim, Bergen and Stavanger to establish support points against German counter-attacks. The operations were cancelled in mid-March 1940 when Finland signed a peace treaty with the Soviet Union.

In France this decision led to the fall of the Daladier government. The new government increased the pressure on the British to mount a new campaign in Scandinavia. After hard negotiations they agreed to lay mines along the Norwegian coast on 8 April. This was to force German shipping out into international waters where they were more open to attack. At the same time, an army force was set up in Great Britain to be sent to Norway if there were signs that the Germans intended landing on the Norwegian coast. The British believed that the chances for such a counter-attack were small.

During the first months of the war, the German admiralty had tried in vain to convince Hitler of the necessity of capturing bases on the Norwegian coast. The navy, fearing it would be locked up in the Baltic, wanted more scope for attacking England and for securing control over the North Atlantic.

It was only after the leader of the NS, Vidkun Quisling, had visited Berlin in December 1939, that Hitler ordered his chiefs of staff to look into the possibilities for a German occupation of Norway. In his conversations with Hitler, Quisling had proposed that Norway and Germany join forces to fight Jews and Communists. Arguments of this kind can have impressed Hitler, because they fitted in with his ideological vision of the creation of a Arch-German Nazi Europe with a common front against communist Soviet Union.

The *Altmark* affair convinced Hitler that Norway was unable to defend her neutrality. Preparations for an invasion were intensified, and by the beginning of March 1940, operations against Denmark and Norway had highest priority. On 3 April the first ships in the invasion fleet sailed northwards from German harbours. The invasion date was set for 9 April.

Norwegian government that they would allow their own naval vessels to operate in Norwegian waters. Norwegian protests were without result. In February of 1940, the British went into action. The destroyer *Cossack* attacked the German merchant ship *Altmark*, which had taken cover in the Jøssing Fjord near Egersund. The *Altmark* had 300 British prisoners-of-war on board. Seven Germans were killed when the British boarded the ship and freed the prisoners. Two Norwegian coastguard ships in the fjord at the time did not intervene in the episode.

After the Soviet attack on Finland in November 1939, the British and the French began planning military action in northern Scandinavia. They decided to land troops in Narvik to move eastwards, take control of the iron mines in Kiruna, and help the Finns in the Winter War. The western allies counted on Germany trying to prevent this development. They therefore

War and Occupation 1940-1945

The Campaign 1940

Late in the evening of 8 April, patrol boat Pol III *was on duty in the outer Oslofjord. Lieutenant Hans Bergan stood look-out on the bridge, when two ships with unlighted lanterns suddenly emerged from the darkness. Bergan roused Captain Jens Welding Olsen, who immediately telegraphed the chiefs of staff that foreign warships were on their way up the fjord. The captain then ordered warning shots fired at the invaders,*

after which the Norwegians rammed one of the unknown ships and sent up three signal flares. A German officer shouted to the Norwegians to surrender. When they refused, the Germans opened fire, hitting and seriously wounding Captain Welding Olsen. He was placed in a lifeboat which sank upon being lowered to the water, carrying the captain with it. The German invasion had claimed its first Norwegian casualty.

German soldiers take cover behind a tank during the fighting in Valdres in April 1940. The attack on Norway cost the Germans about 5300 killed, wounded or missing in action. Allied casualties were about 4900, most of them British.

Norwegian soldiers man a machine gun during the campaign in the spring of 1940. 860 Norwegian soldiers and about 300 civilians were killed in the campaign lasting from 9 April to 9 June.

During this one day, 9 April, the Germans took all their objectives along the coast. Their attack came as a surprise and resistance was weak. Only Oscarsborg Fort outside Oslo afforded the invaders any problems. The fort opened fire, hitting and sinking the cruiser *Blücher*. On board this ship were key personnel and special troops who were to have taken control over the capital city. The sinking of the ship gave the king, the government and members of the Storting an opportunity to escape. They fled first to Elverum, where the Storting authorized the government to carry on the affairs of state independent of the legislative body until the country had re-won its freedom.

From a military point of view, the Germans nonetheless had good reason to be satisfied with the attack against Norway. For the first time in history, army, navy and air force worked together in a coordinated operation, with troops and equipment transported by air and sea. The German military machine again demonstrated its power. Resistance had been wiped out by means of superior fire power from automatic weapons, tanks, artillery and bomber planes.

Despite the superior forces opposing them, the government chose to fight. Having been forced to take sides, it now chose to support Great Britain. A negotiated settlement with the Germans had at any rate become unthinkable after Vidkun Quisling had proclaimed himself prime minister and Hitler had decided to support him. The government pinned its faith on the Allies and their promise to come to the rescue.

British troops did land in Åndalsnes and later on in Namsos, where they were supported by French alpine troops, but the efforts of these allied soldiers were in vain. They were too few, too poorly trained and too poorly equipped. The failure of this operation led to fall of the British government, with Winston Churchill replacing Neville Chambelain as prime minister.

After only three weeks the Germans secured control over southern Norway, but fighting continued in and around Narvik. There British, French, Polish and Norwegian forces had managed to drive the Germans out of the town and isolate them in a mountainous area near the Swedish border. This was the first successful land-based military ope-

German soldiers advancing at Ringerike. Klekken Hotel has been hit and is burning.

ration carried out by Allied troops during the Second World War. But despite the fact that the German units were about to be defeated, the allied supreme command decided at the beginning of June to end the siege. Hitler's attack on France and the Benelux countries made it necessary to transfer forces to the continent.

On 7 June 1940, the royal family and the government left for Britain to continue the war efforts from there. Five years were to pass before they could return to a liberated Norway.

German Occupation Policy

When the Germans launched their attack on Norway, they had hoped to establish an adminstration of occupation in agreement with the government, as had been the case in Denmark. This plan was abandoned because when they failed to capture the government and the royal family. In the confusion of 9 April, Quisling improvised a coup government which was approved by Hitler. This only increased the will to resist. One week later the Quisling government was replaced by an Administrative Council to manage civilian rule in the occupied areas. The Supreme Court appointed the council which was made up of representatives of the state administration and the major organizations in business and industry.

At the same time Hitler set up a Reich Commisariat headed by Josef Terboven, to act as the centre of power for the German occupation administration for the duration of the war. Terboven began negotiations with members of the Administrative Council, the Supreme Court, the important business organizations and the presidium of the Storting. His aim was to replace the Nygaards-vold government with a Council of State approved by the Storting. Because it was generally believed that Germany was winning the war, the Norwegian negotiators went to considerable lengths, but still avoided submitting to the German demands.

In September of 1940 Hitler decided that the discussions were to stop. The Administrative Council was disbanded and all political parties other than the NS were banned. Terboven proclaimed the king and government to have been deposed and replaced by a new cabinet commisariat dominated by

Opposition to the Germans and the NS was expressed in many amusing ways. This cover of a Norwegian weekly magazine made fun of Hitler's help to Quisling. It resulted in the editor being sent to a German concentration camp.

the NS. The NS party and Quisling were now able to carry out a Nazi revolution.

Norway played an important part in German military arrangements during the entire war. Hitler called the country a "place of destiny" where the war might well be determined. Fearing an allied invasion in the north, he built strong defence fortifications along the entire coast. The occupation forces numbered at most about 430,000 men. Norway was an important deployment area for the war efforts aimed at the Soviet Union, while fierce attacks were launched from air

Soviet prisoners-of-war in a slave labour camp in northern Norway. By the time of the liberation, there were over 100,000 Slav prisoners in Norway, some 87,000 of whom were Soviet. Many were sent to new work camps when they got home while an unknown number were executed.

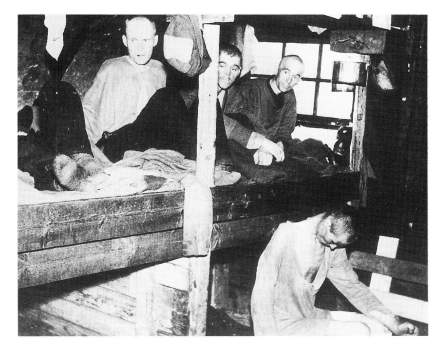

The German «scorched earth» tactics in Finnmark and northern Troms counties caused serious problems for the civilian population. This family had to build a temporary home from a wrecked boat.

resistance people lost their lives in the initial phases of the occupation. More than 30,000 people were imprisoned and about 8000 were sent to concentration camps in Germany. Among these were 760 Jews, of whom only 25 survived. German and Norwegian Nazis gave free rein to their racistist attitudes in slave labour camps set up for Russian, Polish and Serbian prisoners-of-war. More than 17,000 prisoners died of malnutrition, disease and/ or maltreatment, and many were executed. The support enjoyed by the NS during the 1930s was for the most part due to the economic crisis, to fear of communism and to dissatisfaction with parliamentary democracy. When the party had its historic opportunity during the war, about 55,000 people became members. Many were convinced not only of the rightness of joining in the fight against communism, but also that Germany would win the final victory. About 7000 Norwegians served with the Germans on the eastern front, and between 800 and 1000 of these were killed in combat. When the Nazis took over local and national government, some civil servants chose membership in the NS as a way of keeping their jobs. Some young members joined because of the appeal of the party's militarism and radical programme, while others joined because their parents were members.

field and naval bases against the North Atlantic convoy routes.

The German armament industry made good use of Norwegian metals. The aircraft industry secured aluminium and magnesium, while ammunition factories got ample supplies of pyrites.

Although the Germans did not treat Norwegian civilians with the same brutality as in most other occupied countries, the war years were characterized by political suppression and violence unparalleled in modern Norwegian history. About 2000

Not only NS members collaborated with the occupants, however. Many companies carried out work for the Germans, while thousands of workers found employment on German construction sites. And some 9000 Norwegian women bore children to German fathers.

These posters show important features of Nazi propaganda. The NS wanted women to join a new women's movement. The party also warned against the consequences of the royal family and the Nygaardvold government cooperating with the British. They also ran an intense campaign to enlist Norwegian youth to fight the Soviet Union on the German side.

VIDKUN QUISLING

Vidkun Abraham Lauritz Quisling was born in Fyresdal, Telemark, in 1887. In 1911 he took his final examinations at the College of Military Studies with the highest grades in college history. After serving as an officer with the Chiefs of Staff, he was appointed military attaché in Petrograd and Helsinki. Between 1922 and 1926, he was engaged in League of Nations humanitarian relief work in the Soviet Union under Fridtjof Nansen. At this time Quisling had great sympathy for Soviet policy and tried – without success – to establish relations between the Labour Party and Norway's Communist Party.

When he returned home in 1929, he had changed his political views and became a strong anti-communist spokesman. He held the post of Minister of Defence in the Agarian Party governments in 1931 to '33, avidly defending the demands for Norwegian sovereignty over Greenland. After resigning his ministerial post in 1933, Quisling founded a new party, *Nasjonal Samling* (National Unification), taking the Italian Fascist party as a model. During the 1930s, Quisling and the NS became more and more influenced by German national-socialism.

In 1939, Quisling had contact with the head of the NSDAP foreign policy office, Alfred Rosenberg, and with Admiral Erich Raeder. Quisling went to Berlin, where he was introduced to Adolf Hitler. This was the start of his close cooperation with the Germans Nazis.

From the start of World War II and up until the summer of 1945, Quisling carried out several actions liable to the maximum penalties of the law. In September 1939, he had tried in vain to enlist the support of Hitler for a Nazi coup, and just prior to the invasion of Norway, he had supplied German officers with military information. On 9 April 1940, he carried out the only *coup d'etat* in newer Norwegian history, when he deposed the Nygaardsvold government in a radio broadcast and cancelled mobilization.

During the war years, Quisling attempted to change the Norwegian political system. He annulled municipal self-government, headed the country's only legal party and took over the authority given King and Storting by the Constitution. He also led the campaign to recruit Norwegian youth for combat service for the Germans, and he participated both in the persecution of the Jews and in the murder of Norwegian resistance people.

Historian Magne Skodvin has characterized Quisling in this way: «Quisling was both extremely intelligent and extremely learned. At the same time, there was something unrealistic over his intelligence, and he was given to intensive speculation. He was no great orator or organizer, and he seems to have had little ability for positive co-operation. As a politician, he was almost strikingly helpless. His almost messianic conceit and sense of call contributed to distancing him from political realities.»

Quisling was executed before a firing squad on 1 October 1945 after his appeal against the dealth penalty had been refused by the Supreme Court. In many languages of the world, the name «quisling» has become a synononym for those who join the ranks of their countrys' enemies.

Vidkun Quisling in 1942, viewing a parade in Oslo in honour of the police company of the Norwegian Legion about to be sent to the Eastern Front.

Resistance at Home

When the NS took over as the "state-authorized" party in the autumn of 1940, Quisling was determined to gain control over the public administration. He also wished to take over all national organizations and, in keeping with fascist models, subordinate them to a national assembly. Still another of his goals was a Norwegian-German peace treaty, which would assure the country a place in a "Greater Germanic" Europe. In keeping with these plans, a new Norwegian army was to be established and brought into the war on the German side.

These attempts at Nazification failed completely, mainly because Quisling had struck against the bedrock of Norwegian democracy. A wide-spread civil resistance movement grew up as people realized that their most basic human rights were at stake. The autumn of 1940 saw the resignation of the Supreme Court. The national board of the Sports Association retired, while individual sports club members boycotted all official

The hydrogen factory in front of the Vemork power station was completed in 1929. Norsk Hydro used the hydrogen to produce ammonia according to I.G. Farben's method. Heavy water, which was produced in the cellar of the building, was needed by the Germans for their attempts to make atomic bombs. The heavy water plant was destroyed in a sabotage attack carried out by a group of Norwegian Commandoes in 1943. The factory was torn down in 1977.

The NS set up a separate children's organization, the «Children's Hird», in order to raise youngsters in the spirit of the new age.

sporting events in protest against Nazi reorganization. Shortly afterwards, the country's bishops dissociated themselves from the new rulers, and in the spring of 1941, many business and industrial organizations did the same. In order to break this civil resistance, Terboven declared a state of emergency in Oslo. Two trade union officials were executed while other leaders were replaced by NS members. This in turn led to members withdrawing from the Nazified unions. Civil resistance reached a peak in 1942. Teachers refused to join the Nazified teachers' association. Tens of thousands of parents, who would not accept school children being organized in a National Socialist youth movement, smothered the authorities with letters of protest. The Germans retaliated with mass arrests of teachers, but when this merely intensified the will to resist, the NS was forced to abandon its offensive against schools. This failure was an important reason for German loss of faith in the NS' ability to achieve a National Socialistic revolution in Norway. In the autumn of 1942 Hitler began to regard Quisling with growing doubt.

A formal Resistance Movement gradually emerged, whose leaders established close contact with the government in exile in

London. Towards the end of the war, they were able to prevent Norwegian youth being called up for German labour or military service. This terminated Quisling's hopes of creating a national army.

It was only in the final phases of the war that military resistance predominated. The building of a secret army, *Milorg*, capable of carrying out action against the powerful German military machine, took time. A general fear of German reprisals had to be overcome. Weapons and equipment had to be smuggled in from abroad, and personnel had to be trained.

In 1943 military and civilian activities were coordinated under leadership of the Resistance. That same year Milorg was officially recognized by its government in London and by the allied military leadership. In both 1944 and 1945, Resistance forces carried out sabotage attacks against railways and fuel stores. Such attacks did not, however, become a dominant feature of the Resistance Movement. Allied orders specified that Milorg was to hold a state of preparedness in case of invasion. The Norwegian Communists criticized this policy. They agitated in favour of guerilla warfare, carrying out a number of sabotage attacks on their own.

Resistance Abroad

London became headquarters for Norwegian resistance efforts abroad. The Nygaardsvold government had quickly taken control over the merchant fleet, maiking it into "the world's largest shipping company", *Nortraship*,

to transport all types of supplies for the allies, and in doing so becoming a lifeline for Great Britain. But at great cost: 570 ships were sunk and over 4500 seamen lost their lives.

Seamen lived with constant fear. At any moment a torpedo might sink the ship. A tanker loaded with petrol would become an inferno of flames. Crews on ammunition ships were no better off. They knew that a direct hit by a torpedo almost always resulted in a deadly explosion.

Many who did manage to get aboard a lifeboat or float still did not survive. They risked being shot at by enemy planes or ships. Many died of exposure to cold, others of heat and thirst.

Shipping incomes enabled the government to build up military units. Norwegian naval vessels took part in sea battles in the Atlantic and the North Sea. Pilots were trained in Canada and took part in air battles over Great Britain and on the continent. Army units were set up in Scotland and in Sweden for use in a possible invasion of Norway.

During the first war years, relations between Sweden and Norway were extremely strained. The Swedish government had allowed transit of German troops and supplies and had delayed recognizing the Norwegian government in exile until 1943. Hundreds of refugees had been returned to Norway, and Swedish support of the Norwegian resistance struggle was censored. It was only when German war efforts faltered that the Swedes changed their policy towards Norway. They ceased deporting refugees and allowed establishment of Norwegian military units on Swedish soil. They also intensified their humanitarian assistance.

A fishing boat manned by the «Shetland Commandoes». The naval group sailed in deepest secrecy between Norway and Shetland during the war, transporting refugees, secret agents and military supplies. 10 boats and 44 commandoes were lost during transport operations.

The Resistance Movement

When the Germans invaded in 1940 they demanded an end to all opposition, and acceptance of a German occupation. These demands were refused by the King and the government. The fighting in southern Norway lasted three weeks, but the struggle continued in the Narvik area until 7 June. Then the government and the royal family crossed to London to carry on the war.

In Norway the Germans set about reorganising the country along Nazi lines with the help of Vidkun Quisling and NS. But this was thwarted by people in the worlds of sport, the Church, education and various trades and professions who combined into a broadly-based resistance movement. Towards the end of the War the resistance leadership cooperated closely with the government in exile in London to form a clandestine army, Milorg. In May 1945 the Germans laid down their arms, and on 7 June the King and the government returned to a liberated Norway.

Norwegian merchant seamen operating on all the seven seas made Norway's most significant contribution to the Allied victory over Hitler's Germany. 570 ships were sunk and over 4500 men lost their lives.

King Haakon and Crown Prince Olav were the most powerful symbols during the struggle against the Germans and the Norwegian Nazis. The photograph shows them during an air raid near Molde in April 1940.

A soldier of the Norwegian brigade during exercises in Scotland. In 1945 the Norwegian army in Great Britain numbered about 4300. The navy had 51 vessels and about 7500 men.

About 3300 escaped to Great Britain

⊕ The Norwegian fighter squadrons
⚙ Norwegian military forces
✈ Air bases
⚓ The Navy
⚓ The coastal artillery

Pilots were trained in the «Little Norway» camp outside Toronto in Canada. By the end of the War the two Norwegian fighter squadrons in the RAF had shot down roughly 200 German aircraft.

Civil resistance

Sports

In the autumn of 1940 the Nazis disbanded the sports clubs and associations and replaced them by a new Department of Sport and Labour Service. Young Norwegian sportsmen and women protested. They refused to take part in competitions held by the new, Nazi association. The public boycotted Nazi sports meetings. Many athletes organised illegal sporting events. Often the members of the banned sports clubs would become the nucleus of the local branch of the military resistance, Milorg.

The Church

In the spring of 1942 the bishops and almost all the clergy in the Church of Norway resigned from their official state positions in protest at the Nazification process. Parish work was continued clandestinely. The photograph shows a Nazi church service, with just one person in the congregation.

The Schools

1100 teachers were arrested in 1942 and 650 of them sent to do forced labour in Finnmark county because they refused to join their Nazified union.

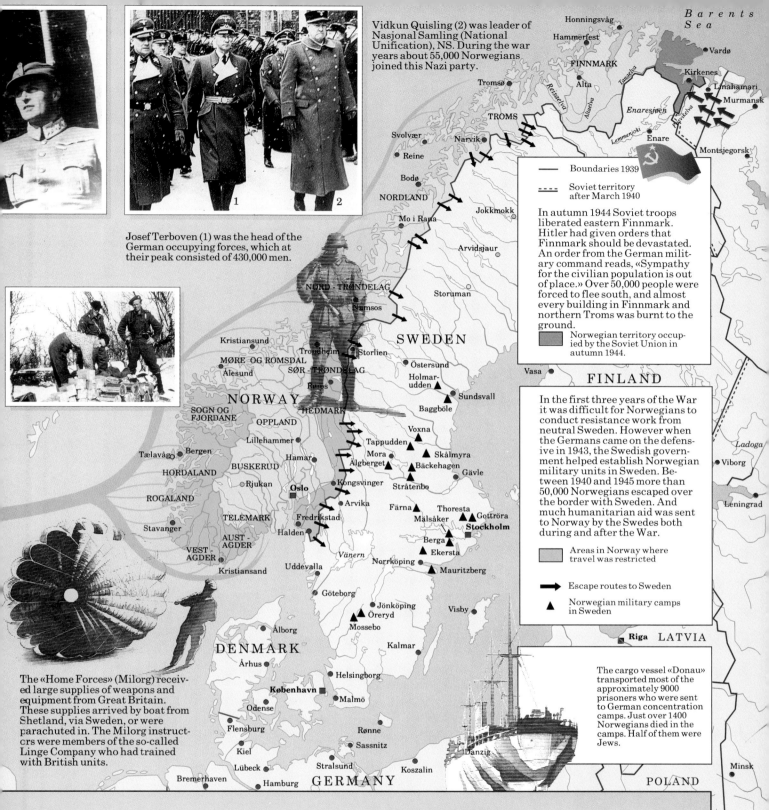

Vidkun Quisling (2) was leader of Nasjonal Samling (National Unification), NS. During the war years about 55,000 Norwegians joined this Nazi party.

Josef Terboven (1) was the head of the German occupying forces, which at their peak consisted of 430,000 men.

— Boundaries 1939

- - - Soviet territory after March 1940

In autumn 1944 Soviet troops liberated eastern Finnmark. Hitler had given orders that Finnmark should be devastated. An order from the German military command reads, «Sympathy for the civilian population is out of place.» Over 50,000 people were forced to flee south, and almost every building in Finnmark and northern Troms was burnt to the ground.

▓ Norwegian territory occupied by the Soviet Union in autumn 1944.

In the first three years of the War it was difficult for Norwegians to conduct resistance work from neutral Sweden. However when the Germans came on the defensive in 1943, the Swedish government helped establish Norwegian military units in Sweden. Between 1940 and 1945 more than 50,000 Norwegians escaped over the border with Sweden. And much humanitarian aid was sent to Norway by the Swedes both during and after the War.

▓ Areas in Norway where travel was restricted

➤ Escape routes to Sweden

▲ Norwegian military camps in Sweden

The «Home Forces» (Milorg) received large supplies of weapons and equipment from Great Britain. These supplies arrived by boat from Shetland, via Sweden, or were parachuted in. The Milorg instructors were members of the so-called Linge Company who had trained with British units.

The cargo vessel «Donau» transported most of the approximately 9000 prisoners who were sent to German concentration camps. Just over 1400 Norwegians died in the camps. Half of them were Jews.

The Press

Immediately after the invasion the Germans introduced strict censorship. They controlled the content of newspapers and took over broadcasting. From 1941 only Nazis were permitted to have radios. Throughout the country people began producing illegal newspapers. The Germans and NS made great efforts to clamp down on this. But despite many arrests the Nazis could not stop information from the government in London and from the resistance movement reaching the majority of the population.

The Intelligence Service

The Allies needed information about the Germans. In cooperation with the Norwegian military command in London they charted the enemy's military camps, airfields, troop movements, defences and shipping activities. Several intelligence organisations built up a network of agents throughout the country. Many women tapped the Germans' telephone lines. Secret radio transmitters and couriers smuggled out news to Sweden and Great Britain.

A scene of joy on Oslo's main street, Karl Johan, during the liberation celebration in May 1945.

The government supported the Resistance Movement with money, weapons and equipment. They also placed great weight on keeping up morale both at home and abroad. King Håkon's and Crown Prince Olav's tireless efforts gave the government added authority. They travelled constantly to encourage seamen and soldiers. Their radio broadcasts helped boost morale at home in Norway, and in them Norway's cause had its foremost champions with the allies.

The Liberation

People living in northern Norway were those hardest hit by war actions. Bodø and Narvik were severely damaged in 1940, and in 1944 eastern Finnmark was subjected to heavy bombing by the Soviet air force. A total of 328 air raids hit Kirkenes. La Valetta on Malta is the only European town to have suffered more raids during the war.

In the autumn of 1944 Soviet forces took the offensive in the north, forcing German troops to retreat from Finnmark and northern Troms counties. On their way south, the Germans burned over 10,000 buildings and destroyed boats, roads, bridges and quays. Nothing of value was to be left to the Red Army. The inhabitants were also forced to flee but not all of them were evacuated by force. Those who managed to hide cheered the Soviet forces as they advanced into eastern Finnmark in October 1944.

That next spring in 1945 there were still more than 360,000 German soldiers in the country. Enormous destruction and loss of life were feared if they refused to surrender. Great relief was felt on 8 May 1945 when the Germans laid down their weapons without a fight.

With the coming of peace, an extensive legal process was started against those who had collaborated with the enemy. Nearly 53.000 people were convicted of treason, som 23.000 of whom were sentenced to prison. Quisling and 24 other Norwegians were executed. 12 Germans were shot as war criminals.

The marks left by the war were obvious during the first postwar decades. Seamen were among those especially hard-hit by war experiences. Many of them were troubled with mental problems for the rest of their lives, and most waited for years before being granted a decent war pension. Families of those who were tried for collaboration also experienced hardship because the Nazi stamp stayed with them.

The war years proved a turning point in national security and foreign policy. The German invasion had destroyed any policy of neutrality and disarmament. Wartime cooperation with the allies became a solid foundation for closer ties to the Western powers after 1945.

The fight against the Nazi dictatorship led to an increase in the prestige of the free and democratic institutions, as well as to a reduction in class antagonism. Wartime economy helped farmers, fishermen and whole towns free themselves of debt, and the unemployed to find work. At the same time, the resistance struggle had forged a national unity that would be of vital help in the coming reconstruction of the country.

From Liberation to EC-struggle

BYGG LANDET!

TRYGG SEIREN

DET NORSKE ARBEIDERPARTI

A Labour Party election poster for the 1945 general election, showing that the party intended go in for the building of more power stations and new industry in order to get the country on its feet again after the war.

On 7 June 1945, five years to the day after he had been forced to flee the country, King Håkon VII set foot once again on Norwegian soil. Endless cheers rose as the king, the very symbol of national unity in the struggle for freedom and democracy, stepped out on to the quay in Oslo.

Resistance during the occupation had brought people more closely together in a feeling of solidarity that became strengthed by the tremendous work of reconstruction. This feeling was most clearly expressed in 1945, when all the political parties stood for election on the same platform, the *Joint*

Programme. The programme's clearly social democratic stamp indicated the extent of the ideological supremity achieved by the Labour Party over the other parties.

The Joint Programme, which gave chief responsibility for social development to the state, has formed the basis for the mixed-economy system followed by Norway since 1945. Working together with private business and industry, the state was to provide the conditions necessary for strong economic growth which would ensure the population of improved standards of living and greater security. The Programme also emphasized the necessity of fighting unemployment and of equalizing living conditions.

As was the case in most other European countries, the war had radicalized the population. In the 1945 elections, the Labour Party received the clear majority it needed to form a government on its own. Barring a period of three weeks in 1963, the party remained in power for the next twenty years.

EINAR GERHARDSEN

Gerhardsen (1897–1987) was a man of the people. He grew up in modest circumstances in Olso without more formal education than primary school. He became shop steward of his trade union and secretary of the Labour Party during his years as a road construction worker. He later became a member of the party's sentral committee and chairman of its youth organization. After having accompanied the government during the 1940-campaign, he became a leader of the civilian resistance movement. This led to his being arrested and sent to a concentration camp. After the liberation, he took over as mayor of Oslo and was also chosen chairman of the Labour Party. In the summer of 1945, he succeeded Nygaardsvold as prime minister and formed a coalition government which remained in office until the elections that autumn.

It soon became obvious that Gerhardsen possessed just those personal qualities necessary to leading the reconstruction of the country. He lived in an ordinary apartment from which he walked to work every day. He was a passionate lover of outdoor life. He took great care in keeping in touch with people from all walks of life regardless of political opinion. With his unassuming nature and plain way of speaking he gained respect in wide circles. In addition he had the ability to listen and to find compromizes in difficult matters. When a decision had been reached, he spared no effort to put it into effect.

Gerhardsen became the symbol of the cooperative and social welfare policies of the first post-war years. By the time he resigned as prime minister in 1965, he was recognized as the «father of his country», with a position as one of the greatest statesmen in Norwegian history.

In a European perspective Einar Gerhardsen is regarded as having held a leading position in the social democratic movement comparable to that of such leaders as Sweden's Tage Erlander and West Germany's Willy Brandt.

Reconstruction and Economic Growth

The burned and devastated areas of Finnmark and northern Troms counties were given highest priority in reconstruction work. The areas were full of dangerous landmines, and providing proper housing and the necessary supplies to the inhabitants would be time-consuming. The authorities decided, therefore, that only men capable of working would be allowed to return that first year. This prohibition on travel proved a complete failure against the homesickness of the evacuees. Thousands of families left the south in the summer of 1945 to head north. Living at first in sod huts, beached boats, shacks and barracks, it was not until the beginning of the 1950s that most were able to move into permanent housing.

From 1945 to 1990, the population grew from 3.1 to 4.3 million people. The continued fall in the death rate led to an increased number of aged. This increase in life expectancy was the result of improved public health facilities, nutrition and housing. Effective, new medicines against infectious illnesses, especially tuberculosis, were of prime importance.

When the war ended, many people feared that the country would be hit by a post-war depression comparable to that following World War I. This was not the case. Starting in 1945, Norway experienced a remarkable economic growth which would place the country among the world's richest idustrialized nations.

Reconstruction work proceeded more quickly than had been expected. By 1945, both the GNP and industrial production had surpassed pre-war levels and up to 1950, Norway's rate of economic growth was the highest in Europe. The government used a ration system to limit private consumption. This meant that imports of ships and machinery, for example, had priority ahead of bananas and private cars. These regulations were still not enough to prevent an explosive growth in the manufacture of consumer products. The government was particularly displeased by the unhampered growth of companies making toys and ornaments.

The great demand for new production equipment from abroad led to an acute foreign exchange crisis in 1947. American Marshall Aid was therefore literally "heaven-sent". From 1948 on, Norway received about 400 million dollars in aid. These funds were not only used for raw materials and machinery. The Americans arranged study tours to the United States to   enable Norwegian companies to learn about modern industrial technology and rationalization. The aid programme also provided the basis for an official research fund in technology and science, and for a Norwegian institute of productivity.

Despite increased productivity and record-high investments, the Norwegian GNP had a slower rate of growth than that of most other European countries during the 1950s. One reason was that some segments of industry encountered more competition. As a participant in the Marshall Plan organization OEEC, Norway was obliged to allow the import of foreign pro-

Norwegian stevedores unloading motor oil shipped from the USA under terms of the Marshall Aid programme.

ducts. This was a blow to producers of consumer goods, who had flourished during the 1940s due to high customs barriers and import restrictions. Some companies were forced to curtail when the demand for many products was met. A scarcity of labour and of capital also hampered growth.

The period between 1945 and 1973 saw a new boom in shipping. In 1968 Norwegian ships amounted to about 10 per cent of the world's tonnage. Over half were supertankers, but several shipowners had also acquired new specialized vessels such as container ships and car carriers. The number of seamen reached a high of about 57,000 in the mid-1960s. After this the number gradually decreased, due mainly to the rapid modernization of the merchant fleet.

The Active State

Production of aluminium at Årdal in 1948. The Germans started construction of the smelting plant during the war. The company expanded production greatly in 1954 with opening of a new plant at Sunndalsøra.

In order to make a strong start in reconstruction, the Labour Party decided to make use of the experiences gained in British and American war economies. Both Great Britain and the USA had utilized official planning to produce weapons and equipment for the fight against Fascism. Could similar methods be used to reach the goals of the Joint Programme?

Such questions were important, as the new government had determined to retain a great deal of public control over business and industry. The rationing system was maintained, as was the strict control of foreign trade, prices and wages. Official approval of all building, repair work and industrial production was required. These restraints on trade were accepted by private business as long as reconstruction made them necessary, but legislation proposed by the government to continue such economic control *after* completion of reconstruction work led to sharp protests.

Extreme opposition from the non-socialist parties, the Federation of Norwegian Industry and from other important organizations forced the Labour Party to withdraw these proposals in 1953. In the years that followed, the party chose to cooperate with business and industry rather than confront them.

Just after the war the Labour Party started the building of new state-owned industrial concerns. The most important of these were the iron works at Mo i Rana and the aluminium works at Årdal and in Sunndalsøra. Enterprises of this kind were never a major element of the party's industrial policy, however. Of far more importance was government support of private business. Good examples of this are the North Norway Plan in 1951 and the Regional Develop-

mental Fund in 1960, which opened for the transference of extensive amounts of state funds to companies in outlying districts. This was also the case with the special agreements between the state and the important organizations in agriculture and fishing.

The Labour Party was interested in the extensive building of hydroelectric power plants and of communications. In 1950 nearly 420,000 people lacked electricity. Twenty years later that number had sunk to about 1000.

The fact that business and industry had freer scope in the 1950s did not mean that the Labour Party had given up its hopes of steering economic development. The party sought the advice of economic experts, among them Minister of Finance Erik Brofoss. He in turn consulted with Ragnar Frisch and Trygve Haavelmo, both later Nobel laureates in economics. And members of the Cabinet and of the Storting set about learning the elements of economic theory, along with all the relevant terminology and phraseology.

Members of the Storting felt fairly helpless as they listened to Brofoss present these new economic theories in his famous budget speech of 1946. Within a few years, however, the concepts of a national budget and of long-term planning were accepted by every political party. The important business

organizations even hired their own economists, who worked closely with the government experts.

In using this new knowledge, the government hoped to acquire a general survey of the country's labour force, supplies of raw materials and means of production. It also wanted an impression of the full and coherent scope of Norwegian economy. What effect did the activities of private and state-owned companies have on "Norway Inc."? How could the national budget best be used to reach the goals of the Joint Programme? It was questions like these economists hoped to answer in their calculations.

As the 1950s progressed, the government relied increasingly on this *macroeconomic* control over the economy. Direct governmental intervention in individul companies was replaced by *indirect* methods. The government influenced demand and production by means of taxes and excises. For example, high excises were introduced on automobiles to save foreign exchange. Subsidies in the Budget kept food prices low so that wage demands would not be too high. The government kept the interest rate low to increase investment in business and industry, and had legislation passed giving the state the authority to restrict loans from private banks. New state banks, such as the

Most of the railway system was electrified during the first 24 post-war years. Here a meeting of the old and the new is shown taking place at Nelaug station on the Southern line in 1949. The last steam locomotives were taken out of service in 1970.

Housing Bank, the State Educational Loan Fund and the Post Office Savings Bank, helped the authorities decide which projects were to receive loans.

The Labour Party was also interested in providing inhabitants with improved cultural activities, in order to link the country's districts and people more closely together. The establishment of such institutions as the National Touring Theatre, the Travelling Art Gallery and the National District Cinema, show that the state accepted more responsibility for the presentation of dramatic, pictorial and cinematic arts.

While employers were given a freer rein, the Labour Party kept its influence over the trade union movement. The leaders of the Trade Union Federation helped by ensuring modest wage demands and preventing strikes. Still, it would not be correct to say that trade union wings were clipped in these first two post-war decades. As long as the conditions of wage-earners in "the Norwegian duck-pond" continued to improve, there was nothing to ruffle feathers about.

Far right: Girls wearing their student caps, fotographed during enrollment ceremonies at the University of Oslo in 1958.

Below: «Rock and roll» at a club in Oslo 1957.

Social Welfare

When the war ended, there was general agreement that the class struggles, unemployment and social distress of the inter-war years should not be allowed to resume. Many of the ideas on which the new welfare state was based came from the British "Beveridge Plan". This proposed that public assistance was not to be limited to society's underdogs. Any citizen who experienced insecurity or financial need had a right to support. The welfare systems were to be financed by and coordinated in a national insurance fund.

When the country's economy improved faster than expected, the Storting used the opportunity to build up an increasingly fine-meshed social safety net. Child benefits were introduced in 1945, giving parents and guardians of more than one child below age 15 a fixed, monthly sum of money. Health insurance became compulsory in the 1950s, while qualification for an old-age pension no longer depended on a means test. Welfare for workers and children improved. New measures were advanced for helping the mentally retarded, those with occupational injuries and the mentally ill. The 1964 law covering social care gave the municipal welfare boards new duties. They were not only to provide support for the needy, but also to ensure that people were able to help themselves.

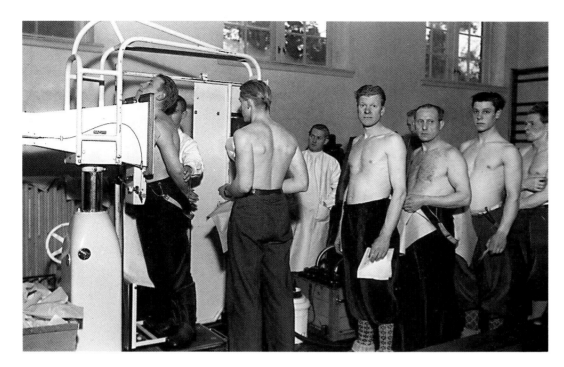

The National Mass Radiography Service was established in 1948 in order to examine large groups of the population in the fight against tuberculosis. Together with BCG-vacination, X-ray examinations led to the virtual eradication of the feared disease in the space of some twenty years.

Stability

The relative strength of the political parties did not vary appreciably during the 1950s and '60s. This political stability had its basis in the feeling of unity that grew up during the war years and the reconstruction period. The country also benefited from rising international trade conditions. The mass unemployment of the inter-war years had vanished and most people experienced increasing prosperity and social security. This meant that the main goals of the Joint Programme had been met, and for this the Labour Party was given credit.

The general agreement on growth and welfare policies shows clearly that idealogical differences between the parties had lessened. It was even maintained that ideology was dead and that party programmes had lost their perspective and purpose. A radical critic of the Labour Party expressed his preference for the slogans of the inter-war years such as "Down with pulpit, purse and throne!" He sneered at the '50s motto about "Solidarity for peace and progress!", saying that this was "just as round as a bun, and as warm and cosy as a duvet. They might as well say Happy Christmas and a prosperous New Year!"

Criticism of this kind was rare and had little effect. Both the Labour Party and the non-socialists moved towards the centre to attract the fastest-growing group of voters -

the white-collar workers. Another sign was when the Agarian Party changed its name to the Centre Party in 1959.

An important reason for the new political stability of the post-war years was the growth of the *corporate system*. The government and the state administration began working in close cooperation with the various interest groups. This meant that these organizations were consulted on matters concerning them. They could comment on proposed legislation and take part on official boards, committees and councils. The Norwegian Shipowners' Association, for example, had considerable influence on Norwegian shipping policy, while farmers' organizations could influence legislators as to agriculture's need of high import duties and restrictions. In many cases the Storting accepted solutions jointly worked out by administration experts and the organizations. This meant that a number of questions which might have caused serious conflict were withdrawn from party politics.

In contrast to what had been the case in the inter-war years, the post-war period was characterized by broad agreement on defence and foreign policies. As relations between the super powers deteriorated, fear of the Soviet Union increased, and the Labour Party joined with the non-socialists in a common front against the Norwegian Communists. This truce also made for improved cooperation on domestic matters.

DAILY LIFE IN THE 1950S

A man who grew up near Sarpsborg relates:

"I was born in 1946 as one of 70,727 Norwegian children born that year, the largest number ever in the country's history. We are often called the tangible results of the liberation.

Housing was desparately short at the end of the war. Dad was one of the lucky ones. He was able to rent rooms in a former German officers' mess bought up by a newly rich packaging manufacturer. I grew up there with my parents and my sister.

Almost all my pals lived in the former German barracks on the other side of the road. While we had our own bathroom, with lavatory, washbasin and shower, they had to make do with an outdoor privet, wash bowl, zinc tub and chamber pot. But things improved for them too. Several of the barrack families bought plots of land in the neighbourhood. With cheap loans from the newly started Housing Bank, they started building their own homes. Excavating was usually done with pick and shovel, while friends pitched in to help with the building.

My mum was a housewife, like most other married women in the '50s. I remember how pleased she was with all our new labour-saving household appliances. After we could afford to buy a washing machine, she stop-ped having to struggle with the old boiler, washboard and sinks in that cold, damp cellar. Our new refrigerator saved us kids from long walks with a milk pail to the dairy. Now we started buying bottled milk that didn't sour in the summer heat.

Even though chocolate, sugar, meat and coffee were no longer rationed in the early '50s, there were still lots of products we couldn't find in the shops. So we squeezed ourselves into one of the neighborhood's few private cars and headed for Strømstad in Sweden. The car belonged to an army officer who had brought it home after attending courses in the USA. We felt like royals as we swept into the backyard with the Studebaker's boot filled with tins of pineapple.

It was easy to see who people were in the '50s. White-collar jobs still had a lot of prestige, and those who had taken their A-levels usually wore their student caps on 17 May, Constitution Day. Workers wore overalls to work and farm children smelt of cowsheds. Everyone dreamed of buying a new car, but most had to make do with a moped, a motor cycle or an old used car.

Very few of the kids at our school went on to secondary school. There was competition to get in and anyway, higher education cost money. Most of us just wanted to start working as soon as possible.

The USA was our great ideal. We admired and copied Americans, never worrying about being influenced. The newsreels showed us that the USA was protecting us against the Soviets. After watching cowboy films, we all played at being Roy Rogers or Hopalong Cassidy, but the new comics brought Donald Duck and the other Disney figures to compete with our western heroes.

Blue jeans were a hit with all of us teenagers. Boys put aside their plus-fours and girls hung their skirts in the wardrobe. We pulled on our Lees or Wranglers and lit up a Camel. We chewed American chewing gum, drank Cokes and played rock 'n' roll on the jukebox. What a future we could look forward to?"

A worker at the Emaljeverket plant at Hasle in Oslo, proudly demonstrating a Norwegian washing machine, the "Evalet", in 1953.

Christianity, Contraception and Abortion

The post-war years also had their share of disagreement on cultural policies. The Labour Party and the Christian Democrats disagreed vehemently on matters of belief and sexual morals. Soon after the liberation, the Christian community attacked the government for providing funds for information on contraception, particularly when such information was given to unmarried women.

When the government later agreed to a distribution of condoms among soldiers stationed as occupation forces in Germany, a new battle started. A nationwide protest action led by the Christian community managed to collect som 440,000 signature protesting distribution. The government did not give in, as the Labour Party would not accept that the measure could undermine sexual morality. Limiting of venereal disease and unwanted pregnancies were of far more importance.

But the Christian community received more support for it views when the Labour Party presented plans for reducing religious education in primary schools. More than 750,000 people protested against the measure in what was the country's largest protest action, and the plans were shelved.

The abortion question also roused controversy. The women's organization of the Labour Party again demanded, as they had in the inter-war years, a new law on abortion that would allow induced abortion on social grounds. Even though the number of illegal abortions rose during the 1950s, the men leading the Labour Party would not support the women's proposal. The new Abortion Act of 1960 showed clearly that the government had yielded to the views of the Christian community and the medical profession: neither low income, inadequate housing or other social conditions were regarded as sufficient cause for abortion. Hospital doctors were given absolute authority to determine abortion applications.

The Abortion Act created dissent, and the abortion conflict flared up again in the 1970s.

Orientation towards the West

The optimistic hopes of peace raised by the liberation were soon replaced by new fears of war. When the communists seized power in Czechoslovakia, and the Soviet Union demanded bases in Finland, the alarm sounded in Norway. Foreign and defence policy would have to follow a new course.

During the first two post-war years, Norway had relied on the new world organization, the UN, to keep the peace. The government hoped to be a bridge-builder on the international scene. Norway would evade block politics and avoid military alliances. At the same time, there was general consensus on strengthening the nation's defences.

The foundations for such bridge-building soon began crumbling. 1947 saw the forming of a sharp breach between East and West. The Cold War had begun.

Norway could not play an active role as mediator in this situation. The country was too weak, both economically and militarily. Norwegian policies in the UN were passive and cautious.

Most Norwegians had had great sympathy with the Soviet Union due to its efforts in liberating Finnmark. But attitudes had begun to change as early as in the autumn of 1946. Suspicions were aroused when this powerful eastern neighbor demanded Norwegian-Soviet military bases on Svalbard. The government rejected this demand and strengthened the country's military cooperation, never completely discontinued, with the western powers. Most of Norway's military purchasing was with Great Britain, and from 1947 on, Norwegian forces under British command had also been part of the occupation army in Germany. Contacts with American and British intelligence had also increased during this period.

Norway took an important step westward in 1947 when the government decided to accept Marshall Aid. It was an easy decision. The country's most important trading partners had done the same, and foreign exchange was in short supply.

The coup in Czechoslovakia early in 1948 provoked an intense anti-communist campaign. Prime Minister Einar Gerhardsen led this crusade against "the enemy within". The Norwegian Communist Party (NKP) had attracted new supporters during the

Trygve Lie was Minister of Foreign Affairs from 1941 to 1946, when he was elected as the first Secretary General of the United Nations. In the early 1960s he was first Minister of Trade, and later Minister of Industry.

Below, right: Norwegian troops took part in the occupation of Germany between 1947 and 1953. The soldier in this photograph from 1948 had just arrived in Schleswig.

war. Due to its active efforts in the resistance and its new social democratic peace programme, the NKP won 11.9 per cent of the vote in the 1945 general election. The party was not able to keep this position for long, however. As early as in 1946, the Labour Party under its secretary Haakon Lie, had begun to register and remove communists from positions of responsibility in the trade unions. This anti-communist campaign led to mass withdrawls, and inner disagreements further weakened the Communist Party. The situation was not helped by NKP support of the Soviet Union in the cold war and by its adoption of a more revolutionary course. Within a short time the party had been reduced to a tiny, isolated sect in Norwegian politics.

When confrontations between East and West grew critical in 1948, negotiations were opened between Norway, Sweden and Denmark concerning a Scandinavian defence union. These negotiations led nowhere. The Swedes wanted an independent alliance, while Norway was interested in establishing ties to the West through arms purchases and a firm guarantee of support in case of war, a policy that had to be agreed upon in time of peace.

After the collapse of Scandinavian negotiations, the view that country's security could be safeguarded only through membership in NATO gradually gained acceptance. Wide-

spread scepticism continued in the Labour Party, but when the prime minister overcame his doubts, his opponents fell into line.

Having joined NATO, the government placed great importance on reassuring the Soviet Union. The so-called Bases' Declaration stated that Norway would not allow foreign troops or atomic weapons to be based on Norwegian territory in peacetime. In the years that followed restrictions were also placed on military activity in Finnmark. This

policy was intended to prevent the Soviet Union from increasing pressure on Finland.

Norway also wished to demonstrate a will to defend herself. Allocations of funds for defence increased sharply, and both the conscript army and the reserve were expanded. Norway used relatively large sums on defence in the 1950s compared to other NATO countries. In this same period, Foreign Minister Halvard Lange gained regard as one of the alliance's most respected statesmen.

The policy on bases did not prevent NATO forces from taking part in short-term manoeuvres on Norwegian soil, nor did Norwegian authorities check allied ships as to whether they had atomic weapons on board when they visited the country. The armed forces also built early-warning systems and stocks of weapons for allied reinforcements. Planes and rockets capable of carrying atomic warheads in times of crisis were also procured. NATO's North Commando was established in Oslo.

Starting in the late 1950s, American espionage planes operated from Norwegian airfields. These flights took place without the approval of the government, becoming publicly known only when a U-2 plane headed for Bodø was shot down over the Soviet Union in 1960.

Norway rejected plans for a Nordic customs union and was critical of cooperation with the EEC. Norwegian business and industry feared competition from Swedish

In 1960 the united States supplied four Nike-batteries for the defence of eastern Norway. These ground-to-air missiles could hit enemy planes flying beyound the range of ordinary anti-air-craft artillery. The Nike-battalion was disbanded in the late 1980s.

industry and Danish agriculture. Many Norwegian politicians had an ingrown scepticism concerning supranational organizations. It was not until 1960 that Norwegian industry made serious efforts to compete on an international scale. This was when Norway joined the west-European, British-dominated free trade association, EFTA, whose aim was the reduction of customs duties among having member nations. The organization had no supranational authority, no common external customs barriers, nor did it include agriculture or fishing.

The head of Milorg, Jens Christian Hauge, was Minister of Defence from 1945 to 1952. Here he is seen at Sola Airfield near Stavanger in 1951, when Norway received new fighter planes from the USA. On Hauge's left, NATO's Commander-in-Chief, Dwight D. Eisenhower. The officer standing behind Hauge is Lauris Norstad, who was head of the American air force in Europe.

Defence

King Christian IV established a Norwegian army in 1628. From 1750 onwards officers were trained at the Military Academy in Christiania. Most of the crews of the Dano-Norwegian fleet were Norwegians.

After 1814 Norway had her own defence forces and when the union with Sweden was dissolved in 1905 the country had a strong defence.

Defence was neglected after the First World War. When the Germans attacked in 1940, the country had little possibility of defending herself. Norway became a member of NATO in 1949. The Norwegian defence system has always been based on a popular army. All males were still conscripted for national service in 1995.

Akershus Castle in Oslo, about 1300.

When a man was conscripted everyone on the farm had to help. Men and servants forged and sharpened weapons, while women sewed clothes and prepared food for one to two month.

THE NAVY
King Hans founded a joint Dano-Norwegian fleet in 1510. Today the Coastal Artillery is an important element in naval defence.

King Christian IV's warship *"Den norske love"*

"Lovendahls gallei", 1712.

THE ARMY
Foot soldiers have always been the backbone of the Norwegian popular army. Up to 1854 only farmers were conscripted into the army.

Conscription was a system of defence that was used both on land and at sea. The farmers supplied ships, crews, soldiers and food. The king organised the conscription system

Conscript ship.

King Hakon V (1299-1319) built more fortresses than any other king, including Akershus, Vardøhus and Bahus castles.

Norwegian infantry soldier, early eighteenth century.

Ski divisions were first established in 1720, two in the north and two in the south.

Ski soldier, 1800.

Farming families sought refuge in local forts in times of war. The forts were built in positions easily defended. When the enemy approached, the farmers let fires (beacons) on the neighbouring settlements.

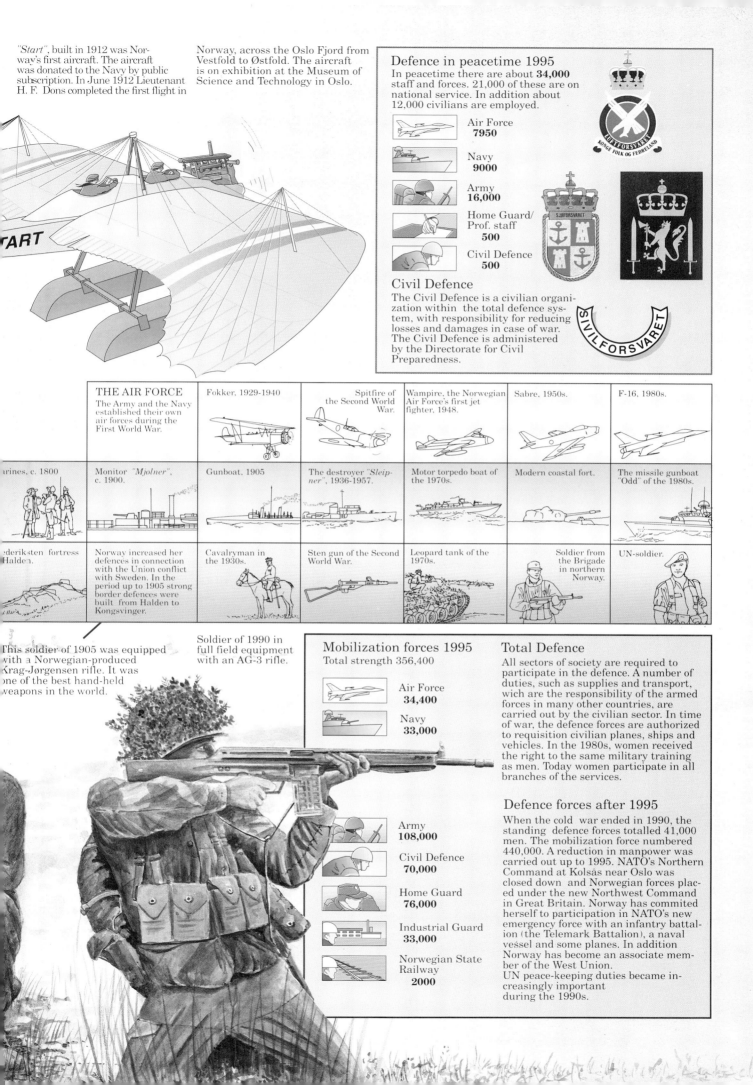

"Start", built in 1912 was Norway's first aircraft. The aircraft was donated to the Navy by public subscription. In June 1912 Lieutenant H. F. Dons completed the first flight in Norway, across the Oslo Fjord from Vestfold to Østfold. The aircraft is on exhibition at the Museum of Science and Technology in Oslo.

Defence in peacetime 1995

In peacetime there are about **34,000** staff and forces. 21,000 of these are on national service. In addition about 12,000 civilians are employed.

Air Force
7950

Navy
9000

Army
16,000

Home Guard/
Prof. staff
500

Civil Defence
500

Civil Defence

The Civil Defence is a civilian organization within the total defence system, with responsibility for reducing losses and damages in case of war. The Civil Defence is administered by the Directorate for Civil Preparedness.

THE AIR FORCE

The Army and the Navy established their own air forces during the First World War.

Fokker, 1929-1940

Spitfire of the Second World War.

Wampire, the Norwegian Air Force's first jet fighter, 1948.

Sabre, 1950s.

F-16, 1980s.

...rines, c. 1800

Monitor *"Mjolner"*, c. 1900.

Gunboat, 1905

The destroyer *"Sleipner"*, 1936-1957.

Motor torpedo boat of the 1970s.

Modern coastal fort.

The missile gunboat *"Odd"* of the 1980s.

...ederiksten fortress Halden.

Norway increased her defences in connection with the Union conflict with Sweden. In the period up to 1905 strong border defences were built from Halden to Kongsvinger.

Cavalryman in the 1930s.

Sten gun of the Second World War.

Leopard tank of the 1970s.

Soldier from the Brigade in northern Norway.

UN-soldier.

This soldier of 1905 was equipped with a Norwegian-produced Krag-Jørgensen rifle. It was one of the best hand-held weapons in the world.

Soldier of 1990 in full field equipment with an AG-3 rifle.

Mobilization forces 1995

Total strength 356,400

Air Force
34,400

Navy
33,000

Army
108,000

Civil Defence
70,000

Home Guard
76,000

Industrial Guard
33,000

Norwegian State Railway
2000

Total Defence

All sectors of society are required to participate in the defence. A number of duties, such as supplies and transport, wich are the responsibility of the armed forces in many other countries, are carried out by the civilian sector. In time of war, the defence forces are authorized to requisition civilian planes, ships and vehicles. In the 1980s, women received the right to the same military training as men. Today women participate in all branches of the services.

Defence forces after 1995

When the cold war ended in 1990, the standing defence forces totalled 41,000 men. The mobilization force numbered 440,000. A reduction in manpower was carried out up to 1995. NATO's Northern Command at Kolsås near Oslo was closed down and Norwegian forces placed under the new Northwest Command in Great Britain. Norway has commited herself to participation in NATO's new emergency force with an infantry battalion (the Telemark Battalion), a naval vessel and some planes. In addition Norway has become an associate member of the West Union.
UN peace-keeping duties became increasingly important during the 1990s.

Scandinavian Airlines System, SAS, opened its first route between Scandinavia and the USA in 1946. The company was the first to start flights between Europe and Japan over the North Pole in 1957.

A new Socialist Alternative

A clear majority of Norwegians supported NATO during the '50s. Small groups opposing membership did still exist in the labour movement. They protested against rearmament and expressed dissatisfaction with the way Labour Party leaders prevented an open discussion on foreign and defence policy. They also disliked the fact that the party had become less socialist and cooperated more with private business and industry.

Opponents of NATO had some success in the late 1950s. Many of them participated actively in the western European anti-nuclear campaigns. The 1961 Labour Party congress resolution opening for the placement of nuclear weapons on Norwegian territory if war threatened was completely unacceptable to them. In protest they established a new party called the Socialistic People's Party (SF).

The party programme showed that the thoughts on neutrality and disarmament of the inter-war years still lived on. The formation of the party was in itself a sign that the worst frigidity of the cold war had begun to thaw.

To general surprise, the SF managed to win two seats in the Storting in the 1961 general election. The Labour Party had now acquired a troublesome rival on its extreme left.

Scandinavian Cooperation

Even though efforts to create a Scandinavian customs union and a Nordic defence association had failed, ties between the Scandinavian countries became stronger after the war. In 1952 the national assemblies of Sweden, Denmark, Iceland and Norway resolved to establish a new cooperative organization, which Finland joined three years later. The *Nordic Council* (Nordisk Råd) consists of members of the national assemblies and governments, who meet annually to discuss matters of common interest. The Council cannot pass binding resolutions, but its recommendations have usually been implemented, as in the 1950s when compulsory use of passports between the Nordic countries was abolished. A common labour market was also established, guaranteeing workers who moved to some other Nordic country the same rights to social benefits as the country's own citizens. The Council's greatest significance is as a body where Nordic politicians can exchange ideas and compare notes.

Contacts between organizations and public authorities in the Scandinavian countries also increased markedly after 1945. The trade union movement can serve as an example. When new reforms were proposed, it became common practice to seek advice from sister organizations in the other Nordic countries. In case of labour conflicts, financial support would usually be available from these same groups.

The Scandinavian countries cooperated closely in the UN. They were more assured of being listened to by the large countries when they operated as a group with joint opinions. Nordic military units also began to cooperate closely during peace-keeping operations.

Most people became better acquainted with the other Scandinavian countries through holiday and leisure time activities. In the 1950s, increasing numbers of Norwegians had their first taste of foreign travel by visiting Sweden and Denmark. Exchange of television programmes started in 1960, and people living near the border could view Swedish programmes.

The Scandinavian Airlines System, SAS, was established in 1946 with the Swedish, Norwegian and Danish governments as chief shareholders. Although the company was a success, it did not establish a precedent for other and future Nordic projects. It was only after the Scandinavian countries joined the free-trade organization EFTA in 1960-61, that serious economic contacts were established.

Norway and the Third World. From Kerala to NORAD

Norway has long had close ties with the third world. Norwegian merchant ships began calling at overseas harbours in the 1700s, while the first Norwegian missionaries went to Asia and Africa early in the next century. Norway was among the first countries to establish bilateral development programmes. In 1952 the Storting allocated funds for a Norwegian-Indian fishery project in Kerala. The initiative came from the leaders of the Labour Party, who hoped to give opponents of NATO something new to think about. Other considerations were of greater importance once the Storting had planned the first aid programmes. Many politicians were interested in using aid projects to stem the tide of communism, while others stressed the importance of showing Christian charity and solidarity with the world's poor.

In 1962 the Aid to India was replaced by the Norwegian Development Aid. The organization was renamed NORAD six years later, and in 1984 became part of the new Ministry of Development Cooperation.

When aid is compared in proportion to the GNP, Norway has been among those countries giving most. Approximately half the funds were given directly to poor, priority-aid countries in Asia and Africa. The remainder was used in the UN system and by private humantarian organizations.

Norwegian aid was meant as assistance to ordinary men and women. Most funds were outright gifts, rather than loans, and very little was tied to the use of Norwegian products and services. Starting in the 1970s, private companies became more involved with the developing countries. This was a result of the increasingly large exports credits granted by the Storting.

A Norwegian-built fishing boat off Kerala in India in the early 1950s.

The "Golden Sixties"

"New inventions, new production methods, new raw materials open un-thought-of possibilities for increasing our prosperity. [...] We must adopt policies enabling our country to utilize these technical advances [...] Then we can meet the future with confidence and optimism."

This quotation from the 1967 election campaign can serve as an example of the faith most people had in economic growth. Optimistic belief in continued prosperity also marked the 1960s. It was only towards the end of the decade that critical voices warned about the unfortunate results of growth. But before these voices were raised, the country had experienced an unprecedented growth in prosperity.

During the years between 1960 and 1973, industry experienced a boom, taking advantage of an expanding international economy and succeeding in the tough competition brought about by free trade in EFTA. Foreign investments increased greatly, especially in energy-intensive industry. In the late 1960s, Norway had become Europe's foremost exporter of aluminium as well as the world's foremost exporter of ferro-alloys. Many companies which had traditionally produced for the domestic market proved capable of selling their products abroad. The engineering industry was particularly successfull.

The rapid growth of industry led to expansion in the retrail trade and in the transport and construction sectors. It came as no surprise, therefore, that the demand for manpower increased. Fortunately there was an available reserve. An increasing number of married women took paid employment in the 1960s. Many of them wanted to increase their family incomes in order to buy new material goods. It was also easier for women to start working because, on the average, they bore fewer children than before. Use of the new contraceptives, made it easier for women to decide if and when they would bring children into the world.

The symbol of the new prosperity was the private automobile. After October 1960 permits were no longer necessary in order to purchase cars. The next few years saw thousands of proud first-car-owners take to the roads. Their desire to drive did not fade even though the number of traffic accidents increased dramatically.

Norwegian television was officially started in 1960. During the 1960s about 900,000 Norwegians bought TV-sets. Because the Norwegian Broadcasting Company was the only channel available, these daily television programmes unified the population in a remarkable way. This characterized daily life right up to the 1980s, when cable TV and parabol antennas were introduced and made choice of different channels possible.

A family in Fredrikstad proudly showing off its new Ford Consul in 1960, the year restrictions on purchase of new cars were lifted.

DAILY LIFE IN THE 1960S

Sverre Eriksen from Hamarøy in Nordland county tells of his experiences of this decade:

"I was born in 1949 and grew up in a rural district. Our township had had about 3500 inhabitants at the end of the war, but in the early 60s over 1000 people, or about every third person, moved away. Some moved to larger towns in Nordland, especially to Mo i Rana, a newly built industrial town with an iron works and a coking plant. Others went to Oslo.

These people had made a living by combining work on their smallholdings with fishing, or by working on road construction. This became well-nigh impossible as time passed, so that many of the men moved to town to get jobs in industry. They came back for their families and the farms were deserted. The district I lived in was nearly depopulated. My dad owned a little auto company with a lorry and a school bus. So he was one of the few who didn't have to leave to find work.

My old buddies came back to visit and had become real townies with sharp clothes and haircuts. In order to hold their own with their new friends in town, some of the lads had started wearing their hair long, just like the foreign pop artists did. Old jerseys and boots were replaced by pointy shoes and brown suede jackets. The girls wore cardigans and skirts with two pleats in the front and two in back.

With time the tourist trade began to expand and that meant something more to do. During the summer we sat longside the dusty high-

way and wrote down registration numbers of passing cars. The grandest of all was to write the number of a foreign car that happened by. We met a little of the excitement of foreign countries when camping tourists came along with their tiny tents, and they were happy enough to meet young people who could speak some English or German. By this time some of the neighbors, those who were still left, began learning to drive and bought little cars - NSU-Prinz, DKW-Junior, Wartburg, IFA, FIAT 600 and whatever they were called.

I began at secondary school and went on to the two-year municipal junior form held in an old German barracks in town. We had a lot of lessons and went to school six days a week. During the winter we got home to our folks at weekends only. Like as not I strapped long-distance skateblades on my winter boots and spent the day on the frozen pond just near where I lived. Speed skating was the grandest sport, we all thought so, and as kids we cut out sports photos from the newspapers and magazines and pasted them in rough books. If we ever did get to see the newsreels it was the sporting events we were most taken with.

At age sixteen I had to leave my home district to begin at sixth form in grammar school in Narvik. We spent all our spare time on the Beatles, the Rolling Stones, the revolution and Mao. I daresay I became one of those 'sixty-eighters'."

The Non-Socialists take the Helm

After the 1965 general election, and for the first time since the war, the four non-socialist parties, were able to form a majority government. This was not the result of steadfast efforts in opposition, as the four parties had not managed to agree on a vote of no confidence in the Labour Party until 1963. Prior to that they had not even been able to present a clearly alternative government to the voters. This was mainly because the Labour Party's pursuit of a moderate centre policy had made it unnecessary for the non-socialists to join forces.

As long as this situation prevailed, the non-socialists were forced to emphasize the differences between them and to preserve the old lines of demarcation. The Christian Democrats were especially concerned with demonstrating their distinctive features. The party had achieved its breakthrough as a new nationwide, non-socialist alternative in 1945. It wished to be regarded as a guardian of Christian morals – bringing a message straight from God – raised above class struggle and petty political bickering. The Liberal and Centre Parties were both uneasy over the voters they lost to the Christian Democrats.

The Centre Party defended the interests of rural districts and of agriculture, often coming into conflict with the Conservatives, who represented urban culture and had close relations with industrial and shipping interests. The Liberals were split into a social liberal and a liberalistic wing. The social liberals took over during the 1950s. They approved of Labour's economic policies but were sceptical to Christian Democratic views on cultural matters. In the early 1960s, the question of Norway's possible participation in the EEC also led to difficulties concerning cooperation between the non-socialists. The Conservatives advocated full membership, the Centre Party was against while both Liberals and Christian Democrats were divided. It was only after the French president, de Gaulle, had vetoed expanding the Common Market in 1963 that the parties became capable of joining forces against Labour.

In the 1961 general elections the Labour Party and the non-socialists had won an equal number of seats in the Storting, while the new radical leftist party, the Socialist People's Party (SF), had won two. The Labour Party government would have to resign if and when the SF and the non-socialists agreed on a vote of no confidence. This was the case in 1963, when Labour Party industrial policies opened for a non-socialist government. Firstly, the Labour Party was attacked for having granted several million *kroner* to a state-owned company without seeking the consent of the Storting. Secondly, there was dissatisfaction with the inadequate information given by the government to the national assembly concerning a mining accident at King's Bay on Svalbard. In the opinion of the opposition, the Gerhardsen government had become too arrogant.

Even though the government led by John Lyng of the Conservatives was forced by Labour and the SF to resign after only three weeks in office, the fact of its very existence had a deep psychological effect. The forming of a government drew the non-socialists closer together, contributing to their agreement on a common political platform. In the 1965 general election they won a majority in the Storting, and Per Borten of the Centre Party formed a non-socialist government.

The Borten government followed the same course that the Labour Party had set. State welfare and other areas of public activity continued to expand. This was expensive, and taxes rose. The non-socialist government introduced compulsory nine-year schooling, a value-added tax and a national insurance scheme.

In 1963, John Lyng, parliamentary leader for the Conservative Party, formed the first non-socialist government since the war. Here he is shown on his way to the speaker's platform in the Storting during the debate over Kings Bay in 1963. This debate was the first to be transmitted over television.

This, the country's greatest social reform, took effect in 1967. The Law on National Insurance provided for a coordination of most of the old insurance regulations. It ensured that all citizens would receive pensions in case of old-age, sickness, injury or unemployment. Aid would also be given to pregnant women and to those who had lost their guardians or parents. Divorced, separated and single parents were also covered by the law.

Both employees and employers were required to participate in financing the national insurance scheme. When these payments proved insufficient, national budget allocations to the insurance scheme rose sharply. During the '60s and '70s the health services were given priority. The Hospital Act of 1969 made over responsibility for building and managing of hospitals to the counties, although most funding came from the state. Many elderly people were cared for in public nursing homes built by municipalities who also employed nurses and home care workers.

John Lyng of the Conservatives was foreign minister in the new government. He continued his predecessor, Halvard Lange's loyal support of NATO, but several of his initiatives created dissatisfaction in his own party. He worked for political détente between east and west, taking several journeys to eastern Europe. Lyng opposed America's bombing of North Vietnam, and advocated NATO intervention against the military leadership of Greece in 1967. When the USA refused to consider this option, Norway joined the countries raising charges against the Greek government in the Human Rights Commission of the European Council.

Centralization

Although Norway did not experience the same extent of urban growth as on the Continent, an unprecedented mass movement occurred in the population after 1945. At the end of the war, approximately half the population had lived in towns and communities with over 200 inhabitants. 25 years later, this figure had increased to nearly two-thirds. This did not result in whole districts becoming depopulated, as was the case in Finland and Sweden. Women still

living in the areas from which people had moved bore more children than elsewhere in the country, while those who moved settled in larger towns in the same district.

Those who moved further chose on the whole to settle in south-eastern Norway. Most of these people came from the north and the west coast. Most were under thirty and the majority were women. While many small communities in mountainous or forested areas were hard-hit by this migration,

Nyksund in Nordland county was one of the many fishing towns along the coast that suffered depopulation during the 1960's and '70s.

A farm being vacated in Tafjord, Møre and Romsdal county, in autumn 1957.

The tractor is a good symbol for the extensive agricultural modernization after the war. By 1965 there were more tractors than horses on Norwegian farms.

the most serious effects were felt in the small towns along the coast northwards from Trøndelag. All were typified by lack of industry and poor communications.

This "mass removal" was the result of profound changes in agriculture, forestry and fishing. Starting in the 1950s, mechanization in agriculture accelerated. Most farms had water and electricity installed, making for radical change in farm women's daily routines. Wood-burning stoves were thrown out, new household appliances appeared in the kitchen, the back-breaking carrying of water pails ceased, and milking machines took over in the cowshed. Farmhands had to find new jobs while the need for help from farm women and children virtually disappeared. Many farmers took paid jobs in addition to running a farm.

Farmers were able to persuade a majority of the Storting to pass laws protecting agriculture from foreign competition. Politicians also voted large sums in agricultural subsidies, in an effort to reduce depopulation and to prevent the country from becoming too dependent on imported food supplies. Norway had the lowest domestic production

of agricultural products of any country in western Europe, and most people felt that the modest amount of land under cultivation (about three per cent) should be maintained. The best farms had to be kept intact in case of war or crisis. In the early 1970s, government subsidies to agriculture were higher than the average of the OECD countries. Switzerland and Japan were the only countries place higher than Norway on the lists of statistics.

Even though close to half of all Norwegian farms were abandoned between 1945 and 1975, this did not lead to an appreciable reduction in the area under cultivation. The more successful farms took over land from those that were abandoned and clearing of new land continued. However, much of the country's best farm land was lost when cities and communities expanded their boundaries. The majority of the remaining farms converted to specialized production based on grains or animal husbandry.

New technology also appeared in forestry. The back-braking toil using axes, handsaws and barking spades ended when woodsmen

began using chain saws and barking machines. This mechanization process led to thousands of forestry workers losing their jobs.

During the 1930s, fishermen had pushed forward legislation banning the building of new trawlers. They feared that modern boats would destroy their livelihood, and that at a time when unemployment was high. The situation changed after the war. Politicians now meant that fishing would have to become more efficient and that catches ought to be delivered to filleting factories, freezing plants, fish-meal factories and fish-oil plants. Such products could be sold abroad and increase the country's export earnings. Fish processing companies required – and got – deliveries from the new trawlers which supplied raw materials year-round by taking catches far out to sea.

The demand for fish products increased markedly as grocery shops installed freezers and families bought home units. Frozen fish became the most valuable Norwegian export product of the '50s. Frozen food companies marketed their products through the sales organization *Frionor*, which built

up a network of freezing sales units throughout western Europe. Foreign interests entered the fishing industry in earnest in 1962, when the Swiss company Nestlé bought *Findus*, the country's largest freezing plant owner.

Work in fisheries became less dangerous and more manageable in the first post-war decades. A new hoisting device – the power block – lifted modern ring nets on board the boats. Echo-sounders and sonars made finding fish easier. Weather forecasts became more reliable. New equipment in lightweight nylons and plastics saved the fisherman from much heavy lifting.

Modernization in the fishing industry led to a steady decline in the number of fishermen. The first to go were those who combined farming with fishing, many of whom also chose to leave their smallholdings.

This new techology led to an unprecedented increase in catches. But were the sea's resources inexhaustible? By the 1960s signs began showing that they were not. Many species of fish, such as winter herring, tuna, and mackerel were threatened by excessive fishing. Norwegian fishermen had to resort to inferior types of fish such as

Log-floating in the Mistra River in 1949. The Trysil River was the last where logs were floated. This stopped in 1991.

capelin. Many also began fishing off Iceland and Greenland and in the Barents Sea.

The development of communications partly determined where people were to live and work. Although the railway's northern line was extended to Bodø and electric locomotives replaced the old steam engines, it was highways that were given highest priority. Main roads were asphalted to withstand the heavy lorries that captured much transport of goods from railways and ships. The number of lorries rose from 21,000 in 1950 to 70,000 in 1975.

Construction of new air fields began for earnest in the 1960s. SAS had to compete for passengers on domestic routes with other airlines. The two most important were Braathens SAFE and Widerøe. By the mid-'70s, the airlines were carrying a total of almost four million passengers per year.

Many small communities hard-hit by people moving away lost out when communications were improved. Those living in such places often experienced that ferry and bus routes were discontinued, or that the railway station and the post office were closed down. Automation of the telephone network led to many women switchboard operators losing their jobs.

When the war ended there were 744 municipalities in Norway. Twenty years later the number had been reduced by three hundred, as many towns had been joined together in larger municipalities. The new road system had made many of the old boundaries irrelevant. Many of the smallest towns had lacked the financial resources to carry out all the tasks imposed on them by the central government. These included building schools, welfare offices and planning authorities. New laws required that municipalities plan housing, industrial parks, waterworks and sewage systems.

This joining together of municipalities led to intense discussion in many local communities. Agreeing as to where the new administrative centre would be located was especially difficult. It was these centres that got most of the new jobs and the best services.

The Education Explosion and the Young People's Revolt

Starting in 1960, any municipality that wished to do so was allowed to introduce nine-year compulsory education. The old junior forms and secondary schools were replaced by modern comprehensive schools. Nine-year compulsory schooling for all was passed by the Storting in 1969.

The development of the compulsory nine-year school made higher education available to more young people than ever before. The numbers of sixth form vocational school pupils grew rapidly, while universities and colleges were swamped with students. New universities opened in Trondheim and Tromsø in 1968 and the first regional colleges in the following year.

As was the case with young people in other western countries, many Norwegian teenagers developed highly critical opinions of the affluent adult, society of the 1960s. The Anglo-American pop industry, which gained a solid foothold, provided youngsters with new fashions and new ideals. The social atmosphere became freer and respect for all types of authority fell. Television gave these teenagers a broader view of the world. They were the first generation to observe war and starvation in the safety of their own homes. This media shock created frustration and rootlessness among the young. Some also reacted against the materialism and status seeking of their parents' generation.

Misuse of hashish and marijuana began in student circles in the mid-1960s. Such drugs gained rapid popularity among the Norwegian hippies who had their headquarters in the park around the Royal Palace in Oslo. Drug abuse spread from here to municipalities in other parts of the country.

As the universities filled to overflowing, the authorities proposed that old open curriculum should be replaced by a stricter system with fixed courses and more examinations. Such proposals were based on a desire to shorten the length of studies and to adapt them to the needs of business and industry. The students went on strike and held demonstrations in support of freer, more socially critical studies. Inspired by the spirit of revolt at American and European universities, the students went to the attack authoritarian unversity administration. These

A rock concert at Holmenkollen in the early 1970s.

Below:
Two representatives from the Norwegian Marxist-Leninists , Tron Øgrim and Pål Steigan were presented for Chairman Mao Tse Tung in 1970.

protests brought results. Student representatives joined the governing bodies of the universities.

American offensives in Vietnam raised sympathy for the cause of the developing countries. Many young people saw the war as indicative of wealthy countries' responsibility for the suffering and repression of the third world.

The most uncompromizing among the socialist students, the Marixt-Leninists, concluded that the capitalistic system in Norway ought to be overthrown by armed revolution. They regarded Mao's China as their great ideal. After some of them had discontinued their studies and "proletarianized" themselves, they gained influence in some local trade unions. They led "wildcat" strikes, focussing attention on workplaces with low wages and poor working conditions.

The Green Movement

During the 1960s, the drawbacks of rapid economic growth became apparent. Overtaxing of resources had led to a suspension of Norwegian whaling in the Antarctic. Herring disappeared from the North Sea and mackerel catches were greatly reduced. Emissions from industry, agriculture and sewage threatened life in lakes, rivers and fjords. Air pollution increased dramatically. Acid rain from Great Britain and the Continent ruined thousands of fishing lakes in southern Norway, while poisonous pesticides disturbed natural cycles. Refuse tips exanded, as did the demand for electricity. This resulted in increasing numbers of waterfalls, rivers and lakes being harnassed to provide electrical power. Europe's last remaining wilderness areas were in danger.

Pollution and exploitation of natural resources increased the importance of environmental protection. The Norwegian Society for the Conservation of Nature

Skiers in the Rondane National Park, Oppland county.

Emissions of pollutants were common in the 1970s. The photograph shows the Smelting Plant in Eydehavn. During the '80s, the company invested huge amounts to reduce pollution, as did other sectors in Norwegian industry.

headed the voluntary effort, demanding that the authorities take action.

In 1962 the Storting passed a resolution creating the country's first national park in the mountain area of Rondane. In following years new areas were permanently listed as protected against exploitation. The real breakthrough for environmental protection occurred during the 1970 European Natural Conservation Year, with the passing of a new nature conservancy act and a new water pollution act. In this same year a group of environmentalists used civil disobedience for the first time. They tried to stop construction of a project to harnass the waters of the Mardalsfossen, northern Europe's highest waterfall. The police removed the demonstrators, but for the first time publicity was focused on the question of developing hydroelectric power and several waterfalls were later protected against development.

In 1972 the new Ministry of the Environment was given chief responsibility for the government's environmental and natural resources policy. Experts at the ministry prepared a mass of laws and regulations which helped to improve the environment in a number of respects. National measures alone were not enough. In the '70s and '80s, Norway increased her efforts to achieve international agreements on the environment.

The EC-struggle

In 1970 the Borten government began negotiations on Norwegian participation in the EC. However, the coalition broke up the following year because of disagreement between the non-socialist parties on the

European question. A minority government led by Trygve Bratteli of the Labour Party then negotiated a full membership agreement. The agreement was rejected in a referendum in 1972, and was thereafter replaced by a free-trade agreement for industrial products, which was entered into in 1973.

Opponents of the EC had a strong dislike of giving up Norwegian sovereignity to the supranational bodies in Brussels. They were also against EC plans for an economic and political union in Europe, disliking the fact that elected bodies had too little say in the EC. Many people opposed the EC philosphy of growth, an opposition that included much of the criticism raised against Norwegian post-war society by the Liberals, environmentalists and student dissenters. The principles establishing the free flow of goods, services, capital and labour seemed frightening. There was wide-spread fear that Eurpean capital, particularly German, would dominate Norwegian industry. This would lead to further depopulation of rural districts and to increased exploitation of Norway's natural resources and environment. The fears of this development were strengthened when the EC refused to give Norwegian farmers and fishermen special protective measures.

Opponents organized themselves in an effective peoples' movement which took the advantage in the struggle to win opinions. The most important groups were composed of farmers, fishermen, radical socialists and trade union members. They were also supported by groups of Christian laymen, abstainers and supporters of New Norwegian.

The country's leaders supported EC membership. They emphasized that the EC would strengthen peace, create greater economic growth and ensure Norway of greater influence on the development of Europe. Supporters also stessed the importance of following Great Britain's and Denmark's examples. These arguments by a majority of the members of Storting, led by the Conservatives, the government and the Labour Party leaders did not win through, even though they had the support of most of the important captialists, the leaders of

the Trade Union Federation and most of the daily newspapers. Nor was there help in Prime Minister Bratteli's threats to resign if the voters did not follow the government's recommendations. A majority of 53 per cent voted "no".

The struggle over the EC disturbed party politics. On the left, the Labour Party lost support, the leftist socialists gained and the Marxist-Leninists founded a new party, the AKP (m-l). On the non-socialist side, a new liberalistic party came into being, later adopting the name *Fremskrittspartiet* (Progress Party). Norway's oldest political party, the Liberals, split up and lost increasing numbers of voters.

The popular movement against membership in the Common Market attached great importance to mobilizing the coastal population during the discussion over Norwegian membership in the 1970s.
The supporters of membership concentrated their efforts in urban areas.

Norway in the Age of Petroleum

The Miracle of Oil

The search for oil in the Norwegian sector of the North Sea started in 1966. A great many companies flung themselves into prospecting for "black gold", but gave up one by one. By the autumn of 1969, Phillips Petroleum Company was the sole survivor. In the company's very last exploratory well, the drill column on the Ocean Viking platform hit oil. In 1970 expert opinion ascertained that not only was the find commercially profitable, but that it was among the world's ten largest.

As early as in the 1960s, the Storting had passed legislation ensuring strict state control as well as high income from the petroleum industry. A special petroleum directorate, later subordinated to the Ministry of Petroleum and Energy, was given responsibility for implementing the new regulations. To prevent Norway's becoming a mere exporter of oil and gas, the authorities backed the establishment of a national petroleum industry, to participate in exploration, production and processing of petroleum resources in cooperation with foreign companies. The enormous investments and high risks involved made sharing of responsibility desirable. Norwegian politicians gave the state oil company, Statoil, a preferential position with considerable shares in future discoveries, while Norsk Hydro, in which the state was majority share-holder, and privately-owned Saga Petroleum were also invited to participate.

Offshore petroleum production proved risky. An uncontrolled blowout on the Ekofisk field in 1977 resulted in spillage that endangered the Norwegian coast. American experts managed luckily enough to stop the leakage after only eight days, thus preventing an environmental catastrophe. An accident like this forced the authorities to tighten oil pollution preparedness, but did not lead to a lessening of tempo in exploration and/or production.

The value of crude oil and gas production rose rapidly and in 1984 reached a national economic high of 18.5% of the GNP. In 1990 Norway surpassed Great Britain as Europe's largest petroleum producer, and by the mid-1990s, Norway was second only to Saudi Arabia in oil exports.

Petroleum production set industry and research enormous tasks. Norwegian engineers developed advanced methods for seismic oil exploration, systems for horizontal oil drilling, and also constructed wholly-automatic robot installations for oil and gas production on the ocean floor. The most spectacular monuments to this new technology were the gigantic platforms. In the spring of 1995 the world's largest production platform was towed out to the Troll field, at that time Europe's largest offshore gas field.

Considered in proportion to investments, oil production did not create many new jobs. This new industry required highly qualified workers who were familiar with modern technology. In the early 1990s about 20,000 people, or about 1 per cent of the total work force, were employed in the petroleum industry. Many were based in Stavanger, which had become the country's petroleum capital.

Statoil's turnover during the 1980's lay between 80 and 90 billion *kroner*, or 10 to 12 per cent of the GNP. The company was the money-making machine in Norwegian economy. Given operating responsibility for large oil fields, such as Statfjord and Gullfaks, they also established subsidiary companies in other countries. Statoil bought up petrol station concerns in neighboring countries, acquired two refineries and became part-owner of several pipeline projects in the North Sea.

Opposite page:
Oil-platform at Ekofisk
field.

Norway as an Oil Nation

In 1969 the Phillips Petroleum Company discovered oil on the Ekofisk field. The Storting decided that the state should play a key role in this new industry and Statoil was founded. The state company received large shares in new discoveries and became involved in the exploration, production and refining of oil and gas. Foreign companies and the Norwegian companies Norsk Hydro and Saga Petroleum also took part in the oil boom.

Oil activities also benefited Norwegian business and industry onshore. The petrochemical industry was established and the production of platforms and equipment brought increased employment. Oil production had its dangers, however. In 1980 the Alexander Kielland platform capsized and 123 people died. However this accident did not prevent exploration off the North Norwegian coast. The first promising gas discoveries were made on Tromsøflaket in 1981.

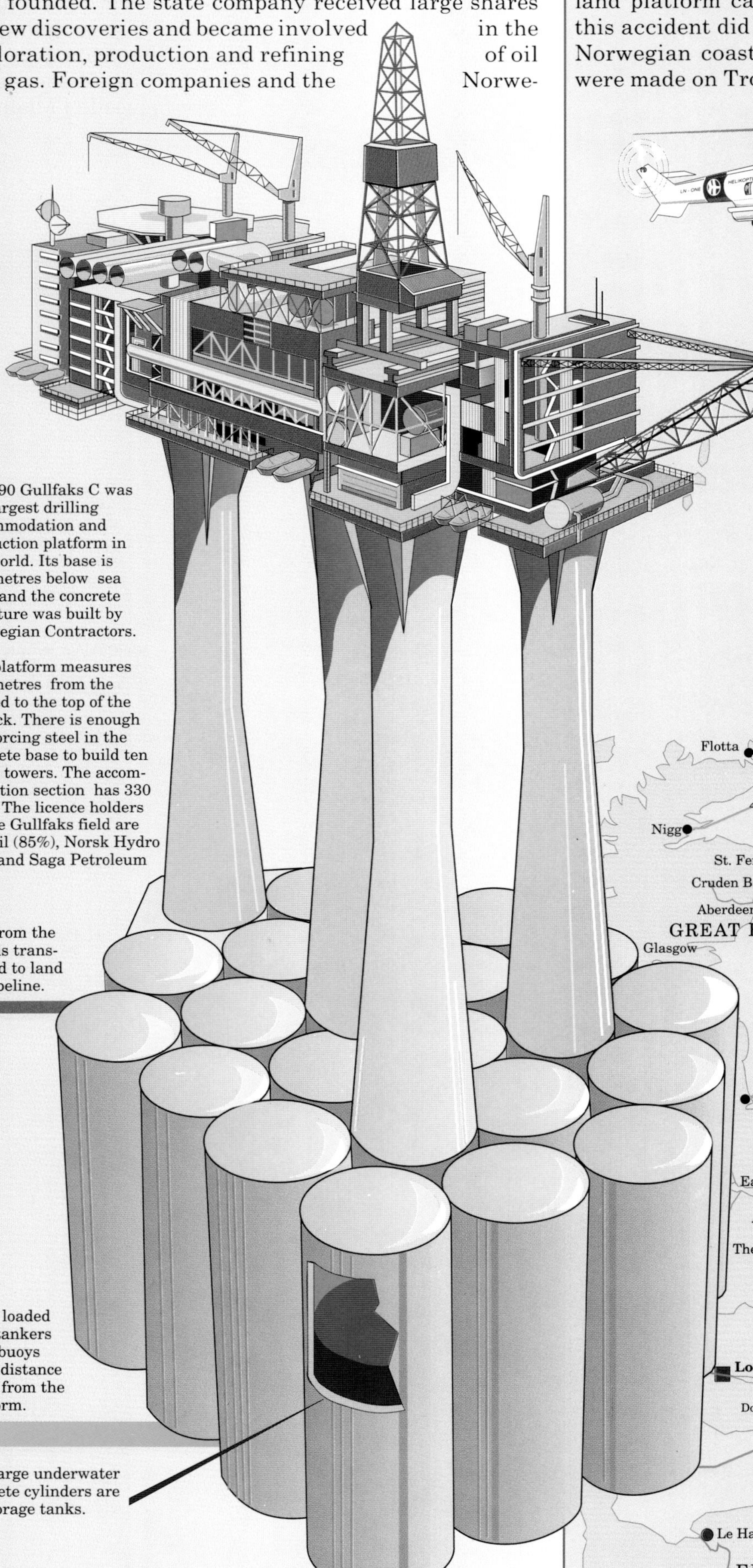

HELIKOPTER SERVICE
LN-ONE

In 1990 Gullfaks C was the largest drilling accommodation and production platform in the world. Its base is 217 metres below sea level and the concrete structure was built by Norwegian Contractors.

The platform measures 380 metres from the seabed to the top of the derrick. There is enough reinforcing steel in the concrete base to build ten Eiffel towers. The accommodation section has 330 beds. The licence holders on the Gullfaks field are Statoil (85%), Norsk Hydro (9%) and Saga Petroleum (6%).

Gas from the field is transported to land by pipeline.

Oil is loaded onto tankers from buoys some distance away from the platform.

The large underwater concrete cylinders are oil storage tanks.

In 1993 about 79,000 people were employed in the petroleum industry itself. Some 12,000 of them were women, and about 3800 were foreign citizens.

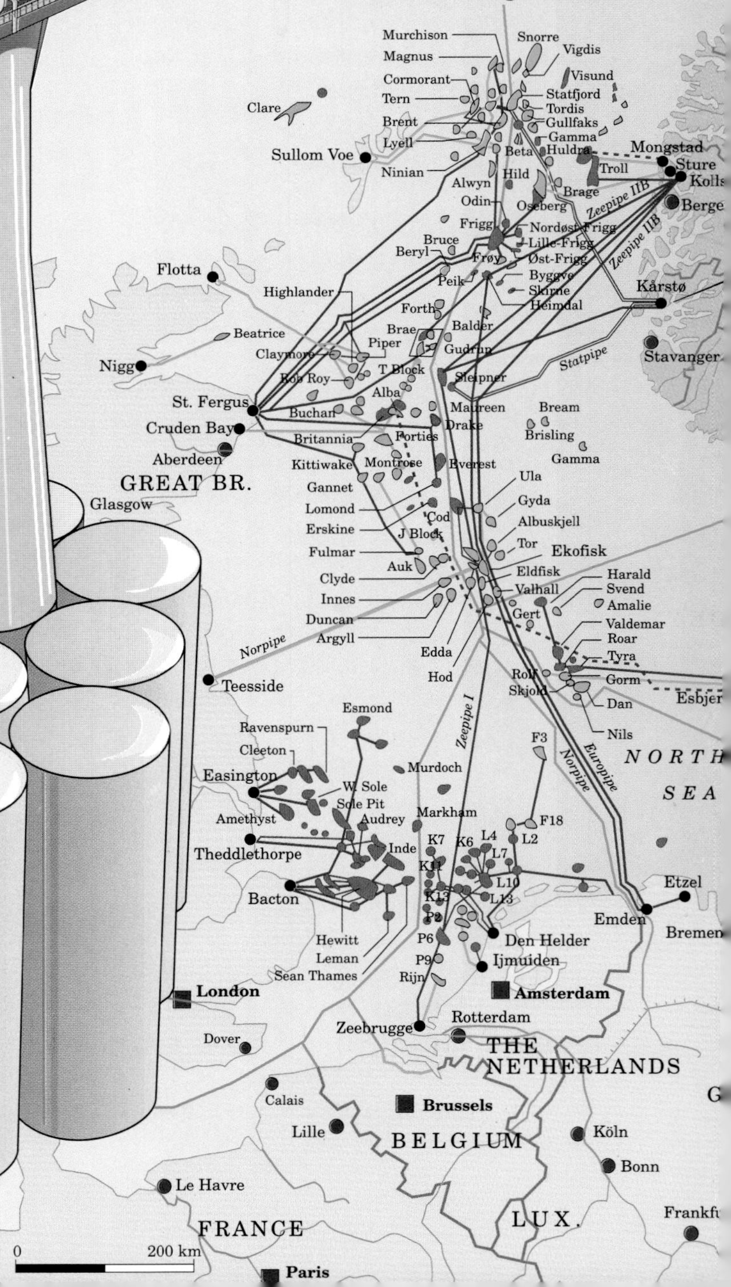

Murchison
Magnus
Cormorant
Tern
Brent
Lyell
Ninian
Snorre
Vigdis
Visund
Statfjord
Tordis
Gullfaks
Gamma
Beta
Huldra
Hild
Mongstad
Sture
Troll
Brage
Oseberg
Alwyn
Odin
Frigg
Zeepipe IIB
Nordøst Frigg
Lille-Frigg
Øst-Frigg
Bruce
Beryl
Frøy
Peik
Byggve
Skirne
Heimdal
Kårstø
Stavanger
Clare
Sullom Voe
Flotta
Highlander
Forth
Brae
Balder
Piper
Beatrice
Claymore
Gudrun
T Block
Nigg
Rob Roy
Alba
Sleipner
Statpipe
St. Fergus
Buchan
Maureen
Bream
Cruden Bay
Drake
Brisling
Britannia
Forties
Aberdeen
Kittiwake
Montrose
Everest
Gamma
GREAT BR.
Ula
Gannet
Glasgow
Lomond
Gyda
Erskine
Cod
Albuskjell
J Block
Fulmar
Tor
Ekofisk
Auk
Eldfisk
Harald
Clyde
Valhall
Svend
Innes
Amalie
Gert
Duncan
Valdemar
Argyll
Roar
Norpipe
Tyra
Edda
Hod
Rolf
Skjold
Gorm
Dan
Esbjerg
Teesside
Esmond
Nils
Ravenspurn
F3
Cleeton
Zeepipe I
NORTH SEA
Murdoch
Easington
W. Sole
Sole Pit
Europipe
Amethyst
Audrey
Markham
F18
K7
K6
L4
L2
Inde
L7
Theddlethorpe
K11
L10
K13
L13
Bacton
Etzel
Emden
P8
Bremen
Hewitt
Leman
P6
Den Helder
Sean Thames
P9
Ijmuiden
Rijn
London
Amsterdam
Zeebrugge
Rotterdam
Dover
THE NETHERLANDS
Calais
Brussels
Lille
BELGIUM
Köln
Bonn
Le Havre
FRANCE
LUX.
Frankfu
Paris
0
200 km

In the 1970s and 1980s several oil and gas pipelines to Great Britain, West Germany and the Norwegian coast were built. The Snøhvit field is the largest gas discovery on Tromsøflaket to date. The oil companies have not yet found it profitable to start production.

Tromsøflaket **Finnmark vest**

Snøhvit
Askeladden   Albatross
Alka   Alke
Hammerfest

Tromsø

NORWEGIAN SEA

Narvik
Kiruna

Bodø

Mo i Rana

Luleå

Norne
Haltenbanken
Heidrun
Midgard
Tyrihans Nord
Mikkel
Draugen

Tjeldbergodden
Kristiansund   Trondheim

NORWAY

Oslo
Drammen

Stockholm

BALTIC SEA

SWEDEN

Gothenburg

Ålborg

DENMARK
Århus

Copenhagen   Malmö

Kiel

Sassnitz

Hamburg

Berlin

Leipzig

POLAND
Lodz

Dresden   Wroclaw

CHECH REP.
Praha

Krakov

The petroleum sector's share of gross national product (as a percentage of GNP)

%
1976 -78 -80 -82 -84 -86 -88 -90 -92 -93

State petroleum-derived revenues from taxes and excises

Bill. 1994-*kroner*   Percentage of total state revenues %

- Tax and excise revenues
- Percentage of total revenues

1978 -80 -82 -84 -86 -88 -90 -92 1994

Natural gas exports in 1993
Total 24.7 bill Sm³

France 23,1%
The Netherlands 11,0%
Belgium 10,3%
Spain 0,8%
Great Britain 18,2%
Germany 36,6%

Crude oil sales 1993
Total 110.5 mill. *Toe*

Germany 11,1%
Norway 20,0%
The Netherlands 14,4%
Great Britain 23,8%
France 7,4%
Denmark 2,8%
USA 5,6%
Other 8,7%
Sweden 6,2%

The installations at Kårstø, just outside Haugesund, process condensate gas from the Statfjord and Gullfaks fields. Liquid gas is transported by ship, while dry gas goes by pipeline to Emden in Germany.

The first Norwegian-built drilling platform, Ocean Viking, was completed in 1967.

Production forecasts according to field

200 Millions of tons
180
160 Heidrun
140 Troll / Sleipner
120
100 Other fields
80 Gullfaks incl. Tordis   Frigg area
60 Ekofisk area   Snorre
40 Oseberg
20
Statfjord incl. Satellites
1994 1995 1996 1997 1998 1999 2000 2001 2002 2003 2004

STATOIL   HYDRO   saga

Naval Challenges

As a result of international conferences on the law of the sea in the 1970s, Norway was assured of a continental shelf of some 1.5 million km^2 and an economic zone of about 2 million km^2. No other European nation, with the exception of the then Soviet Union, controlled as large an area of the ocean. This extension of offshore territory led to a conflict with the Kremlin concerning boundaries in the Barents Sea. Pending a permanent settlement, a temporary agreement was signed concerning distribution of fishery resources in the disputed areas off the coast of Finnmark.

The question of the utilization of offshore areas around Svalbard were not clarified. Norway claimed that the provisions of the Svalbard Treaty on equal rights for all signatory nations as to exploitation of natural resources, did not apply beyond four nautical miles from the coast. Within the remainder of the 200-mile zone around the islands, Norway claimed the same control as on the continental shelf and in the economic offshore zone. Until 1995 only Finland and Canada had given support to the Norwegian claims.

Norway established a fishery protection zone around Svalbard in 1977. Countries that had fished in these waters earlier were given quotas and were required to report catches. Most countries respected these Norwegian regulations, but the Soviet Union refused to send reports. In 1994 Icelandic trawlers began fishing operations in the Svalbard zone. Several of these vessels were seized by the Coast Guard and later fined in Norwegian courts.

The petroleum finds and the country's new sovereignity over large offshore areas increased Norway's economic and strategic importance. The Soviet military presence on the Kola Peninsula had the same effect, as did the increased striking power of the Soviet Northern Fleet in the 1970s. NATO's ability to come to Norway's assistance in case of war or crisis again came under discussion. This resulted in an agreement between Norway and the United States for advanced defence warehousing of heavier weapons for an airborne Marine brigade in Trøndelag. Norway also signed agreements establishing support bases for American air force and naval forces.

Above:
Soviet troops during winter manoeuvres on the Kola peninsula.

Right:
American troops landing in northern Norway during a NATO exercise in the 1980s.

New Reforms

After the 1973 and 1977 general elections the Socialist Left again were on the balance in the Storting between the non-socialist block and the Labour Party. As the largest single party, Labour formed three successive minority governments, seeking support from different parties.

In governing position, the Labour Party was obliged to show consideration for the intense public discussions that had raged during the EC-controversy concerning the basic values of Norway's post-war society. These had reflected much of the social criticism of the young people's revolt and the green movement. After the national referendum, demands for democratization, decentralization and environmental protection were raised. Oil revenues gave politicians excellent means for effecting reforms.

In 1972 the Storting had passed an act on industrial democracy which ensured employees of large companies representation on the board. They were also represented in the new corporate assemblies which determined policies for the companies' development. Five years later, the old Workers' Protection Act was replaced by the Storting with a new Working Environment Act. This act gave workers better protection against dismissal, and tightened rules governing overtime, and the physical and mental aspects of the working environment. In 1978 an agreement was reached ensuring employees full wage compensation in case of sickness.

The winds of reform also touched the school system, as changes were made in education for young people between 17 and 19. A new comprehensive secondary school replaced the old *gymnasium*, vocational schools and business schools. After passage of the Secondary Education Act in 1974, comprehensive schools grew up all over the country and pupils were allowed to choose between academic courses and practical, vocational subjects.

The EC-controversy brought a greater understanding of the problems facing agriculture and rural areas. The Storting passed a staged plan for farmers which ensured them higher incomes and proper holiday arrangements. The national assembly also arranged for the transfer of partial authority

from the central administration in the Oslo to counties and municipalities.

Increasing numbers of women sought higher academic education during the 1960s. By the end of the decade nearly a third of the university students were women. Women academics were also influenced by the general atmosphere of social criticism. This led to the founding of the first feminist groups based on the American Women's Lib movement.

The new feminist movement attacked the traditional pattern of sex roles which forced women to be passive and submissive. The rebellious women established small groups all over the country in order to expose how women were oppressed in a male-dominated society. One result of this criticism was that many women divorced their husbands.

The feminist movement also increased its efforts for equality between the sexes. Political parties were obliged to ensure women of

Top: The peculiarily Norwegian *russ*-celebrations for pupils finishing twelve years of school, have roots reaching back to the last century. The tradition lived on despite the replacing of the old gymnas by the upper secondary school in the 1970s.

Above: A procession marking the annual International Women's Day on 8 March 1977.

more positions of responsibility and higher rankings on the lists of candidates. The number of women in representative bodies increased substantially. A climax was reached in 1981, when Gro Harlem Brundtland became the countrys' first woman Prime Minister.

The Allodial Act on land tenure was amended in 1974, giving female and male heirs to family farms equal rights of inheritance. The Equal Status Act four years later also improved women's positions, in that it forbade sex discrimination and made equal pay for equal work mandatory. Employers were no longer allowed to differentiate between men and women concerning employment, promotion or dismissal. An ombudsman for equal status was given the task of ensuring that these regulations were respected.

The most important question for the new feminist movement in the 1970s was the demand for women's right of decision on abortion. The Abortion Act of 1960 had led to great dissatisfaction because hospital physicians who dealt with applications for abortion did not follow an accepted code of practice, while illegal abortions put women's lives in danger. This led to renewed and vigourous demands for women's right to determine abortion. The Christian community rose up to fight for "unborn lives", collecting some 600,000 signatures in support of their appeal. They were unsuccessful. The Law on Termination of Pregnancy was passed in 1978 with the support of the Labour Party and the Socialist Left.

Laid-up tankers near Karmøy, Rogaland county, during the shipping crisis of 1975.

Anti-inflationary Policies

The international ecnomic recession caused by the oil crisis in 1973, led to drops in production and unemployment in many parts of the world. Norway proved an exception because the government used anticipated oil revenues to keep the wheels moving. Large foreign loans also helped business and industry weather the crisis.

The government also reduced taxes and used large sums on new reforms. Between 1974 and 1977, real incomes increased and unemployment was kept under control. During this period Norway had a higher rate of growth than most other OECD countries. This proved a mixed blessing.

By 1977 the foreign debt had reached NOK 100 billion - over half the GNP. At the same time Norwegian goods lost out on world markets. The increase in wages and affluence had gone too far and strong measures had to be introduced to cut costs. The government reduced aid to industry and shipping, froze wages and prices, and devaluated the *krone*. Other vital problems awaited solution. Norway had become increasingly dependent on oil revenues and with unstable oil prices, calculating state incomes had become more difficult.

The crisis in the '70s was a hard blow to shipping. As the price of oil rose, the demand for tanker tonnage sank. Most Norwegian shipowners had new, expensive ships without long-term freight contracts. Before long, half the tanker fleet had been laid up. These problems spread to the shipbuilding industry. By the late 1970s, many shipyards had had to close down or adapt to new activities. Those that started producing equipment for the new petroleum industry managed best. In the same way, shipowners who invested in specialized ships, cruise ships, oil platforms and supply ships had the least problems.

Several shipping companies were soon on the brink of bankruptcy. State intervention to the tune of billions of *kroner* started to prevent foreign shipowners from buying portions of the fleet at bargain prices. This support proved insufficient, however, and the state lost huge sums. The crisis in shipping was long-lasting. Many shipowners could not pay back the huge state loans and many of them failed.

A stir was created when it became known that the shipping company that had received most state support, the Hilmar Reksten company, had concealed a huge fortune abroad. The government engaged a staff of expert lawyers who hunted this concealed fortune. By 1993 several hundreds of millions of *kroner* had been found, the whole of which was returned to the treasury.

A shipping crisis as serious as that of the 1970s would have been a catastrophe for the Norwegian economy in earlier times. Norway was fortunate in that large oil revenues could replace the loss of foreign exchange from shipping.

Immigration

The rapid economic growth in the '60s lead to a manpower shortage, and for the first time in many years Norway experienced an immigration surplus. Most of these immigrants, many of whom were experts in the petroleum industry, came from western Europe and the United States. In the 1970s the infusion of people from south-eastern Europe, Asia and Africa increased. This coincided with the closing of boundaries in many western European countries.

The growing influx of unskilled labour from poor countries led the authorities to pass stricter immigration laws in 1975. Nevertheless, the number of foreigners continued to rise in the following years. The petroleum industry still had need of skilled labour and many immigrants used their right to bring their families to Norway. In the years before and after 1980, the country accepted several thousand Vietnamese refugees, most of them rescued from boats by Norwegian merchants ships.

Third world immigrants had difficulty finding work and were more often affected by unemployment than Norwegians. Even though many were well-educated, they usually had to take low-status jobs in industry and service. Their housing was often of poor quality.

Immigration became a test of Norwegian tolerance. People with little education and few contacts with immigrant workers were particularly sceptical. The most militant went so far as to attack immigrants' shops and spread racist propaganda. Such groups

never received popular support, however. Towards the end of the 1980s, there was an increase in the number of asylum seekers from developing countries devastated by war and terror. Processing applications was time-consuming, so that the authorities set up temporary shelters all over the country. This new wave of immigration created more fear of foreigners in the population, particularly in groups that previously had been most in favour of immigration, such as young people and students. This development was an effect of rising unemployment and of social problems.

Although Norway has granted more money to international refugee aid than most other European countries, relatively few refugees and seekers of asylum have been accepted here. By 1993 the total of such immigrants had reached 37,000. At the end of that year about 162,000 foreign citizens lived in Norway. Just over half were European, about 28 per cent had an Asiatic background, while North Americans and Africans amounted to about 7 per cent each.

Asylum-seekers at Østerdalen, Hedmark county, in the summer of 1990.

The Sami People demand their Rights

After the war the authorities abandoned their hard "Norwegianization" policy and declared that they wished to protect Sami culture, language and way of life. Because the Sami lacked a proper organization and an effective political leadership with clear-cut goals, however, Norwegian authorities did little to implement the new policies.

There were many reasons why the Sami had difficulties in organizing themselves. They had been discriminated against and suppressed for hundreds of years. Many of them had renounced their Sami background and moved away from Sami districts. They were few, they lived in different countries and they spoke different languages.

The reindeer-herders, who founded their own association in 1948, were the first to build up a proper organization. In the mid-1950s Sami people from Sweden, Finland and Norway formed a Scandinavian Sami association, and in 1964, the government set opp the Norwegian Sami Council, which was given advisory status in Sami matters. Four years later an organization was established with the express purpose of getting Sami to agree to a joint political platform. However, it proved impossible to gather a majority of the Sami people into one and the same organization.

Starting in the 1950s government grants

to education among the Sami increased. In the two following decades, well-educated and self-confident leaders emerged to make the Sami organizations more effective. Many were inspired by the work of the World Council for Indigenous People (WCIP) founded in 1975. The rapid industrialization of the post-war years increased pressure on the Sami cultures. Increasing numbers were alarmed by the intrusion of the Nordic states into areas which the Sami had controlled for thousands of years.

The state energy authority decision to develop the Alta-Kautokeino waterway in the early 1970s marked the end of patience. The Sami joined forces with environmentalists to stop construction machines. This campaign gained the support of indigenous people in other countries and attracted international attention. In 1981 the government sent in a large police force to remove the demonstrators, and construction of the power plant could begin.

The Alta incident forced the authorities to be more attentive to Sami demands. One result of this change of view was the establishment of a separate Sami assembly, the *Sameting*, in 1989. The Storting passed an amendment to the Constitution that same year stating that the Norwegian state had responsibility for protecting the Sami language, culture and way of life.

A review of Sami right of ownership to land and water proved time-consuming. Early in 1994, the Committee on Sami Rights submitted a recommendation denying Sami demands. The Sami Assembly protested energetically against the committee's conclusion and had the government evaluate the matter once more.

Demonstrators being stopped by the police during the Alta protest action in October 1981.

The Conservative Swell

After having been supported by increasing numbers of voters in the 1970s, the Conservatives received 31 per cent of the vote in 1981, the best result ever achieved by the party.

The success of the Conservative Party showed that the swing to the right taking place throughout the western world had also reached Norway. The Conservatives had built up an effective party organization during the '70s and recruited many new members, attracting a majority of the voters who had lost their political roots during the EC controversy. Those who had supported the Labour Party now had less difficulty in supporting the Conservatives, whose image had also become more social democratic. Moreover, the two parties had cooperated closely in promoting EC-membership.

The Conservatives profitted from the reduction in industrial workers, farmers and fishermen, traditional supporters of the Labour Party and the Centre Party. The party also profitted by the growth of urban culture and middle-class values, while the class solidarity of the labour movement became weaker. Growing numbers of people moved into towns and cities and the number of white-collar workers increased. This meant that the counter-cultures - the temperance movement, lay Christianity and the New Norwegian movement - lost support and that the Conservatives made inroads into groups normally voting with the Liberals and the Christian Democrats, particularly in southern and western districts.

In the general election of 1985 the Conservatives again won over 30 per cent of the votes cast, but experienced a severe fall in the 1989 and 1993 elections. After all the returns in 1993, the Consveratives were left with the support of only 17 per cent of the electorate.

NEO-LIBERALISM TAKES ROOT

When the Party of Progress (*Fremskritts- partiet* or *FP*) was founded in 1972, one of its main objectives was the furthering of a «sharp decrease in taxation, excises and public encroachment». This new party, which drew inspiration from a Danish tax- refusal movement, was a result of dissatis- faction with the Conservatives' centre poli- cies. As the Conservatives gradually increas- ed cooperation with the parties of the centre, a growing need was felt for an alter- native giving greater scope to the dynamics of the market-place and to private initiative.

Up until the mid-1980s, between 1.9 and 6.3 per cent of the electorate voted for the Progress Party. The party was so often harri- ed by inner conflict that its rapid demise was constantly predicted. This was proven wrong. At the municipal elections of 1983, the Progress Party won support all over the country, and at the general elections two years later it won 13 per cent of the votes. At this time the Conservatives and the Progress Party were supported by slightly over 35 per cent of the electorate, a result showing that the swing to the right in Norway culminated in 1989.

Supporters of the Progress Party were not only disgusted by high taxation. They also opposed growing state and municipal enga- gement in all manner of affairs and their increasing need of revenues. In this form of criticism the party was inspired by the *neo- Liberalistic* policies of Margaret Thatcher and Ronald Reagan.

Norwegian neo-Liberalism was a reaction against the welfare and equality policies adopted after 1945. The Progress Party felt that the authorities had become too eager to "prop up" too many people, and that individuals instead ought to be paid accor- ding to their efforts.

The party gained support among those who opposed aid to developing countries and who were critical of immigration from the third world. People who were sceptical to the feminist movement were also willing to vote for the Progress Party.

The leader of the Progress Party, Carl I. Hagen, must be given the much of the credit for its success. He had a winning personality, used simple language and was a success on television. Hagen represented a new, fresh style with appeal to people grown tired of the old parties.

The Progress Party lost much of its sup- port in the early 1990s, winning only 6.3 per cent of the votes in the 1993 general elections. This decline indicates both that the international move to the right lost ground and the the party was weakened once again by inner antagonisms.

The Willoch Period 1981-1986

After the 1981 election the non-socialist parties were unable to form a coalition government. Negotiations stranded when the Conservatives refused a Christian Democrat demand that the Abortion Act be revoked. The Conservatives then formed a government alone, with Kåre Willoch as prime minister. The Christian Democrats took two years to recover from the wounds of defeat on the abortion question, but by summer of 1983 the desire to govern had reawakened. They entered the government together with the Centre Party.

Willoch's minority government had set out "to re-establish growth in the Norwegian economy". It reduced taxes, did away with many official regulations, and allowed market forces more leeway.

Public rent control was abolished, and most people living in public housing developments were given an opportunity to purchase their homes. The government also stimulated the stock-market. It became easier for foreigners to invest in Norwegian stocks and bonds, while people buying shares in unit trusts received tax deductions. The turn-over at the Oslo Stock Exchange rose rapidly to record heights.

The non-socialist parliamentary majority also agreed to dissolve the state broadcasting monopoly. New local radio stations came on the air starting in 1982, and private companies began building cable networks for both local and satellite television broadcasts.

By the mid-1980s the government had managed to pay off the nation's foreign debt, but this was not enough to balance the economy. The number of unemployed rose steadily, reaching 80,000 (5 per cent) in 1984. Both the Labour Party and the centrist parties demanded that the Willoch government increase public spending so that unemployment might be reduced.

The foreign debt began to increase again in 1985. At the same time private consumption exploded. This was a consequence of the government's abolishment of state regulations on private loans. People bought new cars, household appliances and luxury items as never before, most purchases being financed by bank loans. The banks also lent enormous sums to the retail trade and to speculators on the stock exchange and the property market.

Kåre Willoch, parliamentary leader of the Conservative Party, being cheered by workers outside the Storting after the 1981 election victory. During the 1980s, the Conservatives won votes from groups of traditional Labour supporters.

Newly rich young people who made fortunes in the hectic boom period of the '80s were nicknamed *japper*, based on the American term y*aps* or *young aspiring professional*s. Many of them worked in finance, advertizing or fashion.

The economic situation worsened with the dramatic fall in oil prices, and foreign exchange brokers began selling off Norwegian *kroner*. During the winter of 1985-86 the Bank of Norway used NOK 28 billion in support of the *krone*. The deficit on internal accounts grew and the Willoch government was forced to raise taxes and cut state expenditures. The Progress Party would not, however, accept an inrease in petrol excises. When the Labour Party joined them, the government demanded a vote of confidence and was forced to resign.

The Labour Party formed a minority government, led by Gro Harlem Brundtland, which remained in power until the 1989 general election. A new non-socialist government then took over with Jan P. Syse, Conservative, as prime minister.

Economy and Environment in the Age of Petroleum

The fact that Norway became an oil-producing country had vast consequences for the national economy. The high wages paid in the petroleum industry raised prices and wages in the mainland economy, so that competing on an international scale became difficult for some sectors of industry. Especially hard-hit were labour-intensive companies, such as shoe and clothing factories, where little specialized knowledge was required and value added in production was low.

From 1973 to 1993, industry's share of the GNP sank by about 1/3 and about 100,000 jobs in industry were lost. The total Norwegian industrial production in this same period remained almost unchanged, while that of western Europe increased by over 30 per cent.

The decline in industrial employment was also influenced by the new technology, especially computer technology, which companies began using. Jobs were also lost when companies were merged with one another. This tendency was also noticeable in retail trade, in banking and in insurance.

After the Labour Party's efforts on behalf of state-owned industry in the 1970s, a change of attitude became apparent in the following decade. Political willingness to support companies operating at a loss declined under rightist influence. A number of state-owned companies, including the Labour Party's old showplace project, the Norwegian Iron Works, were shut down.

One sign that Norwegian economy was becoming more internationalized between 1970 and 1990 was the fact that eleven Norwegian industrial concerns became multi-national companies. At this time a company was regarded as multinational if it owned at least three production units outside the mother country and had an annual turnover of at least two billion *kroner*. Examples of Norwegian companies increasing their foreign activities are Norsk Hydro's building of fertilizer factories, Statoil's purchases of chains of petrol stations, Kværner's expansion in ship-building, and the establishment of foreign factories by pharmaceutical companies Apothekernes Laboratorium and Hafslund Nycomed.

In a European sense, these Norwegian multinationals were small. Statoil and Norsk Hydro, for example, placed 46th and 48th respectively in a list of Europe's fifty largest companies published in 1990.

In the 1980s Norwegian shipowners registered a growing number of their vessels under flags of convenience. This was due to

When Gro Harlem Brundtland (1939) took over as prime minister in 1986, eight women became cabinet ministers, a higher percentage of women than in any other government in the world.

The M/S *Americana*, owned by A/S Ivarans Rederi, was the world's first combined cruise and container ship. The ship was registered in the Norwegian International Ships' Register (NIS).

high costs in Norway and harder international competition. Shipping incomes and the number of Norwegian seamen both sank dramatically. Maritime traditions and the many land-based jobs were in danger of disappearing.

Amid strong protests from the Norwegian Seamen's Union, the Storting passed an act establishing the Norwegian International Ships' Register (NIS). Shipowners could now enter into wage agreements with foreign seamen without participation from Norwegian trade unions. This saved shipping companies millions in wages per ship.

The Registry was a success. After only three years, NIS covered over 850 ships totalling 38 million dwt. Foreign exchange earnings from shipping again increased, with positive effects for land-based industry. In 1989 Norwegian shipowners bought goods and services from their country's industries for almost 10 billion *kroner*. By the early 1990s, Norway had become an international centre for shipbrokerage and maritime insurance.

The expansion of the NIS-fleet was not without problems, however. Several serious accidents raised questions concerning the quality of the oldest ships and the standards of the crews. As a result the authorities expanded the Norwegian Ship Control, while shipowners increased grants for the training of officers.

During the 1980s increasing numbers of people again began moving from northern Norway. Between 1980 and 1985 the area's population fell by about 10,000, a tendency

that continued. These depressing figures resulted from a crisis in fisheries. Pessimism was especially wide-spread on the coast of Finnmark, with growing demands that the government take measures to help the situation. At the 1989 general election, the people of Finnmark returned a representative on a new northern party list. This was clear warning to the established parties, who approved tax reductions and other economic advantages for these inhabitants of the far north.

Optimism returned to Finnmark in the early 1990s. Cod fishing again became profitable, and with the Cold War over, the government set about establishing economic and political contacts with Russia and the other Arctic nations. The principles for this Barents area cooperation were set forth in the Kirkenes Declaration signed in 1993.

The stock market crash in 1987 marked the end of the '80s boom and the beginning of a deep crisis. Labourers were laid off, retail companies went bankrupt, the property market collapsed, construction companies went into liquidation, and banks and insurance companies were on the verge of failure. The Labour Party government introduced deflationary measures with higher taxation and interest rates, and passed legislation to limit wage increases. Private consumption fell as did requests for loans. Private banks lost more and more money. Several of the larger banks faced bankruptcy by the beginning of the 1990s. The state poured in billions to get the banking business back on its feet, but this aid came at a price: The state acquired a majority share in several of the largest merchant banks.

Oil revenues gave Norway an exceptional politico-economic freedom of action. While the other OECD countries were forced to reduce state expenditures after 1987, Norway was one country using the greatest proportion of the GNP on public expeditures and having the greatest share of the labour force in the public sector. The largest number of new jobs in this sector of the economy were established in municipalities, especially in health, welfare and education, and by far the greater number were jobs for women.

As the first country in the world, Norway established a Ministry of the Environment in 1972, with principal responsibility for drawing up new laws against pollution. This legislation had positive effect. Emissions of sulphur dioxide, CFC's (refrigerants and aerosols), lead and soot were reduced, while the quality of water in rivers, lakes and fjords improved. An important victory was won in the early 1980s when Norway's largest lake, the Mjøsa, was saved from serious pollution by algae.

Several problems remained to be solved, however. Much of the population lacked good quality drinking water. Asphalt dust caused by use of studded tyres was a nuisance in towns and cities. This was also true of the huge clouds of smoke that billowed in over eastern Finnmark from a nickel works in Russia. The rising production of oil and gas also led to a rise in emissions of carbon dioxide, even though this development was defended by environmental authorities. They argued that Norwegian exports of gas helped replace cokes and atomic energy in other countries, thus reducing the sum total of carbon dioxide emission in Europe. Conservationists did not agree with this view. They claimed that Norwegian gas made energy economizing and use of renewable energy unprofitable, thus contributing to a higher total consumption of energy.

Pollution from Great Britain and the continent continued to strike the country. Between 1980 and 1990, there was a doubling of areas whose lakes no longer contained fish because of acid rain. Analyses of fish samples taken at extreme depths showed clearly that ocean currents along the coast carried far too large amounts of environmental poisons.

Norway wished to prove herself an innovator in international work to improve the environment. Gro Harlem Brundtland was therefore an opportune choice as leader for the UN Commission on Environment and Development, which presented the "Brundtland Report" in 1987. The commission launched the ambitious plan of a "viable" development, meaning that the world must stive for a development "which satisfies today's needs without destroying future generations' possibilities for fulfilling theirs."

Characteristics of Social Development after 1980

In the early '80s it was generally accepted that poverty and social need had been wiped out in Norway. Before long social scientists found this to be a myth. An survey carried out in 1985 showed that about 5 per cent of the population – approximately 200,000 people – could be designated as *newly poor*. The majority of these were old people, single parents, the disabled, and young people without a job.

The number receiving disability pensions grew rapidly in the '80s, rising from 150,000 in 1977 to 230,000 in 1987. One reason was that older people had difficulty in adjusting to the new demands of working life. By 1987 fully one-third of all Norwegians reaching retirement age (67) were already on disability pensions. During the '80s national health insurance expenses soared from 1/8 to 1/5 of the GNP.

Social security payments increased. By 1991 they were more than seven times those in 1980 - calculated according to fixed rates, while the number of persons receiving social security had almost trebled between 1980 and 1990. The marked rise in unemployment and in housing costs must take much of the blame for this increase. An industrial worker had to pay about five times his annual wage to buy a new house in the 1980s; in the 1950s he would have managed with one year's income. With expenses like this, it comes as no surprise that many of the unemployed could not manage on their unemployment benefits.

Social Security, painted by Odd Nerdrum (1944-) in 1973, gives a good idea of the loneliness suffered by many old people in the Norwegian welfare state.

Unemployment started increasing again in 1987, reaching about 170,000 by 1991. This meant that unemployment included nearly as large a portion of the labour force as in the worst inter-war depression years. The difference now was that as many as 58,000 of the unemployed were temporarily employed or were taking part in training courses organized through state employment measures.

There was widespread anxiety in the 1980s over the rapid rise in crimes of violence and narcotics, while both children's officers and temperance boards had much more to do. The fact that more people committed suicide was not a good sign either.

Statistics show in addition that the number of divorced and single parents continued to rise. More women took paid employment, wage differences between the sexes continued to decline, and from 1981 on, there were more women than men studying at universities and colleges.

Although social and economic problems still existed towards the end of the 1980s, the life of the average Norwegian was undoubtedly marked by greater material prosperity and social security than at any previous point in history. At the same time international statistics give cause for reflection. In 1953 Norwegian women and men had the highest average life expectancy in the world. In 1988 they were not even listed among the ten countries ranked highest on those same statistics.

On the other hand, Norway was among the countries ranked highest in the UN survey of quality of human life carried out in the early 1990s. These reports are a total evaluation of living standards in all the countries of the world, based on life expectancy, level of education, purchasing power, GNP, division of incomes, equality of the sexes and welfare benefits.

NOBEL'S PEACE PRIZE

Alfred Nobel (1833-1896) of Sweden is known as the founder of the modern explosives industry due to his discovery of dynamite. He owned factories in several countries and built up a considerable fortune. In his last will and testament from 1895, he declared that his fortune was to be set aside in a fund, the interest on which was to be used as «an award to those who in the past year had done the most good for mankind». This interest money was to be divided into five equal parts. The prizes in physiology and medicine, physics, chemistry and litterature were to be awarded by Swedish institutions, while responsibility for the last prize, the Nobel Peace Prize, was given to an independent committee appointed by the Norwegian Storting. A limited number of persons have the right to propose candidates to the Peace Prize; among these are the members of the Nobel Committee, members of various nations' national assemblies, members of the International Court of Justice in The Hague and former prize winners. The Peace Prize was awarded for the first time in 1901 on the anniversary of Afred Nobel's death, 10 December. Two men shared the prize: Jean Henri Dunant (1828-1910) of Switzerland, founder of the Red Cross, and Frederic Passy (1822-1912) of France, founder of France's first association for peace.

Just why the honour of awarding the prize was given to Norway has been a matter of some discussion. One explanation can be that Nobel wished to reduce the union controversy. It is also possible that he wished to honour the Storting because it approved international arbitration in 1880 and because it supported the interparliamentary movement.

According to its statutes, the Nobel Peace Prize shall be awarded to persons or institutions which have "most advanced the cause of brotherhood among peoples and the abolishment or lessening of standing armies, and the establishment or spread of peace assemblies". Over the years, the Nobel Committee has chosen a broad interpretation of this provision, taking into considera-tion all actions for the promotion of peace. Willy Brandt of Germany, who won the prize in 1971 for work of reconciliation between east and west, and Mikhail Gorbachev, of Russia who won in 1991, are examples of winners who satisfy the letter of the provisions. Mother Theresa (1979) of India received the prize for her work among the poor in Calcutta's slums. The struggle for human rights had been accepted as a criterium for being awarded the prize, and Andrei Sakharov of Russia in 1975, Lech Walesca of Poland in 1983, opposition leader Aung San Suu Kyi of Burma in 1991, and Nelson Mandela of South Africa in 1993, are examples of this. As the then chairman of the Nobel Committee stated in 1983, concerning human rights and the Nobel Peace Prize: "The testament does not make mention of this, but the testament was written in a different aera. Today we realize that peace cannot be established unless freedom is fully respected."

Gro Harlem Brundtland greeting Nelson Mandela after the awarding of the Nobel Peace Prize in 1993.

WINTER SPORTS

FEBRUARY 28, 1994 No. 9

TIME

SALVATION FOR SARAJEVO?

The Flash

Norway superhero
Johann Olav Koss
leads the host country
to a host of medals

Norway has often been called the homeland of skiing, probably because the first competitions took place in this country. The first public ski meet was held in Tromsø in 1843, but it is the people of Telemark, led by Sondre Norheim (1825-1897), who are considered the pioneers of modern sports skiing. These meets first combined downhill skiing with jumping, but around the turn of the century the sport was divided into the jumping, cross-country and alpine events with which we are familiar with today. In 1825 skis were brought to the United States by Norwegian emigrants. Jon Torsteinson Rui (1827-1876) of Telemark – or «Snowshoe Thompson» – gained fame for skiing with his mail bags over the wintery Sierra Nevada Mountains. Norwegians also took the initiative in spreading skiing throughout Central Europe. The first inter-national ski congress was held in Christiania in 1910 under the auspices of the Nor-wegian Ski Association, founded in 1908.

Norwegian competitors have often domi-nated speedskating. The first competitions took place in the Netherlands in the 1800s, but it was when Scandinavia joined in that sports skating became really popular. The first really large skating competition was held in Christiania in 1860, on the icy fjord beneath the walls of Akershus Castle. Norway had several world champions in the inter-wars years. Sonja Henie (1912-1969) was Queen of the Ice, winning Olympic gold medals in 1928, 1932 and 1936, nine world champion-ships and six European championships.

This long history of winter sports forms the background for Norway's having arranged two Olympic Winter Games. The sixth Winter Olympics in Oslo in 1952 had 1178 partici-pants from 30 countries, who competed in 30 disciplines. Holmenkollen Ski Jump was the main arena for the Nordic events, while speedskating was arranged at Bislet Stadium. Hallgeir Brenden, who won the gold medal in cross-country over 18 kilometres, is a good representative for the Norwegian partici-pants in 1952.

When Lillehammer was awarded the 17th Winter Olympics for 1994, the organizers determined to give priority to the environ-ment and to joy in sports, something that was achieved to the fullest. The Lillehammer Games had the greatest number of visitors – a total of 2,000,000 – in the history of the Winter Games. The home country won ten gold medals, eleven silver and five bronze medals. The greatest hero of the Lillehammer Games was speedskater Johan Olav Koss, who won three gold medals and set three world records in the process. He donated his winner's bonus for taking the gold medal in the 1500-metre-event – NOK 225,000 – to the humanitarian organization Olympic Aid.

From the the Chamonix Games in 1924 to the Lillehammer Games in 1994, Norwegian sportspeople have won 73 gold, 74 silver and 64 bronze medals.

Above:
Sonja Henie (1912-1969),
Left:
Hallgeir Brenden (1929)
Opposite page:
Johann Olav Koss (1968)

Norway and Europe in the 1990s

Norway's relations with the European Community came up for renewed discussion in 1990. Together with the other EFTA-countries, Norway opened negotiations with the EC concerning a new economic cooperation agreement (*European Economic Area, EEA*). Their varying attitudes towards the EC again created problems of cooperation among the non-socialist parties. Disagreement as to the EEA-agreement led to the fall of the Syse government, but before this happened they had come to an important decision which was not revoked by the new government: virtually unrestricted transference of foreign exchange and funds, to start in July 1990.

In the autumn of 1991 the Labour Party formed its third minority government with Gro Harlem Brundtland as prime minister. The next year, negotiations were opened with the EC on the EEA. This agreement allowed for the free flow of goods, services, labour and capital between the countries of the EFTA and the EC. A common set of regulations was to ensure equality of competition for business and industry in all member nations. This meant the revision of hundreds of Norwegian laws and regulations, while legislation covering a number of fields would have to be coordinated in the years to come. The agreement did not lead to Norway's becoming a member of the EC's supranational bodies. Nor was the country affected by the EC's common policies in agriculture, foreign affairs or defence, although a majority in the Storting approved a proposal that Norway become an associate member of the Western European Union (WEU), which is the EC's defence policy link with NATO.

While these EEA-negotiations were taking place, Sweden and Finland applied for membership in the EC, which had changed its name to the European Union (EU) after the Treaty of Maastricht came into force. The treaty concerned plans for an economic, monetary and foreign policy union of European states. The Labour Party government decided to follow Sweden's and Finland's examples. After hard negotiations, the membership agreement between Norway and the EU was completed in the spring of 1994. This was the start of an intense debate that focused in general on the same arguments and followed the same fronts as in 1972, but which was carried out in an entirely different European context. When the nation voted in the fall of 1994, a majority of the populations in Austria, Finland and Sweden had already agreed to membership. These results did not affect public opinion, however, and once again a small majority of Norwegians voted against European cooperation based on the Treaty of Rome.

The uncrowned queen of the struggle against Norwegian membership in the EU in 1994 was the leader of the Centre Party, Anne Enger Lahnstein (1949). Here she is cheered by «No» supporters just after the result of the referendrum was announced.

NORWEGIAN EURO-SCEPTICISM

As the only people in western Europe, Norwegians have voted against membership in the European community in two referendums. The strong antagonism towards supranational cooperation shown in these results has an extremely complex foundation.

Norway, lying on Europe's outskirts, has never had the close connections to the continent as have neighboring countries. As a coastal nation, Norway has traditionally been orientated towards Great Britain and the United States. Great Britain was Norway's ankerhold in matters of national security between 1905 and 1945, while the large numbers of Norwegian immigrants to the United States linked the two peoples closely together.

Norway is a young nation, with full national sovereignty dating as late as from 1905. Many Norwegians are therefore particularly conscious of protecting their independence. After having been dominated by Denmark and Sweden in protracted unions, many people feared that the country once again would be ruled at long distance from a faraway centre. These fears were accentuated by the German occupation between 1940 and 1945.

Norway has a long tradition of peace. The country has not been at war with a neighbouring country since 1814, and therefore does not have the same need as the war-torn states of the continent for securing peace through supranational cooperation. On the contrary, many Norwegians believe that Norway can beste serve international peace by becoming an independent link between nations and a generous model for other states.

The profound conflicts between centre and periphery in Norwegian politics deserved special mention. Counter-cultures are of extreme importance in this matter. In mountain districts and along the fjords of the northwestern coast, where New Norwegian and the liberal young peoples' movement have their heart, there is an ingrained scepticism towards industrialization, urban culture, modernization and élitist leadership. Opposition towards a centralized culture is also found in the temperance movement and among lay Christians.

Given their long tradition of self-ownership, powerful organizations and plentiful funds to the campaign against European integration, Norwegian farmers make up the storm troops among the Euro-scepticists. Working with representatives for the counter-cultures, the Socialist Leftists and fishermen, they have twice built up an effective grass-roots movement that has won the majority. The Socialist Leftist opposition to supranationality is rooted in the neutrality policies of the inter-war years and in their opposition to NATO during the cold war. Fishermen have a different point of departure: they are primarily interested in maintaining national control over the immense fishing grounds that Norway ensured herself by means of the extension of territorial waters in the 1970s.

A great deal of the explanation for why the opposition against European integration was not appreciably weakened between 1972 and 1994 can be found in the enormous deposits of oil and natural gas that gave Norway a unique economic strength and freedom of action. From the 1970s and on, Norwegian politicians have allotted huge sums to groups in outlying districts that worked for maintaining national control. Norwegian farmers were assured of the largest subsidies in Europe, while the number of women's jobs in the public sector exploded. Women's marked opposition to EU membership was decisive to the result of the referendum. Many of them were determined to defend the strong ideals of equality that have long been an important element in Norwegian politics. They feared that Norway, as a member of the EU, could be forced to cut expenditures in the public sector, endangering both the welfare state and their own jobs.

Opposition to the EU included other attitudes popular in the early '90s. Increasing immigration had created more fear of foreigners in the general public, while Norwegian triumphs in international diplomacy for peace and during the Lillehammer Games strengthened national self-respect.

The fact that an alternative to EU-membership existed in 1994 should also be emphasized. By assuring the greater part of Norwegian industry and services full admission to the EU inner market, the EEA agreement made it easier to vote "No".

Norway and the world

Norway is a small, rich, democratic, industrialized country in the far north. In 1995 the country had a population of 4.3 million, 88% of whom were members of the Church of Norway. But other characteristics give the country its distinctive stamp:

- Its GNP is among the highest in the world in proportion to population.
- Incomes are relatively evenly distributed amongst the population
- Norway gives more development aid per capita than any other western industrialized country.
- A great many women participate in politics.
- Norwegians drink relatively small amounts of alcoholic beverages.
- The country, with one of the world's longest coastlines, is deeply involved in ocean-related activity, such as fishing, shipping and petroleum production.
- Norway has vast amounts of energy resources, such as hydroelectric power, oil and gas.
- Norway hopes to be a bridgebuilder in international politics, for example as meditator in conflict areas such as the Middle East, Nicaragua and the former Yugoslavia.
- Norway is the only country in Europe where a majority of the population has twice refused membership in the EU.

Norway's first woman Prime Minister, Gro Harlem Brundtland, is often called the "World's Minister of the Environment". In the 1980s she headed the UN Commission on Environment and Development

El Salvador 1991-92

Imports and exports as percentages of the GNP.

Imports
Exports
Oil and gas
Gross income from shipping

NICARAGU
1.11 mrd. k

%
30
20
10

25,64 29,15 34,89 29,60 29,88 29,70 43,11 41,29 44,48 47,29 44,36 36,76
18,03 14,52 9,47 13,40 6,96

1870   1900   1930   1960   1980   1990

Norway became a member of the European Free Trade Association, ETFA, in 1960. Thirteen years later, Norway signed a free trade agreement with EC, which was replaced by the EEA agreement in 1993.

Iceland
NORWAY
Finland
Sweden
Denmark
Great Britain
Ireland
The Netherl.
Belgium   Luxembourg
Germany
France   Austria
Liechtenstein
Portugal   Switzerland
Spain
Italy
Greece

500 km

EFTA countries
EU countries
EFTA and EEA countries

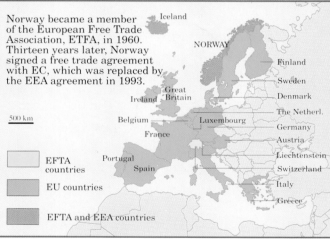

Norway's imports 1950 to 1990

Import value in percentage

| | 1950 | 1960 | 1970 | 1990 |

24
22
20
18
16
14
12
10
8
6
4
2
0

Sweden, West Germany, Great Britain, Denmark, France, The Netherlands, Belgium, Luxembourg, Italy, Finland, Spain, USSR, Canada, USA, Brazil, Japan, Asia (-Japan), America (-USA and Canada), Africa

Norwegian ships' ports of call 1950

New York	1006
Antwerp	811
Rotterdam	789
Hamburg	611
Le Havre	545
Kharg Isl.	507
Baltimore	481
Philadelphia	480
London	433
Hong Kong	410
Gothenburg	400
Singapore	398
Copenhagen	381
New Orleans	381
Curacao	374

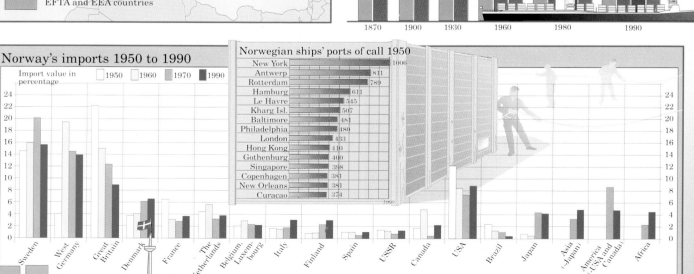

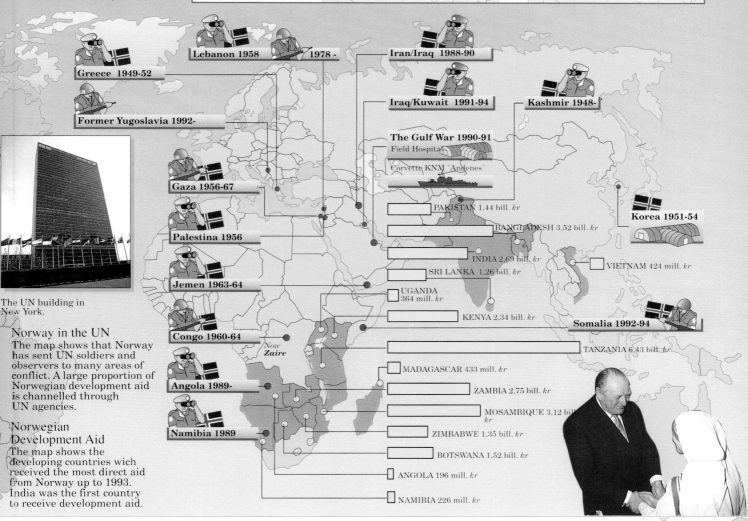

"Today Norway is the largest folk museum in Europe, but at the same time an enormous laboratory of the future". (Hans Magnus Enzensberger, German author, 1984.)

The Nordic Council was established in 1952. Here representatives from governments and national assemblies in the Nordic countries meet to cooperate on matters of common interest.

Norway became a member of the western defence organization NATO in 1949. The map indicates the political and security situation in 1990.

Greece 1949-52

Lebanon 1958 **1978 -**

Iran/Iraq 1988-90

Former Yugoslavia 1992-

Iraq/Kuwait 1991-94

Kashmir 1948-

The Gulf War 1990-91
Field Hospital
Corvette KNM "Andenes"

Gaza 1956-67

PAKISTAN 1,44 bill. *kr*

BANGLADESH 3,52 bill. *kr*

Korea 1951-54

Palestina 1956

INDIA 2,69 bill. *kr*

SRI LANKA 1,26 bill. *kr*

VIETNAM 424 mill. *kr*

Jemen 1963-64

UGANDA 364 mill. *kr*

KENYA 2,34 bill. *kr*

Somalia 1992-94

Congo 1960-64

Now Zaire

TANZANIA 6,43 bill. *kr*

The UN building in New York.

Norway in the UN
The map shows that Norway has sent UN soldiers and observers to many areas of conflict. A large proportion of Norwegian development aid is channelled through UN agencies.

MADAGASCAR 433 mill. *kr*

ZAMBIA 2,75 bill. *kr*

Angola 1989-

MOSAMBIQUE 3,12 bill. *kr*

ZIMBABWE 1,35 bill. *kr*

Namibia 1989

BOTSWANA 1,52 bill. *kr*

Norwegian Development Aid
The map shows the developing countries wich received the most direct aid from Norway up to 1993. India was the first country to receive development aid.

ANGOLA 196 mill. *kr*

NAMIBIA 226 mill. *kr*

A committe nominated by the Storting awards the Nobel Peace Prize. The illustration shows King Olav V congratulating Mother Theresa in 1979.

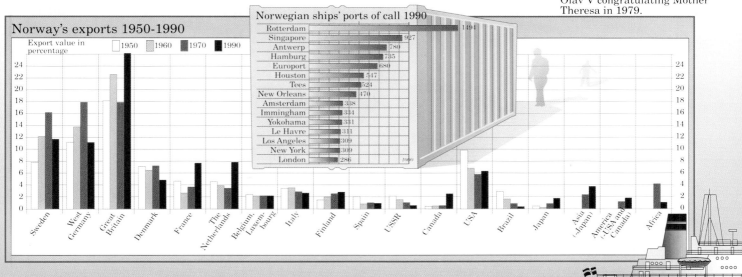

Norway's exports 1950-1990

Export value in percentage
□ 1950 ▨ 1960 ▨ 1970 ■ 1990

Norwegian ships' ports of call 1990

Port	Calls
Rotterdam	1494
Singapore	927
Antwerp	780
Hamburg	735
Europort	680
Houston	547
Tees	524
New Orleans	470
Amsterdam	338
Immingham	334
Yokohama	331
Le Havre	311
Los Angeles	309
New York	309
London	286

Sweden, West Germany, Great Britain, Denmark, France, The Netherlands, Belgium, Luxembourg, Italy, Finland, Spain, USSR, Canada, USA, Brazil, Japan, Asia (-Japan), America (-USA and Canada), Africa

NORWEGIAN KINGS

Harald I Hårfagre	ca. 890 - 940	Magnus III Berrføtt	1093 - 1103
Eirik Blodøks	ca. 940 - 945	Olav Magnusson	1103 - 1115
Håkon I the Good	ca. 945 - 960	Øystein Magnusson	1103 - 1123
Harald II Gråfell	ca. 960 - 970	Sigurd Jorsalfare	1103 - 1130
Danish reign: Håkon Ladejarl	ca. 970 - 995	Magnus IV the Blind	1130 - 1135
Olav II Tryggvason	995 - 1000	Harald IV Gille	1130 - 1136
Danish reign: Eirik Ladejarl		Sigurd Munn	1136 - 1155
and Svein Ladejarl	1000 - 1015	Inge I Krokrygg	1136 - 1161
Olav II (St. Olav)	1015 - 1030	Øystein Haraldsson	1142 - 1157
Danish reign: Svein Knutsson	1030 - 1035	Håkon II Herdebreid	1159 - 1162
Magnus II the Good	1035 - 1047	Magnus V Erlingsson	1161 - 1184
Harald III Hardråde	1046 - 1066	Sverre	1177 - 1202
Magnus II Haraldsson	1066 - 1069	Håkon III Sverreson	1202 - 1204
Olav III Kyrre	1066 - 1093	Guttorm Sigurdsson	1204
Håkon Magnusson	1093 - 1094	Inge Bårdsson	1204 - 1217
		Håkon IV Håkonsson	1217 - 1263
		Magnus VI Lagabøte	1263 - 1280
		Eirik Magnusson	1280 - 1299
		Håkon V Magnusson	1299 - 1319
		Magnus Eriksson	1319 - 1374
		Håkon VI Magusson	1343 - 1380
		Olav IV Håkonsson	1380 - 1387
		Margrete	1388 - 1412
		Eric of Pomerania	1389 - 1442
		Christopher of Bavaria	1442 - 1448
		Karl I Knutsson	1449
		Christian I of Oldenburg	1449 - 1481
		Hans	1483 - 1513
		Christian II	1513 - 1523
		Frederik I	1524 - 1533
		Council of the Realm	1533 - 1536
		Christian III	1536 - 1559
		Frederik II	1559 - 1588
		Christian IV	1588 - 1648
		Frederik III	1648 - 1670
		Christian V	1670 - 1699
		Frederik IV	1699 - 1730
		Christian VI	1730 - 1746
		Frederik V	1746 - 1766
		Christian VII	1766 - 1808
		Frederik VI	1808 - 1814
		Christian Frederik	1814
		Karl II (XIII)	1814 - 1818
		Karl III (XIV) Johan	1818 - 1844
		Oscar I	1844 - 1859
		Karl IV (XV)	1859 - 1872
		Oscar II	1872 - 1905
		Håkon VII	1905 - 1957
		Olav V	1957 - 1991
		Harald V	1991 -

King Harald V and Queen Sonja being blessed by Bishop Finn Wagle in Nidaros Cathedral in Trondheim, 23 June 1991.

NORWEGIAN GOVERNMENTS SINCE 1873

Frederik Stang	21.7.1873 – 31.10.1880	
Christian August Selmer	1.11.1880 – 11.2.1884	
Chr. H. Schweigaard	3.4.1884 – 26.6.1884	
Johan Sverdrup	26.6.1884 – 13.7.1889	Left
Emil Stang (1)	13.7.1889 – 6.3.1891	Right
Johannes Steen (1)	6.3.1891 – 2.5.1893	Left
Emil Stang (2)	2.5.1893 – 14.10.1895	Right
Georg Fr. Hagerup (1)	14.10.1895 – 17.2.1898	Coalition: Right, Moderate, independent Left representatives
Johannes Steen (2)	17.2.1898 – 21.4.1902	Left
Otto Blehr (1)	21.4.1902 – 22.10.1903	Left
Georg Fr. Hagerup (2)	22.10.1903 – 11.3.1905	Coalition: Left, Right, Moderate, Liberals
Christian Michelsen	11.3.1905 – 23.10.1907	Coalition: Left, Right, Moderate, Liberals
Jørgen Løvland	23.10.1907 – 19.3.1908	Coalition: Independents, Left
Gunnar Knudsen (1)	19.3.1908 – 2.2.1910	Left
Wollert Konow	2.2.1910 – 20.2.1912	Coalition: The Liberal Right, Right
Jens Bratlie	20.2.1912 – 31.1.1913	Coalition: The Liberal Right, Right
Gunnar Knudsen (2)	31.1.1913 – 21.6.1920	Left
Otto B. Halvorsen (1)	21.6.1920 – 22.6.1921	Right
Otto Blehr (2)	22.6.1921 – 6.3.1923	Left
Otto B. Halvorsen (2)	6.3.1923 – 30.5.1923	Coalition: Right, The Liberal Right
Abraham Berge	30.5.1923 – 25.7.1924	Coalition: The Liberal Right, Right
Johan Ludwig Mowinckel (1)	25.7.1924 – 5.3.1926	Left
Ivar Lykke	5.3.1926 – 28.1.1928	Right
Christopher Hornsrud	28.1.1928 – 15.2.1928	Labour
Johan Ludwig Mowinckel (2)	15.2.1928 – 12.5.1931	Left
Peder Ludvik Kolstad	12.5.1931 – 14.3.1932	Agrarian Party
Jens Hundseid	14.3.1932 – 3.3.1933	Agrarian Party
Johan Ludwig Mowinckel (3)	3.3.1933 – 20.3.1935	Left
Johan Nygaardsvold	20.3.1935 – 25.6.1945	Labour
Einar Gerhardsen (1)	25.6.1945 – 5.11.1945	Coalition
Einar Gerhardsen (2)	5.11.1945 – 19.11.1951	Labour
Oscar Torp	19.11.1951 – 22.1.1955	Labour
Einar Gerhardsen (3)	22.1.1955 – 28.8.1963	Labour
John Lyng	28.8.1963 – 25.9.1963	Coalition: Right, Left, The Center Party, Christian Democrats
Einar Gerhardsen (4)	25.9.1963 – 12.10.1965	Labour
Per Borten	12.10.1965 – 17.3.1971	Coalition: The Center Party, Right, Left, Christian Democrats
Trygve Bratteli (1)	17.3.1971 – 18.10.1972	Labour
Lars Korvald	18.10.1972 – 16.10.1973	Coalition: Christian Democrats, The Center Party, Left
Trygve Bratteli (2)	16.10.1973 – 15.1.1976	Labour
Odvar Nordli	15.1.1976 – 3.2.1981	Labour
Gro Harlem Brundtland (1)	3.2.1981 – 14.10.1981	Labour
Kåre Willoch (1)	14.10.1981 – 8.6.1983	Right
Kåre Willoch (2)	8.6.1983 – 9.5.1986	Coalition: Right, Christian Democrats, The Center Party
Gro Harlem Brundtland (2)	9.5.1986 – 16.10.1989	Labour
Jan P. Syse	16.10.1989 – 3.11.1990	Coalition: Right, Christian Democrats, The Center Party
Gro Harlem Brundtland (3)	3.11.1990 –	Labour

FOR FURTHER READING

T.K. Derry: *A Short History of Norway*. London 1968

T.K. Derry: *A History of Modern Norway, 1814-1972*. London 1973

R. Popperwell: *Norway. London* 1972

John Midgaard: *A Brief History of Norway*, Oslo 1986

T. Bergh, T. Hanisch, E. Lange and H. Pharo: *Growth and Development*. Oslo 1981

P. Sveaas Andersen: *Vikings of the West. The Expansion of Norway in the Middle Ages*. Oslo 1985

J. Brøndsted: *The Vikings*. London 1970

M. Magnusson: *Vikings!* London 1970

Snorri Sturluson: *From the Sagas of the Norse Kings*. Oslo 1984

J. Andenæs, O. Riste and M. Skodvin: *Norway and the Second World War*. Oslo 1983

J. G. Arntzen and B. Knudsen: *Political Life and Institutions in Norway*. Oslo 1981

O.S. Lovoll: The Promise of America. *A History of the Norwegian-American People*. Minneapolis and Oslo 1984

I. Semmingsen: *Norway to America. A History of the Migration*. Minneapolis 1980

INDEX